AURORA

New Canadian Writing 1980

EDITED BY

MORRIS WOLFE

DOUBLEDAY CANADA LIMITED
TORONTO, ONTARIO

DOUBLEDAY & COMPANY, INC.
GARDEN CITY, NEW YORK

1980

ISSN 0706-7577
ISBN 0-385-15771-1
Library of Congress Catalog Card Number 80-719

Copyright © 1980 by Doubleday Canada Limited

Printed in Canada by Webcom Ltd.
Design by Robert Burgess Garbutt

First Edition

ACKNOWLEDGEMENTS

I'm grateful to Rick Archbold and Janet Turnbull,
my editors at Doubleday, for their advice and
assistance—and especially their patience. This
project meant a great deal to former editor Betty
Corson; I wish her well in her new life and career
in Hawaii. Barbara Track once again (almost un-
complainingly) kept track of all the submissions;
I wish her well too—wherever she is. Michèle
Doucet helped me go through the French entries
and make a final selection. Ivon Owen approved
our choice and copy-edited it. Jennifer Wolfe
and Michèle Doucet proofread the manuscript.

CONTENTS

AURORA

INTRODUCTION

Welcome to the third issue of *Aurora*.

I regret to announce that with this edition we are suspending publication — at least temporarily. The decision to suspend publication of *Aurora* was mine. Doubleday was ready to go ahead with the fourth volume. My editors merely suggested that we switch from fall to spring publication to see if that might help sales — and that we do whatever possible to cut costs. But sales of *Aurora 1979* have been discouraging. We thought the book would do at least as well as volume one, which sold 2,200 copies. (The break even point on a project such as this is roughly 3,500.) The quality of *Aurora 1979* was, if anything higher than that of *Aurora 1978*. *Aurora 1979* was more attractively packaged; it was more favourably reviewed. *Nonetheless,* it sold 1,500 copies. Many booksellers who stocked *Aurora 1978* didn't bother ordering volume two. *Aurora* simply didn't move off their shelves quickly enough. Based on sales of the first volume, we'd assumed that there was a market for a literary annual in book form, more widely distributed than the "little mags" whose circulation averages between 1,000 and 1,500. Now I'm not so sure.

Serious Canadian publishing has for a long time been about books that sell two or three thousand copies — a few hundred more perhaps during periods of popular cultural nationalism. The contiued publication of such books has always been made possible by a comparatively small number of best sellers. That pattern seems to be changing. It wasn't just *Aurora 1979* that had trouble getting into the bookstores this year. Other literary books had trouble too. For example, copies of Jack Hodgins' Governor-General's-Award-winning novel, *The Resurrection of Joseph Bourne* were so hard to find that the CBC news did an item in which a newsman went from Toronto bookstore to Toronto bookstore looking for it. Hodgins' publisher, Doug Gibson of Macmillan, says the economics of publishing have changed so much in the

1

past few years that were Hodgins to come along now, he probably wouldn't get published at all.

As if to underscore that point, Macmillan's new owner, Ron Besse, a Canadian, is fond of reiterating the (now all too prevalent) view that *every* book should be a "profit centre." "What," asks Besse, "is quality writing anyway?" Aren't Harlequins" well writen, with a good simplified vocabulary and a wide readership?" Publishers he thinks spend far too much time looking for books that sell only two or three thousand copies, for books that "can only be understood by a PH.D." The result of this kind of thinking is that mindless non-books occupy more and more space in our bookstores.

My original plan for *Aurora* was to persuade a Canadian-owned house to undertake the project. I didn't even consider approaching a branch plant. But none of the Canadian publishers I spoke to was interested, although Canada Council of Ontario Art Council money would certainly have been available to help underwrite any loss. Doubleday, though not entitled to financial assistance, *was* interested — for a couple of reasons. *Aurora* would be a goodwill gesture; *Noblesse oblige*, if you like. And *Aurora* might bring in some good new writers at a time when developing a more literary list still seemed possible.

Because of *Aurora*, I'm delighted to say, a number of beginning and little-known writers have appeared in print, or in book form for the first time — Guy Vanderhaeghe, David Blostein, David Macfarlane, M. L. Knight, Christine Webb, Bruce Meyer, Gloria Sawai, John Reibetanz, Anne Collins — the list could go on. Contrary to popular belief there are a lot of good unpublished manuscripts around. There are many academics, for instance, who are closet poets and short story writers; it only takes a little encouragement to get them to come out of the closet.

The irony, of course, is that *Aurora* may simply be raising false hopes among such writers: What's the point of being published in *Aurora* if the chances of ever being published in a book of one's own are almost non-existent and *Aurora* itself is having trouble getting into the bookstores? That's a question I want to wrestle with over the next few months while deciding whether I want to continue. Stay tuned. Indeed, feel free to let me know what you think.

I'm not going to comment on this year's *Aurora* other than to say that it's as good as last year's and that I think the poetry is the best yet. I do, however, want to say a few words about two new features. Because it's the end of a decade, I thought it might be useful to invite Northrop Frye, our leading literary scholar, and Robert Fulford, our leading literary journalist, to talk about where they think Canadian culture is in 1980. CBC *Anthology* recorded the conversation and will broadcast it early this fall. An edited transcript appears in this issue. I have also included in *Aurora 1980* an excerpt in French from a novel in progress by Yvette Naubert. It's my belief that enough of *Aurora's* small audience are sufficiently bilingual to warrant doing so.

Happy reading.

Morris Wolfe
June 1980

From Nationalism to Regionalism: The Maturing of Canadian Culture

Robert Fulford talks with Northrop Frye

FULFORD: Culture in Canada in the 1970s expanded enormously in numbers, in everything from the number of books of poetry published to the number of dancers employed. But as the decade ended there was a sense of — maybe not despair, but certainly disappointment that somehow things hadn't worked out as everyone had hoped or expected. Did you get that feeling?

FRYE: I'm not so sure. I think there are other factors such as the growing recognition of Canadian literature outside Canada, and a growing response to it which I find almost miraculous. I don't understand what people on the continent of Europe get out of Canadian literature, but they certainly get something out of it, and it registers as a kind of unified statement to them. With us it's the ordinary entropy which seems to set in with almost any cultural movement after a few years. Perhaps we'll be refreshed by seeing our mirror images coming back to us from other countries.

FULFORD: When I read about the culture of various periods, usually in Europe but to some extent in America, I see again and again the well-to-do playing a part — the person, say, who founds a dance company with her father's millions. Is there something that keeps Canadian private money from being interested in the arts? You don't have in this country the families — one thinks of the Guggenheims or the Rockefellers — who in the United States pour in millions of dollars. One thinks of patrons of the arts throughout European history. Nothing like that seems to happen here.

FRYE: No, it doesn't happen. I think we are basically a country of deficit financing, and we tend to look to government agencies to subsidize culture just as we look to government agencies to set up a broadcasting commission or a national railway or a National Film Board. Consequently, private business seems to feel that's

5

something they pay taxes for anyway and don't need to support further. I think a peculiar feature of Canadian cultural life is its dependence on government assistance.

FULFORD: Peculiar for a democracy anyway. In a democracy it's unusual to find the government as the mainstay, without a powerful equivalent in the private sector. It seems to me, though, that in the period we're talking about, the 1970s, that government has not been as much help as it might have been, even though the federal government spent a lot more money than ever before. The government really hasn't demonstrated strong leadership. I wonder if it would have been different if Pierre Trudeau had been as interested in the development of Canadian culture as he was in renewed federalism and the constitution.

FRYE: I have a notion that the government's attitude to culture should be a fairly relaxed one. It's more a matter of trying to let the cultural imagery of the country emerge, than providing leadership for it. I'm not just sure where government leadership would take it. I think that as a culture matures, it becomes more regional anyway. And whatever a culture does, if it's worth doing, there's going to be a strongly unpredictable element in it. I think the best and wisest government policy is to allow for a certain leeway, to allow for the spontaneity of cultural expression. In the natural course of events the real initiative comes from the creative people themselves. They know what they want to do, and they can go to a foundation, whether it's a government one or a private one as in the States, and say, "Look, I've got a wonderful idea," and the foundation's job is to evaluate the idea and to respond accordingly.

FULFORD: But there *are* things that governments can do. If we talk about the Canada Council, the government by an act of will created that foundation. And then it determined its size. The Canada Council is now — I don't know what — ten times the size it was when it was founded. But it could be fifty times that size. Or it could be half the size. Those are key government decisions made in cabinet and caucus and so on. They may not determine the quality of the cultural life of the country but they determine whether there will *be* one. That is, by saying, "All right, we'll have a Canada Council in 1990 that's five times the size of the present one," they would call into being twenty more dance companies or three opera companies, or a lot more publishing houses, or something like that. So there is a sense in which they *are* crucially involved at least in a quantitative sense.

FRYE: They're involved in the quantitative sense but there's a fine line, I think, between *laissez-faire*, saying the culture can look after itself, which in our case would mean that culture would still be at a pretty undeveloped state, and assuming leadership, actually providing the cultural ideas.

FULFORD: It seems to me in looking at the 1970s that one of the most striking features is the diminishing role of some of our major cultural institutions. Even though some of them have grown larger, they seem less visible. Some of them ended the 1970s less important than they began them. I'm thinking of the National Film Board, which at times seems to vanish from sight; of the Canada Council, which seems dispirited and defensive even though it has grown considerably. I'm thinking of the National Gallery which, to anyone who goes in to see their exhibitions, seems to be a shambles. Major cultural institutions to which we looked for some kind of leadership, or coherence, some way of making our culture accessible and understandable — they seem to be slipping into the background.

FRYE: There are several processes at work there. One is that anyone handling so expensive a medium as television or film tends to get mired in real estate, bureaucracy and vested interest. I hesitate to draw the inference that there is a connection between limited funds and liveliness of intellect, but it *is* true that when these things started (the National Film Board, CBC television) there was a feeling, not merely of starting something new, but of defining oneself over again to society. I think culture always has to have a feeling of *cult* about it. And again I hesitate to say that complete public tolerance of, say, the art of painting, would tend to make painting rather decorative — that is, it would become simply a function of society and not the voice of a creative impulse that is stirring and prodding the society. I think that those things have set in in many respects. The golden days of the National Film Board had a lot to do with its defining itself as an entity in the Grierson days. And similarly with the CBC, where the level in radio, I think, is much higher than the level in television simply because it is more of a minority medium.

FULFORD: What you're suggesting is that one has to have some kind of outsider status in order to come to life. You can't be totally accepted and still remain culturally alive.

FRYE: I think the question of defining oneself as a presence over or against a society is pretty essential for the creative life. I think that it's been an immense advantage to the writers and creative people in Quebec to feel that they were fighting for a beleaguered and threatened language. And I think that separatism is a very unattractive combination of a progressive cultural movement and a regressive political one — and that the cultural side is the *genuine* part of it.

FULFORD: It seems to me that in the 1970s regionalism became the dominating force in the culture. Maybe it was always so, and became a lot more visible in the 1970s.

FRYE: Regionalism is an inevitable part of the maturing of the culture of a society like ours. I think that in this "instant world of communications," as it's called, there is a kind of uniform international way of seeing and thinking which is derived from the fact that everybody is involved in the same technology. Regional developments are a way of escaping from that, developing something more creative. If you want to learn about *American* life from its literature, for example, you learn about it inferentially from what Faulkner tells you about Mississippi and what others tell you about New England or the Middle West. That is becoming increasingly true of Canada, where the conception of Canada doesn't really make all that much sense. "Canada" is a *political* entity; the cultural counterpart that we call "Canada" is really a federation not of provinces but of regions and communities.

FULFORD: To me it was very striking that in the 1970s one began to be able to read poetry and guess what region the poet was from without reading the poet's biography. I don't think that was true ten or fifteen years before.

FRYE: It's an inevitable part of the maturing of the culture. One area after another becomes culturally articulate through its writers. If you want to know about Canada from its culture, look to see what Jack Hodgins has to say about Vancouver Island, or James Reaney or Robertson Davies about southwestern Ontario, or Roger Lemelin about Quebec. If you add up the cultural communities you get a sense of the vitality and variety of Canadian culture.

FULFORD: Can you see a time when there'll be *national* cultural figures? In my lifetime the only people who have done it have been the Group of Seven. They created a kind of art that has strong adherents in every region, and in both language groups.

FRYE: The Group of Seven were really pre-Canadian in the sense that they were imaginative explorers. Their literary counterpart would not be our established writers so much as people like David Thompson and Samuel Hearne. They were the end of a long period of exploratory and documentary painting which plunged into the country in the wake of the voyageur. I think the country we know as Canada will, in the forseeable future, be a federation of regions culturally, rather than a single nation. I think cultural nationalism gets confused about its units and tends to introduce unreal forms of casuistry, that is, what is truly Canadian and so on. The question can be answered more precisely in different terms.

FULFORD: When I've lectured in a different part of the country from the one I live in, Toronto, and when some element of what I regard as cultural nationalism comes into what I'm saying, there's always an objection. I remember a painter in Halifax telling me that my point of view was that of Ontario politics, not Canadian nationalism at all. It had nothing to do with Halifax, he said.

FRYE: I can understand that reaction very well. I was brought up in the Maritimes myself. I think it's been of an immense benefit to Canada first that it went from a pre-national phase to a postnational phase without ever quite becoming a nation, and second that it never tried to be homogeneous, a melting pot. It always let ethnic groups have their own head, culturally speaking, and I think that is of tremendous benefit to the variety of our culture. To some extent the melting pot, the homogeneity, occurs anyway in response to certain social conditions, and it happens all the better if it isn't too much forced from the outside. The process takes longer. There are many elements in Canadian life — I'm thinking of the Ukrainians and the Icelandics, of the Mennonites in the prairies — they have all made a distinctive appearance in our literature and our painting which, I think, is all to the good. Of course, I see it as a minority movement.

FULFORD: But television is the most pervasive conveyor of culture and, many people believe, the most important one. Yet in this period, despite what we've said about regionalism, and in a period which has been characterized as nationalistic, Canadians have watched less and less *Canadian* television and more and more American television. Do you think this is, in any significant way, the fault of the government, or of the CRTC, of which you were a member? Or is it simply a function of North Americanism? Was it inevitable, no matter what we did?

FRYE: I think it was inevitable. I joined the CRTC in 1968, when the new Broadcasting Act made a good deal of sense. And then what happened was the practically autonomous, it seemed, development through microwave and cable satellite and pay TV, of new technology that tends to follow the centralizing political and economic rhythms rather than the decentralizing cultural ones. And every new medium seems to have to recapitulate a history from a very archaic phase to a very sophisticated one. I think in radio and film we're a long way now from Amos and Andy and the Keystone Cops. Television is still pretty formulaic. But mass culture is just *that* — it's what the vast majority of people want. If we speak of Canada being flooded with American programmes, we find that the Canadian viewer is a fish, not somebody who wants to get into a Canadian ark, floating on top.

FULFORD: What happened was that the technology had control of the CRTC, rather than the CRTC having control of the technology.

FRYE: The technology took the bit in its teeth, and there wasn't much that any government regulatory agency could do about it.

FULFORD: Cable made all this American programming available, the people gobbled it up, and nothing you could have done would have changed that.

FRYE: I don't think that anything could really have changed that. But there will be other technological developments in Canada that will again regionalize things, and bring smaller communities into focus.

FULFORD: Then you see the development of a more sophisticated form of television which will encourage a more sophisticated form of culture, namely regionalism.

FRYE: I think it's inevitable that as any medium matures it tends to become more directly an expression of human beings, rather than an expression of mass formulae.

FULFORD: Certainly we can see that with phonograph records. There was a period when there were about four record companies in North America, and they put out a few records every week, and everyone in North America was expected to know about those records and hear them. Then, as the industry became more sophisticated with the development of the LP and cheaper means of pressing, the process became much more sophisticated. In that case, regionalism could express itself through phonograph records. Indeed very sophisticated kinds of culture can express themselves through that medium, while at the same time the million-seller, the gold record and so on reach the mass market. The technology has made possible hundreds of other forms of expression. But I'm interested in pursuing your idea that as culture becomes more sophisticated it also becomes more local or regional. It seems to me that's the opposite of many people's view of culture. Those people see big cities and the development of communication as making it possible to centralize culture.

FRYE: I see increasing regionalism as a way of the creative mind escaping from a centralizing uniformity. I was in New Zealand recently, and in Guyana for a week, and I looked into the literature of New Zealand and of the Caribbean, and I noticed intense regionalism alongside certain ways of handling time and space and characterization which reminded me strikingly of what I've seen in Canadian as well as British and American literature. I think we can take the centralizing aspect of contemporary culture for granted. But it's at that point that the growth towards more and more regionalism begins. If you get on a jet plane, you can't expect a different culture in the place where the plane lands, but you will find different people, and the creative people will be aware of the differences.

FULFORD: In other words, if you go to Guyana you may find as you glance around first of all that everyone watches American television, or American films, but then you will also find an intense local expression.

FRYE: Yes. Although Guyana is not really a clear example, because they don't get American television. But if they did, it would be the same thing as you have here: the mass response is for the mass culture, but within that, little creative pockets form.

FULFORD: I saw an Australian film last year, *Newsfront*, about people working in newsreels in Melbourne — and it was astoundingly like Toronto. People I've known for twenty years were in that film, except they were speaking with an Australian accent and had different faces. They were the same people with the same attitudes and the same views and the same resentment of Los Angeles and the same hope — to create something uniquely their own. That feeling of resistance towards a distant metropolis which is really in control of mass culture came through very strongly.

FRYE: Yes, that's part of the general uniformity of attitude, I think.

FULFORD: A curious thing has happened in a field which I take a special interest in, and that's making films for theatrical distribution. It seems to me that Canada has actually stepped back from the position it held, very shakily, a decade ago, before the Canadian Film Development Corporation came along. The Quebec films of the 1960s were quite interesting, and they had audiences, and I think they'll always be looked at as something important about that period. And there were a few films from English Canada around that period which were interesting too. But we had nothing then that most people would call a film industry. Now we have, but we've gone backwards, because we're not making *Canadian* movies any more. In a curious way the government has helped to set up an imitation Hollywood in Canada. We're making movies that almost no one, even the producers, would claim have anything to do with Canada. Work has been provided for some people. That's about all that can be said for it.

FRYE: Well, I think there's a powerful undertow in both film and television which follows the centralizing political and economic rhythms of the country rather than the decentralizing cultural rhythms. Certainly that undertow has been very evident in both film and television in Canada. The CRTC Canadian content regulations look rather unreal now. And yet I think that the tendency which is built into the technology and into the quality of response has to work itself out, and one shouldn't be too discouraged by finding that these media from time to time relapse into commercial formulas and mass productivity.

FULFORD: In a curious way, what has happened in the Canadian film industry is that it's become an inferior Hollywood. It hasn't developed that edge of creativity which you see in a number of current American filmmakers such as Coppola and Altman. Nothing of that kind has happened in the Canadian context. It's all been imitative, and imitating something that someone saw four years ago.

FRYE: A great many people make the same remark about Canadian television. They would say that it is bad American television and that the best American television is far better.

FULFORD: The matter of films and television opens up the larger question of the Americanization of Canada. Some people believe that only a tiny number of Canadians are touched by anything that could be called Canadian culture. And almost everyone in the country has now been submerged by American culture.

FRYE: The phenomenon that we call mass culture is uniform in the United States and English Canada. I'm not greatly worried about what is called the Americanization of Canada. What people mean when they speak of Americanization has been just as lethal to American culture as it has been to Canadian culture. It's a kind of levelling down which I think every concerned citizen of democracy should fight, whether he is a Canadian or an American.

FULFORD: And yet there is a choice between American and Canadian culture in some areas. For instance, I remember a friend who was teaching in a community college in southwestern Ontario when the War Measures Act was brought in, who discovered that most of what his students knew about the War Measures Act they knew from what Walter Cronkite told them. The fact is that Walter Cronkite, and those broadcasts, are an expression of America, even though it may be a levelled America. And so are movies. Movies can be good or bad expressions of America. They can be levelling, or they can be defining, but they *are* America. And they leave out the reality of Canada.

FRYE: I think that to the extent that they become *genuine* American cultural products, they tend more and more to speak for a smaller community than the United States of America. While Faulkner is not a part of American *mass* culture, he is a very articulate expression of American culture. But the American part is an inference from what he tells you about his corner of America.

FULFORD: Paradoxically, although I'm as worried as anyone about the phenomena we've been discussing, the curious thing is that the Canadians I know are much more Canadian today than they were twenty-five years ago. By Canadian I mean sophisticated to some extent about the different parts of Canada, interested and so on. For instance, my daughter's friends and the students I encounter when I go out to teach, and the young people who come into my office — they know vastly more about Newfoundland, or Alberta, or Quebec than I did when I was eighteen or twenty or twenty-five in Toronto. Something has happened, and I think it's television. Television has worked for a lot of these people.

FRYE: Television does have a profoundly civilizing aspect in that it compels people to look like people. I think of what an abstract notion I had of Eskimos when I was a student at school, or even college, and how that simply disappeared as soon as one began seeing them on television.

FULFORD: You have to accept René Lévesque as a human being when you see him three times a week on the eleven o'clock news.

FRYE: You have to start whittling away your stereotypes.

FULFORD: When the 1970s began we had a crisis in the publishing business which led to a great deal of government activity.

Ryerson Press was purchased by an American firm, McGraw-Hill. The Ontario government appointed a Royal Commission. The Canada Council threw itself into a frenzy of activity. The Secretary of State made various moves. And a publishing community of a kind was created. What's been the result of that? Has it affected you? Has it changed what you're reading in any way?

FRYE: I'm not sure that it has, really. The publishing and selling of books is an economic enterprise; it follows economic rhythms, rather than strictly cultural ones. It didn't worry me too much that certain publishers in Canada were British, like Macmillan and Oxford, because they were working very hard and conscientiously to produce Canadian books. I regret the kind of nationalism that defines a Canadian publisher in artificial terms. A certain amount of takeover is almost inevitable, given the economic conditions. Canadian authors in the meantime seem to continue to get published. And it doesn't worry me too much if a roomful of Canadian schoolchildren is asked who the Prime Minister of Canada is and say Jimmy Carter. What interests me is that Jimmy Carter is reading Peggy Atwood. The growth of Canada as a distinctive presence in the world scene is something that's also going on.

FULFORD: The idea that in Italy and elsewhere there are courses in Canadian literature would have seemed outlandish ten or fifteen years ago. How do you explain that? Is Canada becoming exotic in some way?

FRYE: It's partly that, but I think too it's the maturing of a culture. An immature culture imports its culture. So long as Canada was a colony, the works of British and American literature were brought out to the boondocks and people tried to imitate them. But as a culture matures, it becomes a native manufacture, and eventually it's an export. Canada is now producing a literature which has an imaginative integrity to other countries. I was talking with a professor at the University of Bordeaux who spoke eloquently about Canadian literature as the expression of a people finding its own voice. I assumed he meant French-Canadian literature, but he didn't. He meant English-Canadian writers like Margaret Laurence and Timothy Findley and Jack Hodgins — writers working within a region.

CAROL SHIELDS

Dolls, Dolls, Dolls, Dolls

Dolls. Roberta has written me a long letter about dolls, or more specifically about a doll factory she visited when she and Tom were in Japan.

"Ha," my husband says, reading her letter and pulling a face, "another pilgrimage to the heart's interior." He can hardly bring himself to read Roberta's letters anymore, though they come addressed to the two of us; there is a breathlessness about her letters that makes him squirm, a seeking, suffering openness which I suspect he finds grotesque in a woman of Roberta's age. Forty-eight, an uneasy age. And Roberta has never been what the world calls an easy woman. She is one of my oldest friends, and the heart of her problem, as I see it, is that she is incredulous, still, that the colour and imagination of our childhood should have come to rest in nothing at all but these lengthy monochrome business trips with her husband, a man called Tom O'Brien; but that is neither here nor there.

In this letter from Japan she describes a curious mystical experience which caused her not exactly panic and not precisely pleasure, but which connected her for an instant with an area of original sensation, a rare enough event at our age. She also unwittingly stepped into one of my previously undeclared beliefs. Which is that dolls, dolls of all kinds — those strung together parcels of wood or plastic or cloth or whatever — possess a measure of energy beyond their simple substance, something half-willed and half-alive.

Roberta writes that Tokyo was packed with tourists; the weather was hot and humid, and she decided to join a touring

16

party on a day's outing in the countryside — Tom was tied up in meetings. As per usual, Roberta writes.

They were taken by air-conditioned bus to a village where ninety percent — the guide repeated this statistic vigorously — where ninety percent of all the dolls in Japan were made. "It's a major industry here," Roberta says, and some of the dolls were still manufactured almost entirely by hand in a kind of cottage industry system. One house in the village, for example, made nothing but arms and legs, another the bodies; another dressed the naked doll bodies in stiff kimonos of real silk and attached such objects as fans and birds to the tiny laquered female fingers.

Roberta's party was brought to a small house in the middle of the village where the heads of geisha dolls were made. Just the heads and nothing else. After leaving their shoes in a small darkened foyer, they were led into a surprisingly wide, matted workroom which was cooled by slow-moving overhead fans. The air, Roberta writes, was musty from the mingled straw and dust, but the light from a row of latticed windows was softly opalescent, a distinctly mild, non-industrial quality of light, clean-focused and just touched with the egg-yellow of sunlight.

Here in the workroom nine or ten Japanese women knelt in a circle on the floor. They nodded quickly and repeatedly in the direction of the tourists, and smiled in a half-shy, half-neighbourly manner; they never, Roberta writes, stopped working for a second.

The head-making operation was explained by the guide who was a short and peppy Japanese with soft cheeks and a sharp arfing way of speaking English. First, he informed them, the very finest sawdust of a rare Japanese tree was taken and mixed with an equal solution of the purest rice paste. (Roberta writes that he rose up on his toes when he reached the words *finest* and *purest* as though paying tribute to the god of superlatives.) This dough-like material was then pressed into wooden molds of great antiquity (another toe rising here) and allowed to dry very slowly over a period of days. Then it was removed and painted; ten separate and exquisitely thin coats of enamel were applied, so that the resulting form, with only an elegant nose breaking the white egg surface, arrived at the weight and feel and coolness of porcelain.

The tourists, hulking, Western, flat-footed in their bare feet, watched as the tiny white doll heads were passed around the circle of workers. The first woman, working with tweezers and glue, applied the eyes, pressing them into place with a small wooden stick. A second woman painted in the fine red shape of a mouth, and handed the head on to a woman who applied to the centre of the mouth a set of chaste and tiny teeth. Other women touched the eyes with shadow, the cheeks with bloom, the bones with highlight, so that the flattened oval took on the relief and contours of sculptured form. "Lovely," Roberta says in her letter, "a miracle of delicacy."

And finally the hair. Before the war, the guide told them, real hair had been used, human hair. Nowadays a very fine quality of blue-black nylon was employed. The doll's skull was cunningly separated into two sections so that the hair could be firmly, permanently rooted from the inside. Then the head was sealed again, and the hair arranging began. The two women who performed this final step used real combs and brushes, pulling the hair smoothly over their hands so that every strand was in alignment, and then they shaped it, tenderly, deftly, with quick little strokes, into the intricate knots and coils of traditional geisha hair dressing.

Finally, at the end of this circular production line, the guide held up a finished head and propagandized briefly in his sharp gingery lordly little voice about the amount of time that went into making a head, the degree of skill, the years of apprenticeship. Notice the perfection of the finished product, he instructed. Observe the delicacy, mark the detailing. And then, because Roberta was standing closest to him, he placed the head in her hands for a final inspection.

And that was the moment Roberta was really writing me about. The finished head in her hands, with its staring eyes and its painted veil of composure and its feminine, almost erotic crown of hair, had more than the weight of artifact about it. Instinctively Roberta's hands had cupped the head into a laced cradle, protective and cherishing. There was something *alive* about the head.

An instant later she knew she had over-reacted. "Tom always says I make too much of nothing," she apologizes. The head hadn't moved in her hands; there had been no sensation of pulse or breath, no shimmer of aura, no electrical charge, nothing. Her eyes went to the women who had created this little head. They smiled, bowed, whispered, miming a busy humility, but their cool waiting eyes informed her that they knew exactly what she was feeling.

What she *had* felt was a stirring apprehension of possibility. It was more than mere animism; the life, or whatever it was that had been brought into being by those industriously toiling women, seemed to Roberta to be deliberate and to fulfill some unstated law of necessity.

She ends her letter more or less the way she ends all her letters these days: with a statement which is really a question. "I don't suppose," she says, "that you'll understand any of this."

Dolls, dolls, dolls, dolls. Once — I forget why — I wrote those words on a piece of paper, and instantly they swam into incomprehension, becoming meaningless ruffles of ink, squiggles from a comic strip. Was it a Christmas wish list I was making? I doubt it; as a child I would have been shocked had I received more than one doll in a single year, the idea was unworthy, it was *unnatural*. I could not even imagine it.

Every year from the time I was born until the year I was ten I was given a doll. It was one of the certainties of life, a portion of a large, enclosing certainty in which all the jumble of childhood lay. It now seems a long way back to those particular inalterable surfaces: the vast and incomprehensible war; Miss Newbury with her ivory coloured teeth who was principal of Lord Durham Public School; Euclid Avenue where we lived in a brown house with a glassed-in front porch; the seasons with their splendours and terrors curving endlessly around the middle eye of the world which I shared with my sister and my mother and father.

Almost Christmas: there they would be, my mother and father at the kitchen table on a Saturday morning in early December, drinking drip coffee and making lists. There would come a succession of dark, chilly pre-Christmas afternoons in which the air would grow rich with frost and longing, and on one of those afternoons our mother would take the bus downtown to buy the Christmas dolls for my sister and me.

She loved buying the Christmas dolls, the annual rite of choosing. It's the faces, she used to say, that matter, those dear molded faces. She would be swept away by a pitch of sweetness in the pouting lips, liveliness and colour in the lashed eyes, or a line of tenderness in the tinted cheeks — "The minute I laid eyes on that fact," she would say, helplessly shaking her head in a way she had, "I just went and fell head over heels."

We never, of course, went with her on these shopping trips, but I can see how it must have been: Mother in her claret-wine coat with the black squirrel collar, bending over, peering into glass cases in the red carpeted toy department, and searching in the hundreds of stiff smiling faces for a flicker of response, an indication of some kind that this doll, this particular doll, was destined for us. Then the pondering over price and value — she always spent more than she intended — having just one last look around, and finally, yes, she would make up her mind.

She must also have bought on these late afternoon shopping excursions Monopoly sets and dominoes and sewing cards, but these things would have been carried home in a different spirit, for it seems inconceivable for the dolls, our Christmas dolls, to be boxed and jammed into shopping bags with ordinary toys; they must have been carefully wrapped — she would have insisted on double layers of tissue paper — and she would have held them in her arms, crackling in their wrappings, all the way home, persuaded already, as we would later be persuaded, in the reality of their small beating hearts. What kind of mother was this with her easy belief, her adherence to seasonal ritual? (She also canned peaches the last week in August, fifty quarts, each peach half turned with a fork so that the curve, round as a baby's cheek, gleamed lustrous through the blue glass. Why did she do that — go to all that trouble? I have no idea, not even the seed of an idea.)

The people in our neighbourhood on Euclid Avenue, the real and continuing people, the Browns, the McArthurs, the Sheas, the Callahans, lived as we did, in houses, but at the end of our block was a large yellow brick building, always referred to by us as The Apartments. The Apartments, frilled at the back with iron fire escapes and the front of the building solid with its waxed brown foyer, its brass mail boxes and nameplates, its important but temporary air. (These people only rent, our father had told us.) The children who lived in The Apartments were always a little alien; it was hard for us to believe in the real existence of children who lacked backyards of their own, children who had no fruit cellars filled with pickles and peaches. Furthermore these families always seemed to be moving on after a year or so, so that we never got to know them well. But on at least one occasion I remember that we were invited there to a birthday party given by a little round-faced girl, an only child named Nanette.

It was a party flowing with new pleasures. Frilled nutcups at each place. A square bakery cake with shells chasing each other around the edges. But the prizes for the games we played — Pin the Tail on the Donkey, Musical Chairs — were manipulated so that every child received one — was that fair? — and these prizes were too expensive, overwhelming completely the boxed handkerchiefs and hair ribbons we'd brought along as gifts. But most shocking of all was the present that Nanette received from her beaming parents.

We sat in the apartment under the light of a bridge lamp, a circle of little girls on the living room rug, watching while the enormous box was untied. Inside was a doll.

What kind of doll it was I don't recall except that her bronzed hair gleamed with a richness that was more than visual; what I do remember was the affection with which she was lifted from her wrappings of paper and pressed to Nanette's smocked bodice, how she was tipped reverently backwards so that her eyes clicked shut, how she was rocked to and fro, murmured over, greeted, kissed, christened. It was as though Nanette had no idea of the inappropriateness of this gift. A doll could only begin her life at Christmas; was it the rigidities of my family that dictated this belief, or some obscure and unconscious approximation to the facts of gestation? A birthday doll, it seemed to me then, constituted a violation of the order of things, and it went without saying that the worth of all dolls was diminished as a result.

Still, there sat Nanette, rocking back and forth in her spun rayon dress, stroking the doll's stiff wartime curls and never dreaming that she had been swindled. Poor Nanette, there could be no heartbeat in that doll's misplaced body, it was not possible. I felt a twist of pity, probably my first, a novel emotion, a bony hand yanking at my heart, an emotion oddly akin — I see it clearly enough now — to envy.

In the suburbs of Paris is one of the finest archeological museums in Europe — my husband had talked, ever since I'd known him, about going there. The French, a frugal people, like to make use of their ancient structures, and this particular museum is housed inside a thirteenth century castle. The castle, if you block out the hundreds of surrounding villas and accacia-lined streets, looks much as it must always have looked, a bulky structure of golden stone with blank, primitive, upswept walls and three round brutish towers whose massiveness might be a metaphor for that rough age which equated masonry with power.

The interior of this crude stone shell has been transformed by the Ministry of Culture into a purring, beige-toned shrine to modernism, hived with climate controlled rooms and corridors, costly showcases and thousands of artifacts, subtly lit, lovingly identified. The *pièce de resistance* is the ancient banqueting hall where today there can be seen a wax reconstruction of pre-Frankish family life; here in this room a number of small, dark, hairy manikins squat naked around a cleverly simulated fire. The juxtaposition of time — ancient, medieval and modern — affected us powerfully; my husband and young daughter and I stared for some time at this strange tableau, trying to reconcile these ragged eaters of roots with the sleek, meaty, well-clothed Parisians we'd seen earlier that day shopping on the rue Victor Hugo.

We spent most of an afternoon in the museum looking at elegantly mounted pottery fragments and tiny vessels, clumsily formed from cloudy glass. There was something restorative about seeing French art at this untutored level, something innocent and humanizing in the simple requirement for domestic craft. The Louvre had exhausted us to the glitter of high style and finish, and at the castle we felt as though the French had allowed a glimpse of their coarser, more likeable selves.

"Look at that," my husband said, pointing to a case which held a number of tiny clay figures, thousands of years old. We looked. Some of them were missing arms, and few were missing their heads, but the bodily form was unmistakable.

"They're icons," my husband said, translating the display card. "From the pre-Christian era."

"Icons?" our daughter asked, puzzled. She was seven that summer.

"Like little gods. People in those days worshipped gods made of clay or stone."

"How do you know?" she asked him.

"Because it says so," he told her. "*Icone*. That's the French word for icon. It's really the same as our word."

"Maybe they're dolls," she said.

"No. It says right here. Look. In those days people were all pagans and they worshipped idols. Little statues like these. They sort of held them in their hands or carried them with them when they went hunting or when they went to war."

"They could be dolls," she said slowly.

He began to explain again. "All the early cultures — "

She was looking at the figures, her open hand resting lightly on the glass case. "They look like dolls."

For a minute I thought he was going to go on protesting. His lips moved, taking the necessary shape. He lifted his hand to point once again at the case. I felt sick with sudden inexplicable anger.

Then he turned to our daughter, shrugged, smiled, put his hands in his pocket. He looked young, twenty-five, or even younger. "Who knows," he said to her. "You might be right. Who knows."

My sister lives three hundred miles away in Ohio, and these days I see her only two or three times a year, usually for family gatherings on long weekends. These visits tend to be noisy and clamorous; between us we have two husbands and six children, and then there is the flurry of cooking and cleaning up after enormous holiday meals. There is never enough time to do what she and I love to do most which is to sit at the kitchen table — hers or mine, they are interchangeable — with mugs of tea before us and to reconstruct, frame by frame, the scenes of our childhood.

My memory is sharper than hers, so that in these discussions, though I'm two years younger, I tend to lead while she follows. (Sometimes I long for a share of her forgetfulness, her leisured shrugging acceptance of past events. My own recollections, not all happy, are relentlessly present, kept stashed away like ingots, testifying to a peculiar imprisoning muscularity of recall.) The last time she came — early October — we talked about the dolls we used to be given every Christmas. Our husbands and children listened, jealously it seemed to me, at the sidelines, the husbands bemused by this ordering of trivia, the children open-mouthed, disbelieving.

I asked my sister if she remembered how our dolls were presented to us, exactly the way real children are presented, the baby dolls asleep in stenciled cradles or wrapped in receiving blankets; and the schoolgirl dolls propped up by the Christmas tree, posed just so, smiling brilliantly and fingering the lower branches with their shapely curved hands; we always loved them on sight.

"Remember Nancy Lynn," my sister said; she was taking the lead this time. Nancy Lynn had been one of mine, one of the early dolls, a large cheerful baby doll with a body of cloth, and arms and legs of painted plaster. Her swirled brown hair was painted on, and at one point in her long life she took a hard knock on the head, carrying forever after a square chip of white at the scalp. To spare her shame we kept her lacy bonnet tied on day and night. (Our children, listening, howled at this delicacy.)

One wartime Christmas we were given our twin dolls Shirley and Helen. The twins were small and hollow and made of genuine rubber, difficult to come by in those years of shortages, and they could actually be fed water from a little bottle. They were also capable of wetting themselves through tiny holes punched in their rubber buttocks; the vulnerability of this bodily process enormously enlarged our love for them. There was also Barbara the Magic Skin Doll, wonderfully pliable at first, though later her flesh peeled away in strips. There was a Raggedy Ann, not to our minds a real doll, but a cloth stuffed hybrid of good disposition. There was Brenda, named for her red hair, and Betty with jointed knees and a brave little tartan skirt. There was Susan — her full name was Brown-Eyed Susan — my last doll, only I didn't know it then.

My sister and I committed the usual sins, leaving our dolls in their pajamas for days on end, and then, with a rush of shame and love, scooping them up and trying to make amends by telescoping weeks and even years into a Saturday afternoon. Our fiercely loved dolls were left out in the rain. We always lost their shoes after the first month; their toes broke off almost invariably. We sometimes picked them up by the arm or even the hair, but we never disowned them or gave them away or changed their names, and we never buried them in ghoulish backyard funerals as the children in our English stories seemed to do. We never completely forgot that we loved them.

Our mother loved them too. What was it that stirred her frantic devotion? — some failure of ours? — some insufficiency in our household? She spent hours making elaborate wardrobes for them; both my sister and I can remember the time she made Brenda a velvet cape trimmed with scraps of fur from her old squirrel collar. Sometimes she helped us give them names, Patsy, Gloria, Merry Lu, Olivia.

"And the drawer," my sister said. "Remember the drawer."

"What drawer?" I asked.

"You remember the drawer. In our dresser? That little drawer on the left hand side, the second one down."

"What about it?" I asked slowly.

"Well, don't you remember? Sure you do. That's where our dolls used to sleep. Remember how Mother lined it with a doll blanket?"

"No," I said.

"She thumbtacked it all around. So it was completely lined. That's where Shirley and Helen used to sleep."

"Are you sure?"

"Absolutely."

I remind her of the little maple doll cribs we had.

"That was later," she said.

I find it hard to believe that I've forgotten about this, especially this. A drawer lined with a blanket; that was exactly the kind of thing I remembered.

But my sister still has the old dresser in the attic of her house. And she told me that the blanket is still tacked in place; she hasn't been able to bring herself to remove it. "When you come at Christmas," she said, "I'll show it to you."

"What colour is it?" I asked.

"Pink. Pink with white flowers. Of course it's filthy now and falling apart."

I shook my head. A pink blanket with white flowers. I have no memory of such a blanket.

Perhaps at Christmas, when I actually look at the drawer myself, it will all come flooding back. The sight of it may unlock what I surely have stored away somewhere in my head, part of the collocation of images which has always seemed so accessible and true. The fleecy pink drawer, the dark night, Shirley and Helen side by side, goodnight, goodnight as we shut them away. Don't let the bedbugs bite. Oh, oh.

It happened that in the city where I grew up a little girl was murdered. She was ten years old, my age.

It was a terrible murder. The killer had entered her bedroom window while she was sleeping. He had stabbed her through the heart; he cut off her head and her arms and her legs. Some of these pieces were never found.

It would have been impossible not to know about this murder; the name of the dead girl was known to everyone, and even today I have only to think the syllables of her name and the whole undertow of terror doubles back on me. This killer was a madman, a maniac who left notes written in lipstick on city walls, begging the police to come and find him; he couldn't help himself; he was desperate; he threatened to strike again.

Roberta Callahan and JoAnn Brown and I, all of us ten years old, organized ourselves into a detective club and determined to catch the killer. We never played with dolls anymore. The Christmas before, for the first time, there had been no doll under the tree; instead I had been given a wristwatch. My mother had sighed, first my sister, now me.

Dolls which had once formed the centre of my imagination now seemed part of an exceedingly soft and sissified past, something I used to do before I got big. I had wedged Nancy Lynn and Brown-Eyed Susan and Brenda and Shirley and all the others onto a shelf at the back of my closet, and now my room was filled with pictures of horses and baseball stickers and collections of bird nests. Rough things, rugged things, rough things.

For Roberta Callahan and JoAnn Brown and I desired, above all else, to be tough. I don't remember how it started, this longing for toughness. Perhaps it was our approaching but undreamt of puberty. Or the ebbing of parental supervision and certain possibilities of freedom which went with it.

Roberta was a dreamy girl who loved animals better than human beings; she had seen *Bambi* seven times and was always drawing pictures of spotted fawns. JoAnn Brown was short and wiry and wore glasses and could stand any amount of pain; the winter before she had been hospitalized with double pneumonia. *Double pneumonia*. "But I had the will to live," she told us solemnly. The three of us were invited to play commandoes with the boys on the block, and once the commando leader Terry Shea told another boy, in my hearing, that for a girl I was tough as nails. *Tough as nails*. It did not seem wildly improbably to JoAnn and Roberta and me that we should be the capturers of the crazed killer. Nancy Drew stalked criminals. why not us?

In JoAnn Brown's house there was a spare room, and in the spare room there was a closet. That closet became the secret headquarters for the detective club. We had a desk which was a cardboard carton turned upside down, and there, sitting on the floor with Mr. Brown's flashlight and stacks of saltines, we studied all the newspaper clippings we could find. We discussed and theorized; where did the killer hide out? When and where would he strike again? Always behind our plotting and planning lay certain thoughts of honour and reward, the astonishment of our parents when they discovered that we had been the ones who had led the police to the killer's hideout, that we had supplied the missing clue; how amazed they would be, they who all summer supposed that their daughters were merely playing, believing that we were children, girls, that we were powerless.

We emerged from these tenebrous closet meetings dazed with heat and determination, and then we would take to the streets. All that summer we followed suspicious looking men. Short men. Swarthy men. Men with facial scars or crossed eyes. One day we sighted a small dark man, a dwarf in fact, carrying over his shoulder a large cloth sack. A body? — perhaps the body of a child. We followed him for an hour, and when he disappeared into an electrical supply shop, JoAnn made careful note of the address and the time of entry.

Back in the closet we discussed what we should do. Should we send a letter to the police? Or should we make our way back to the shop and keep watch?

Roberta said she would be too frightened to go back.

"Well, I'll go then," I spoke bravely.

Bravely, yes, I spoke with thrilling courage. But the truth was this: I was for all of that summer desperately ill with fear. The instant I was put to bed at night my second floor bedroom became a cave of pure sweating terror. Atoms of fear conjoined in a solid wall of darkness, pinning me down as I lay paralyzed in the middle of my bed; even to touch the edges of the mattress would be to invite unspeakable violence. The window, softly curtained with dotted swiss, became the focus of my desperate hour-by-hour attention. If I shut my eyes for even an instant, he, the killer, the maniac, would seize that moment to enter and stab me through the heart. I could hear the sound of the knife entering my chest, a wet, injurious, cataclysmic plunge.

It was the same every night: leaves playing on the window pane, adumbration, darkness, the swift transition from neighbourhood heroine, the girl known to be tough as nails, the girl who was on the trail of a murderer, to this, this shallow-breathing, rigidly sleepless coward.

Every night my mother, cheerful, baffled, innocent as she said good night, would remark, "Beats me how you can sleep in a room with the window closed." Proving how removed she was from my state of suffering, how little she perceived my nightly ordeal.

I could so easily have told her that I was afraid; she would have understood, she would have rocked me in her arms, bought me a night light at Woolworths, explained how groundless my fears really were, she would have poured assurance and comfort on me, and ironically, I knew that her comfort would have brought release.

But it was comfort I couldn't afford; at the risk of my life I had to go on as I was; to confess fear to anyone at all would have been to surrender the tough new self which had begun to grow inside me, the self I had created and now couldn't do without.

Then, almost accidentally, I was rescued. It was not my mother who rescued me, but my old doll, Nancy Lynn. I had a glimpse of her one morning in my closet, a plaster arm poking out at me. I pulled her down. She still wore the lacy bonnet on her chipped head, grey with dirt and the ribbons shredded. She had no clothes, only her soft soiled mattressy body and the flattened joints where the arms and legs were attached. After all these years her eyes still opened and shut, and her eyelids were a bright youthful pink in contrast to the darkened skin tone of her face.

That night she slept with me under the sheet, and malevolence drained like magic from the darkened room; the night pressed friendly and familiar through the dotted swiss curtains; the Callahan's fox terrier yapped at the streaky moon. I opened the window and could hear a breeze loosened in the elms. In bed Nancy Lynn's cold plaster toes poked reassuringly at my side. Her cloth body with its soiled cottony fragrance lay against my bare arm. The powerful pink eyelids were inexpressibly at rest. All night, while I slept, she kept me alive.

For as long as I needed her — I don't remember whether it was weeks or months before the killer was caught — she guarded me at night. The detective club became over a period of time a Gene Autry Fan Club, then a Perry Como Record Club, and there must have been a day when Nancy Lynn went back to her closet. And probably, though I don't like to think of it, a day when she and the others fell victim to a particularly heavy spree of spring cleaning.

There seems no sense to it. Even on the night I first put her on the pillow beside me I knew she was lifeless, knew there was no heart fluttering in her soft chest and no bravery in her hollow head. None of it was real, none of it.

Only her power to protect me. Human love, I saw, could not always be relied upon. There would be times when I would have to settle for a kind of parallel love, an extension of my hidden self, hidden even from me. It would have to do; it would be a great deal better than nothing, I saw. It was something to be thankful for.

BILL HOWELL

Prettyoungirl

1

Alone but watching each other
with guarded Victorian amazement
on the ferry deck back
to Halifax from Dartmouth, both of us
pretending we've never been hit
by lightning, the fresh dress
her shape of young wind
billowing into dusk. . . .

2

If I were a friendly footnote
in a world of footprint beaches
I'd wade below her waterline
and swim through all her speeches. . . .

3

She's undoubtedly perceived I'm a poet
(I have that special way of allowing zephyrs
to flutter my cowlick), and maybe
I can kind of throw myself over
that churning stern there
with the offhand hope that she
just happens to be a lifeguard and
her dress drips dry. . . .

4

Love is a conspiracy
invented by poets:

"Pardon me, but do you know
the way to Atlantis?"

"Yes, but I think we'll need
a better line than that
to get there. . . ."

5

I could begin again, I suppose
by comparing her to almost
anything — to a shiver of electrons

like phonelines in spring rain,
or a bridge like a ship so huge
it's docked at either shore.
                              But
ladies invent their own excellence
as they grow into the firsthand words
they choose to hear. . . .

6

If I were an Admiral I'd
invite her to my quarters for
dry sherry and tell her she'd
make a lovely mermaid.
                        And would she
like to become my coat-of-arms. . . .

7

I have amnesia, see, and she
is the first person in seven years
I can maybe recognize, and

does she have a longlost
brother or lover?
                    But she just might
turn out to be my third cousin
twice removed. . . .

8

"Okay, this is the Revolution.
You take this water pistol and tell
everyone to swim for their lives and
I'll overpower the bridge with this
glint in my eye, and then we'll run
with the wind to Tahiti, okay?"
                              "Okay, but
check the food and fuel supplies first. . . . "

9

ATTENTION FEMALE EARTHLINGETTE!!!
I AM KRYXINON, FROM ABSTRACTIONOXYS!!!
THIS FERRYBOAT HAS SUDDENLY BECOME
AN ANTI-GRAVITY TRANSPORTATION AND
COMMUNICATIONS DEVICE BASED UPON
THE PRINCIPLE THAT MAN IS OF THE SAME
ORDER OF MAGNITUDE LARGER THAN AN ELECTRON
AS HE IS SMALLER THAN THE UNIVERSE!!!
YOUR PLANET IS DOOMED!!! COME WITH ME
IMMEDIATELY TO NIRVANA AND BE SAVED!!!

Or at least as far as Clam Harbour Beach. . . .

10

"William," she says to me suddenly,
"it sure is fun, sometimes, being
married to a poet."

                    "Beverley,"
I tell her with an offhand grin, "you
sure look great in that dress."

MICHAEL COOK

The Island of Fire

At the stroke of midnight on the 15th February 1950 Patrick Pearse Coley was yanked kicking and screaming into the mid Twentieth Century. Beyond the immediate confines of Cuckold's Cove, the principal community of the Island of Fire, itself twelve miles across terrible water from the rocky Island of Newfoundland, the event did not appear to be of significance. At least, not for close to two and half decades. The Korean War was at its height. Harry Truman and Louis St Laurent both agreed that the war was a necessary evil and a boost to the economy. Joseph R. Smallwood, the Premier of Newfoundland, having led that ancient colony into Confederation with Canada only ten short months before this nativity, was already plotting to turn the Dominion's latest acquisition into the greatest industrialised nation on earth, adopting the brilliantly simple expedient of giving most of it away to rapacious global industries.

But, in Cuckold's Cove, these events were as nothing compared to the advent of the infant who (so the rumours ran like wildfire about the tiny frame houses bravely facing the Atlantic) had been born with so much black hair on its head that it had to have a haircut before it could be suckled at the breast of its proud mother. Who, it was whispered in the snug kitchens, had a set of parts (a euphemism much neglected nowadays in favour of coarser words) that would not have disgraced a horny teenager. Who, it was roared out in the taverns and the cabs of pick-up trucks and the dark doorways of collapsing fishing stages, looked absolutely nothing like poor Mary (a saint, that woman, a saint), and bore as much resemblance to Sean Coley, Mary's husband and the sup-

Chapter one of a novel in progress.

posed father of the child, as a trout to a whale. Could it be that the ancient prophecy was about to be fulfilled? Had indeed, been fulfilled?

Aunt Mary Ellen donned her crochet shawl, lit three more kerosene lamps, poured herself a cup of black tea from a black kettle that had been stewing on the wood stove for two hours, and shuffled her great weight to the table. She sat on the high backed Captain's chair that had once belonged to Skipper George, her much loved and much haunted husband who had left, despite her remonstrances, to cross to Sheep Island one All Hallow's Eve in the teeth of a force ten gale to pick up a gallon of moonshine (and some said, a sheep or two), and who had never been seen again. Only his favourite chair bumping, nuzzling against the green gray wharf the following morning gave an indication of his fate although some said, in the way of the island, that he had thrown the chair overboard and gone joyously on, out into the Atlantic, freed of his wife and her endless predictions forever.

And indeed Aunt Mary Ellen had never had a mass said for his drowned soul, if it was drowned, and since that day had never even mentioned his name, but that she remembered was manifest, for his chair was the only one she would sit on in the house and its round back, like the spokes of a ships wheel, was polished daily to such a depth that everything in the kitchen was reflected and distorted in mahogany eyes.

There was a murmuring outside the door.

The Eaton's Catalogue wallclock struck one.

The door opened.

One by one, wordlessly, the women of the community filed into the tiny kitchen until it seemed full of strange, misshapen figures cowled against the cold; shadows dancing on the walls like a medieval frieze made fluid in the spirit light.

There was Ida of the nine sons, embittered, so it was said, because none of them had been the awaited one; and Madeline the Fox with the strange eyes that could lure a man up her skirts faster than a gull could swallow a herring; and Eileen the gentle one to whom everyone sent their children when cut or bruised or burning with fever; and Therese, riddled with consumption, and Ruth, rotund as the great cabbages she nursed to gargantuan size on the heads, guts and sound bones of the gap-mouthed cod; and Aunt Lillian, eyes cataract white and rheumy, gone blind from searching for her man who ran out from under her downy arm one hot, long summer's day, ran up into the blazing barrens and disappeared, though she spent every bright day looking for his bones. There were others too, who do not concern us now, the last one of whom closed the porch door carefully, to keep the frost out, and then closed the kitchen door and latched it, to keep all others out — for others there would be but, like the foolish virgins, they had left it too late. And now all in that smoke blackened, tiny kitchen, as if at a signal, stared at Aunt Mary Ellen who in turn looked back at them, one by one and nodded a greeting, her eyes glittering, the black pupils contracting until they seemed to be tiny pools of unfathomable depth, of unspeakable knowledge.

She raised the cup to her lips and drank, slowly. The women waited. So often had they done this before: so often had they filed out as they had come, in silence — the silence of hope fomented into the bitter silence of disappointment. But on this occasion all the omens were right, the time, the hour, the brilliance of the constellations, the remarkable characteristics of the child — if Midwife Green were to be believed — and Ida said she had not been drinking, Ida, who of all people would be the first to discredit the story for reasons already stated.

The tea leaves lay scattered in the bottom of the cup, reflecting in their patterns the constellations of stars reflected in the unnaturally calm sea. Aunt Mary Ellen peered, shook the cup, waited for all motion to subside, peered again. She passed the cup to Madeline the Fox who shook the cup and handed it back. Once more, the moment of waiting for the turbulence to subside, once more the glittering eyes reading the leaves. The women watched, immobile.

Aunt Mary Ellen picked up the cup for the fourth time, held it dramatically against her breast, and then hurled it against the wall. It broke into a myriad pieces — fragments of china clung to the damp edges of trailing skirts.

"It is done," she said. "It is he."

In the Hell's Gate Motel Sean Coley was about to embark upon his thirteenth bottle of Harpoon Ale, a remarkable beer, made only in Newfoundland, distinguished more for its laxative than its alcoholic characteristics. The brewery responsible for Harpoon had been founded by a harassed doctor of Irish origins who had discovered, early in his practice of Medicine in Newfoundland that constipation, or, as it is affectionately known, the state of being hard bound, was the single biggest affliction suffered by a hardy race given to absorbing vast quantities of salt food and very little fruit. In desperation, after several months of dealing with such fundamental problems he surrendered his licence and, after a period in which he struggled with the morality of his decision — he was after all a practising if not a good Catholic — he entered into partnership with a senior Customs and Excise Officer, determined to solve the intestinal ailments of future generations whilst making a fortune at the same time. He was only partially succesful in the first part of his plan, wholly in the second. When occasionally smitten with pangs of conscience, as he rang the bell for the fifteen-year-old freckle-faced maid to bring him his brandy and *gin seng* in bed — a maid it should be said, whose boundless energy and enthusiasm was eventually to cause his untimely demise through overwork and exhaustion (he had made out his own death certificate a month before the occurrence) — he drew comfort from the work of E. J. Pratt, that giant literary figure who had risen to prominence by the simple expedient of selling alcoholic cough mixture to those same hardy, hard bound fishermen around the Bays whilst, at the same time piling up material to feed his creative genius for four decades.

Waiting for the maid, the good Doctor would sometimes lie back on his giant four poster bed and read aloud from Ned's (for in his own mind he had become familiar with him) work.

> I could not paint, nor could I draw
> The look that searched the night;
> The bleak refinement of the face I saw
> In lantern light. . . .

He would wonder whether he, in some small way through the side effects of Harpoon Ale had assisted in easing that look of bleak refinement which he knew, even if old Ned didn't, was caused solely and simply by constipation. The joyful advent of the maid already divested of undergarments, would put a stop to such reflections and one can only wonder had the panting ex-Doctor been more addicted to contemplation than concupiscence, what other exciting literary observations he might have made in the pursuit of the correlation between art and physical ailments. Gauguin's syphilis; Van Gogh's myopia, Chopin's consumption — the list is endless, but it is pointless to speculate. Sufficient to say that, though the Doctor was long deceased his life's work lived on, as events in the Hell's Gate Motel confirmed.

"I'm going to beat the shit out of her when I get home," said Sean.

One of the marked side effects of Harpoon was an increase in belligerance.

"Now Sean, ye can't do that. Poor Mary's done her duty to the Church and to yourself. We can ask no more." Father Gorman, in his secondary role of ecclesiastical barman, spoke gently to his parishioner.

"We!" Sean peered at the priest while assimilating the significance of the pronoun. A thought struck him. His voice rose to the level of outrage.

"And so, ye caperin' cleric, ye're the one who done it. I knowed darn well she were spending too much time in that confessional."

He snaked a brawny arm across the bar and seized the luckless Father Gorman by the throat. In a swiftly executed second movement he lifted him up off his feet, swung him over the bar and thumped him down in front of him. Father Gorman was five feet, four and a third inches, in his clerical boots. Sean Coley was six foot four inches in his socks. When Father Gorman turned sideways he resembled a rather neat, if ineffectual scarecrow. When Sean Coley turned sideways he looked like the side of a house.

"I never thought ye had one," said Sean, towering over the trembling priest. "And if ye have, I don't see how it could have done the job. But we'll soon find out."

So saying, he set about to turn the unhappy cleric upside down but, after a struggle was forcibly restrained by his drinking colleagues and neighbours, most of whom were — if not as big — as hardy as he. They were also enjoying the discomfiture of their friend, had actively encouraged it in the way of men when doubt is cast on the paternity of a child. Of course, in this case there wasn't anything, or anyone physically to get hold of, and even if they did half believe the ancient tale at times, at others they thought it was a bunch of old baloney perpetuated by old crones like Bridie Green or Aunt Mary Ellen up the hill. But Sean had been rising to the bait all night, and no opportunity for a laugh at another's expense was ever turned down in Cuckold's Cove.

"Leave the Father alone," said Pete, Sean's long time friend, fishing companion and drinking partner. "Ye've got it all wrong. The Father here's a good man. Take a look at him."

Sean surveyed the little priest with bleary eyes. Father Gorman, struggling to recover his dignity, stared back, like a fearful yet defiant sparrow.

"I'd go so far as to say," said Pete, winking at his companions, "that never an impure thought, let alone an impure deed has ever crossed his mind, or afflicted his mortal body. He's not like the rest of us."

"True enough Pete, that's true enough indeed, and may God have mercy on your soul. Last orders please."

Father Gorman skipped round behind the bar and began uncapping bottles of Harpoon faster than he could douse the candles at Benediction. He had often pondered the wisdom of running a bar next door to the church like this, but in truth, it was the only way to get these sleveens to contribute to the church upkeep at all, and the women grumbled if he kept ten per cent from the Bingo for day to day expenses and the parish was as poor as a church mouse to begin with. It was unfair. No. It was more than unfair — it was a burden, a cross for which he had not been prepared, and he yearned, often, for the reflective civilised and ordered life of the seminary. His predecessor, who had started it all, had told him that he would have to keep up the bar if he wanted to keep his parishioners' interest in the Church alive, a contradiction in terms but a necessary evil. But, Lord save us, he had no idea how hazardous it could be.

The other men were trying to keep that oaf Coley in order now, praise be to God. He'd been looking for a fight all night and they had goaded him on with tales of prophecies and damnable immaculate conceptions and other such blasphemies. He'd heard that old wive's tale of course, about the new Saviour of Newfoundland coming out of the East — out of Cuckold's Cove. It was ridiculous. If the story ever reached the main island of Newfoundland they'd be a laughing stock. And if it ever reached the Mainland. He shuddered. How could people be so primitive. Of course Sean Foley was the father of his child.

His trouble was that be was probably drunk when he assaulted — no no no — the Church didn't like that word — when he assailed poor Mary and that was that. And she good woman, probably praying all through the terrible experience.

He slammed the bottles on the bar.

"I said last orders, men." He tried to sound authorititive but Sean had dented his windpipe and the words came out in a squeak. Feeling beaten, he leant helplessly across the counter, and the thought flashed into his mind that he had chosen the wrong profession. The dreams of ritual and celebration and mystery and the respect that should be accorded a chosen servant of God were a far cry from this. He raised his eyes and at that moment thought he saw a shaft of light, a finger pointing at his heart and at once felt contrite. Ignoring the men he sank to his knees in a pool of beer in a moment of total submission and acceptance of his task, however humble.

Pete adjusted his lighter.

"The damn thing's always doing that" he said. "Like one o' they flame throwers."

The shaft of light died out on the bottle of dark rum and on Father Gorman but he was too wrapped up in prayer to notice.

Bridget, or Bridie Green as she was known, settled down in the rocking chair by the stove with a sign of satisfaction. In her hand was a glass of Sean Coley's moonshine, warmed with a little hot water, and made more readily digestible by a spoonful of sugar. By her side lay her handbag, a large bell shaped affair made from the hide of a luckless goat that just happened to fall in her well (so she said), stitched onto a frame made from the rib cage of the aforementioned goat. Into that bag went all the implements of her trade: in addition to the acceptable forceps, tweezers, shaving equipment, disinfectant, lint, swabs, swaddling bands, there was a large piece of dried seal meat, cut an inch round and six inches long for the labouring women to bite into as the pains became more severe, and an assortment of little jars filled with ointments and unguents of her own making from formulas which, if her great grandmother spoke true, had their origins in the days of the old Goddess Diana, which in turn were purified anew in the fires of St Bridget, her own namesake in the grove of the sacred oak in the ancient and holy land of Ireland. Nobody knew the ingredients, nobody dared ask, but it was known that at Midsummer's Eve, or St John's Eve as it used to be known, Bridie Green would lock the doors of her house and retire to the kitchen, there to spend many hours boiling up the brews which would make her a year's supply, and for weeks before that she could be seen cutting slips of alder and rown — though few knew that the dogberry boasted a history of magic older than Christianity — and tapping spruce and fir and juniper, and tucking young spotted frogs into the pockets of her billowing black skirts, and chasing butterflies across the barrens, arms outstretched. And when a man killed a sheep or a pig she would walk up to where the animal hung from its wooden cradle and wait for the entrails to be removed before she herself, without a word being said, would cut out the heart and the liver and make off again to her small pointed house on the hill.

And some, who went walking on St John's Eve with their lovers, and others, drawn by an ancient ritual beyond their understanding who just went to walk or bathe in the small lakes up on the barrens reported, on returning home, as the mist clung about the houses and the stars clashed overhead and the sea glowed with phospherous, some of these reported in whispers that they had heard a strange, high singing and looking up towards Bridie's house had seen a bulky figure capering wildly against the sky, naked as the day she was born, capering and occasionally rolling about the dew-wet grass like a young puppy smitten with the ecstasy of life.

Nobody spoke of these things to Bridie, and all agreed that whatever was in those jars could cure anything that could happen to a woman in labour and even if, on occasions, a cure was not effected it was generally agreed that the unfortunate occurrence was either the result of a marital misdemeanour or that God had an overwhelming desire to see the unfortunate woman or child at once, sometimes both together.

And thus Bridie sat at peace in the Coley kitchen, warmed by the shine and comforted by the knowledge that in her handbag lay the long black locks of the infant to be called Patrick Pearse, locks which she would dry carefully and then prise apart, strand by strand, before putting them individually into lockets she would make from the delicate shells extracted from the stomachs of plaice and flounder and sell to the women of Cuckold's Cove — the most potent, the most powerfull charm she had ever had the good fortune to come across.

For this was He. And at last, out of the bleak poverty of Cuckold's Cove, the rejection of its people by successive governments, the exploitation of its fishermen by generations of piratical merchants and, God forgive her but it needed to be said, the continued failure of Mother Church to send anyone but fools and nitwits to guide its flock — out of all this a hero who was destined to lead, not merely Cuckold's Cove, not merely Newfoundland, but this whole great nation of which, if Smallwood was correct, Cuckold's Cove itself was now a part. A hero in the old stamp, a veritable Cuchulain who even now, lay sulking on his mother's breast in the back room, delivered safely, without a hitch, by her own hands. She would be a surrogate mother to him. Why, what would poor Mary — a saint it was true but somewhat simple — what would poor Mary do with such a boy.

The latch was lifted on the outer door.

Bridie started from her reverie. Registered the sound of shuffling footsteps. Nodded. Drained her glass. Folded her arms and waited. The kitchen door opened softly. Led by Aunt Mary Ellen the women of the community, each one now bearing a gift — a loaf of bread, a pot of partridgeberry jam, a bottle of moose meat, a pot of turr soup, a salt cod, a limb of dried caribou, a smoked salmon, a birch junk, a net needle — each one filed in assured finally of their place in history. And the secret shone behind their eyes.

Mary, dozing, was woken by the sound of murmuring voices in the kitchen. Patrick lay asleep on her breast. Her first child. She tightened her arms about him and looked with wonder at his face — no bigger than a sunflower, the old man and the child clearly defined in the features, the future and the present one at the day of birth.

She put her hand down to her stomach, strangely flat, a little tender. For a moment, she felt a sharp pang of loss. She smiled. How foolish. And yet, not so foolish. The living seed protected within her, growing, she had felt whole and contented, had been aware of the blood singing in her veins, of the extraordinary clarity of water and sky, had felt the movement of the grasses beneath her feet and understood the joy of soaring birds. It was over too soon. Now the reality lay in her arms and to him was bequeathed the discovery of life. To her, the certainty of care, the assurance of loss. But not yet. The infant stirred and involuntarily his small, rubbery lips sucked at her breast. Blind, he blindly sucked. Her milk surged, bubbles appeared at his mouth. She marvelled at the strength of his suction, even as her distended stomach muscles cramped and contracted as he pulled.

The voices outside in the kitchen swelled. She could sense the tension and excitement in the sound. She knew why. Hadn't she seen, as in a dream, Old Bridie cutting the hair from her baby's head, mumbling incantations and crooning like an old witch. That's what she was surely, if a good soul. And hadn't she seen her sprinkling something over the poor infant's parts before she wrapped him in cloth and gave him to her to take to the breast. God knows, if she had felt stronger she would have protested, except that she knew Bridie meant no harm. It was all foolishness, this talk of the old tale and the child to be born in Cuckold's Cove who would become a giant among men, a hero, a leader. She remembered, as Sean sucked and pulled, a strange ecstasy creeping over her body, she remembered her grandmother telling her the story. Everyone knew. Everyone had passed it on it seemed, for generations. Why? She wondered. Perhaps it was because in a place where dreams were so few it was necessary to cling to the wisps of dreams without which men and women become strangers to each other and the little world God had chosen for them. The Church had always tried to suppress the tale — considered it blasphemous she supposed.

"Out of the sea," she could still hear her Grandmother's voice, half crooning as Mary brushed her hair by the stove before she went to bed: "Out of the sea, they say, one of the old ones with glittering eyes and arms strong as the wave and a mane of black hair blown like bladderwrack in the wind will come to the dreams of a pure woman in the Cove, and in her dreams he will lie with

her, and she will conceive and bring forth a great hero, and he will
be honoured amongst the men of all nations." It was the stuff to
fill a young girl's head full of romantic notions, but her Grandmother was no romantic as far as Mary was concerned. "Ach,"
she'd go on to say. "It won't happen to you child. You're too
simple. Too simple be far."

Mary had to agree. It wasn't that she thought simply she knew
that, although they didn't. In her head were songs and music and
books and thoughts they knew nothing of, but she couldn't speak
them. In fact, she spoke rarely at all, preferring to smile. And it
wasn't that she didn't understand the things they all understood
about sex — hadn't she always know how things grew and were
made fertile. But she did not understand what they talked about
with many a laugh and a poke in the ribs, or a groan or sometimes
even a curse.

When she had married Sean everyone had thought that he was
crazy — a great, brawling hulk of a man much given to riot and
considerable laughter even when things did not go well. She was
hardly a match for such a gale of masculinity, small, and quiet,
and — well, simple. But she knew what no one else knew about
him which was that at his core there was a terrified small boy who
knew less about growing things than she did, a boy who dared
only come out at night, when locked safely in her arms, one
scared of anything fragile like birds and grass and berries, and
yes, herself. And although she knew they didn't do it, as the
others called it, deliberately, consciously, at night or at morning
labouring over each other like the poor beasts of the field, she
knew also that when they were asleep, locked into each other, his
arms about her like some mighty oak tree, her legs twined about
him like ivy, then they were together, then they were one. Her
dreams were full of this and his also.

She looked at Patrick Pearse and laughed joyfully, and tickled
his sticky chin with her finger.

Of course this was their child.

And if Sean were a god of the sea, which he was during the day,
then he was her God at night also, and let the silly women believe
what they wanted. The only miracle was that Patrick was theirs.
The only prophecy one she had made Sean within days of their
marriage on St John's Eve two years ago. "I will give you a son."

Her instinct warned her that gossip and beer might make a dent in Sean's confidence, but only for a while. Intuitively, she knew that he would rage and bluster as the gossip mounted, and mount it would, for she had heard Old Bridie muttering about the promised one as she pushed for the last time, and she knew that in the kitchen full of women Bridie was showing them the hair she had cut from Patrick's forehead that he might suckle, but all of this was as nothing to her. She would ease Sean when he stumbled home, and show him Patrick and he would come under the spell of that young old face and the blind eyes and all would be well. And if — and she laughed at the thought — if she, simple Mary, had finally put the old story to rest then so much the better. Why Poor Father Gorman might even be able to sleep at night.

"Mary. Mary. Are ye awake now."

Bridie, tapping, insistent, on the door.

"Yes. I'm awake Bridie."

"And himself?"

She looked down. Patrick appeared asleep on her breast, his breathing short, regular, eyes squeezed shut.

"I think he's asleep Bridie."

"They're all here to see you maid. You and Young Patrick."

Mary giggled and composed herself.

Then come on in," she said. "All of you."

There was a jostling in the narrow doorway as they all struggled to be first to get a glimpse of the miracle, the first immaculate conception — well, unnatural conception since you-know-who. Aunt Mary Ellen and Ida nearly fell over each other in their eagerness and everyone forgot poor Lil who walked into the wall and had to be helped off by Eileen though what Aunt Lil expected to see God knows. Madeline the Fox eyed the youngster up with a critical eye, wondering how soon it could be before she could initiate him into the true mystery of life, and Ruth wondered whether he would like cabbage.

Mary, struggling to keep her laughter at bay — necessary because it was also painful — turned her face and looked herself at the face of Patrick Pearse Coley. To her astonishment, it seemed, for one moment, that the milky membrane fell from his eyes and he looked at the assembled gathering with a look of profound horror and distaste. Then the gauze dropped and he became, once more the picture of innocence.

Long after they had all gone, while Mary was waiting for Sean, she peered into the baby's face to see if there was another revelation. But there was nothing. Nothing at all.

A BRIEF ASIDE ON THE HISTORY, GEOGRAPHY AND MYTHOLOGY OF THE ISLAND OF FIRE, REAL AND IMAGINED, FROM THE BEGINNINGS OF TIME UNTIL THE BIRTH OF OUR HERO.

Cuckold's Cove was discovered by either Eric the Red or Leif the Lucky. This is not surprising as almost every part of the main island of Terra Neuve or Terra Nova or The New Found Land, as John Donne described it, was discovered by one or the other of these gentlemen. This assumption is of fairly recent origin and was first put about by Farley Mowat and later confirmed by Dr. Helge Instadt and is now held as truth by every man, woman and child on the island. The occasional questing and questioning tourist who suggests gently that Eric the Red discovered Greenland is likely to be taken on a tour of numerous barren islands which the said Eric is known to have visited, most of which are five or six miles off shore located in treacherous shoal waters which the locals like to navigate in a gale force southerly wind. After such an experience the sight of a lily pond on a calm day has been known to make those unaccustomed to either sacred truths or the water violently ill.

There was another Viking, Thorfinn Karlsefni, but his name doesn't readily lend itself to memory, and a rather predatory female called Freydis whose sexual instincts were such that she killed off all female opposition. She is uninteresting except that she might well have left a few offspring scattered around who inherited her characteristics, Madeline the Fox for instance, and thus she could indirectly be responsible for the popular Cuckold's Cove phrase concerning women or girls with excessive appetites: "She's had more men than I've had hot dinners."

After the Vikings, the tales run, there was John Cabot. As with the case of Eric the Red and Leif the Lucky, most communities on the east coast of Newfoundland claim that he landed there first, and many can recite the history of their communities, right back to that moment in the fifteenth century when the somewhat dull

Caboto put ashore and was greeted by Uncle Walter or Black Joe Kelly or some such with a meal of cod tongues fried in whale oil. Cuckold's Cove has however, the distinction of having a large inscription carved in Bluff Head, that five hundred foot slab of granite rising sheer from the sea, that confirms the presence of the historically accepted discoverer of the New World. Carved about eight feet from the top the inscription reads: "To Ye Inhabitants of ye Cuckold's Cove, many thanks for ye foine times, and ye many gifts to take back to My Liege Lord King Henry, including ye Foine Carved Net Needle. Signed. Gratefully Thine — J. Caboto. Mariner."

It is of course, a matter of recorded fact that the ill-fated John did take back numerous gifts to the rather tight-fisted Henry who, with typical Tudor circumspection had given him permission to go providing that he, Henry, had one-fifth of the spoils. How they divided a net needle into fifths is a matter of conjecture and need not concern us, but the inscription proves to everyone's satisfaction that not only was Cuckold's Cove the first to be discovered, unfortunately as it turned out, by England, but was also in an advanced state of civilisation at that time.

Of the Native Indians little needs to be said, as they do not affect the history of Cuckold's Cove as it was, or is known. For a while, certain persons from the mainland of literary or journalistic pretensions made the claim that the good fishermen of Cuckold's Cove were in the habit of slaughtering the said red Indians at every encounter between them, but anyone who knows the residents of this idyllic community could not conceive of them murdering anything other than each other on occasions when a dispute over a cod trap or a woman got out of hand. This being so, it is unlikely that their ancestors were any different.

At some time or other the little island has been used by Basque Whalers, Portugese Fishermen, French Marauders, English Marauders and pirates of all kinds, including Turks who had a passion for salt fish and fat women, but the basic population, a mixture of Celtic origins from the West Coasts of Ireland and England, with a dash of the Scilly Isles thrown in, remain essentially unchanged. The seasons come and go, winter and summer, winter and summer. They harvest the sea and the sea, in turn, takes its harvest of them. Those who die on land are buried

in the rocky graveyard behind the church on top of Cuckold's
Point, and in winter are mercifully covered with a yard or two of
snow. In summer wild roses and dandelions and raspberry
bushes carefully blind the eyes of the long dead, protecting them
from the vistas of sea that had at once been their curse and their
blessing, men and women alike.

The island is not large, a mere seven miles long and two miles
wide, most of its shoreline so inhospitable that settlement for
fishing purposes is impractical, save at Cuckold's Cove where the
sea breaks in between two fingers of land straining to touch each
other, and the inside, like an inverted palm, makes a comparatively safe harbour even on the wildest days when the Atlantic
throws up some of its oldest waves against the granite walls of
Bluff Head, or they hiss, thirty, forty sometimes fifty feet high
along the marble smooth ledge of Coley's Point, the extremity of
one of the fingers, for when the wind is southerly there is no
protection between Cuckold's Cove and the Antarctic.

Inland, all is barren, scoured by the receding ice aeons ago,
scoured by the wind ever since, and further scoured by the
occasional activity of courting couples legitimate and otherwise
during the few months such activity is practical out of doors.
There are ponds dotting the barrens full of trout, and in the fall,
the ground is ablaze with the colours of partridge and blue and
choke berries and bake apples, and here are carpets of wild
flowers, the creeping snowberry and the insectivorous pitcher
plant of blood red flower, and white flowering cotton grass and
wild blue iris rising from peatland where the water trickles
underfoot even in the hottest weather, and the scent bottle orchid
of strange green flowers and wild lily of the valley with the
bittersweet scent.

It is this strange mixture of beauty and savagery which re-
affirms the Celtic nature of the people of Cuckold's Cove, ancestors of a glorious and barbaric dark past whose blaze now is but a
dim glow in their ancestral homes where the once vivid life of the
spirit is dissected in the dusty tombs of libraries; fed upon by
wordy jackals of dubious origins who falsify the mysteries of time
that they might pretend a common ancestry, and worse, varnish it
with the drab gloss of respectability.

Such hypocritical machinations were already at work as Newfoundland struggled to take its place alongside North America as a God-fearing and, God help us, respectable nation. The inhabitants of Cuckold's Cove were blissfully unaware that already on file in some garishly lit building in the Capital of St John's two hundred sea miles away was a list of names that had to be changed to something more akin with Newfoundland's new standing. Certain clergymen and respected elders had been employed to track down the offending epithets and change them to something more in keeping with Disneyland. Devil's Hole, Famished Gut, Ragged Arse Cove, Hell Cove yes, and even Cuckold's Cove were just a few of the names on that list.

And if nobody knew how it got its name — well, it's an ancient word, a strong word, a mocking word for an activity as old as man and it was often said in Cuckold's Cove, when tales were spread about this one or that one: "What d'ye expect here. We got to keep the tradition alive." And so it was, without self-deception at least, although deception of the occurrence was practised here as elsewhere.

It was into this strange world then, that our hero was born. An unlikely setting one might think, for the rise of a great leader, isolated, pagan at heart as Father Gorman never tired of pointing out, bawdy and self sustaining and proud. The men Viking in temperament, the women Celtic in sensibility, the landscape, elemental: a place possibly to which the Old Gods ran when the New Gods drove them from their haunts of mountain and rock, the citadels of parable in the Old World.

But then — perhaps not.

DAVID DONNELL

What the 19th Century Serfs Did

Got up before the sun and worked all day until they
were dripping with sweat and the earth was cooling
went four acres back to the cottage and drank root beer
six to eight inches shorter than we are but solid
thick-shouldered   earthy   how many of them had blue eyes?
suppers were enormous   very little meat   a thick soup
slabs of bread   potatoes   no eggs   barley was popular
then they sat around for the evening mending tools
putting a new buckle on a piece of harness   children
playing evening games on the kitchen floor and his wife
dishes finished mending clothes making fresh candles perhaps
wheat cakes and to bed early in the straw loft upstairs
takes the neighbor's daughter he married in his arms
quiet, she says to him, the children, giggling to sleep
three of them, who have been watching the horse all day
ah, now, she says, and to sleep, dark spin settling down
dream of the fields, the horse, roots with shapes like heads
mothers who smell like barns, god, apples, broken harnesses
Farrell's daughter's white arms, the cows lowing   the
coming and passage of winter

SUSAN GLICKMAN

Because

Because the day lunges at me
like a big stupid animal that kills
with affection

because too many nights I walk
moonlit beaches
of broken glass

because the voices of friends
cloud the air
and give me fever

I am sitting very quiet now between
four walls.
I am practising home safety.

One table, one chair, one bed with me in it,
planting stars by remote control
turning down the volume and up the brightness

of the bleached and battering world.
Because still I believe; because patience
is a form of revenge.

BRUCE MEYER

Deal Beach

I was a little farther than Arnold
Along the English Channel coast.
Where he saw stars and blind endurance
I saw daylight cloaked in fog
And pure pale breakers
Wearing at England's last defence.
Yes, those armies had fought in the night
And the battleground within my heart
Lay cold and lunar like the beach.
Time had turned the sand to stones
And each pebble cried against each wave.
I would have liked a tranquil bay
A measure of serenity mixed with truth —
But Deal Beach, lined with old hotels
Would not be faithful to the sea
And all the sufferings of love and pain
Were not mine to reject or hold;
Only a cool morning breeze
And the soft faint traces of light
Gave me the happiness that Arnold craved.
And the waters crept slowly around my feet.

EUGENE McNAMARA

Physics of the Solid Earth

yesterday a bee stung me
on my right ring finger —
it is late september but
it's eighty in the shade
and the bees are tired —
all over you can see them
frantic bumping into windows
in this late season's heat

i am tired and frantic too —
everything seems to be
waiting for the change —
now a letter arrives from
someone i used to know
who says i can name her
new sailboat

i think of a boat yearning
to be lifted from the autumn
water and my finger throbs
i think of the sting working
in towards my heart and now
in the library i see a journal
called *physics of the solid earth*
and i am strangely comforted
in these last hours hoping
to sting something anybody
the earth yes the tired earth
is not frantic yes the earth

DAVID HELWIG

Another Fall

A quiet wind in the chimney. A flicker
of fire. History is taking place
(when we speak our eyes don't meet)
somewhere else tonight.

Outside are stars. The ground is wet
and dead leaves lie in the grass. History
is taking place, if at all, somewhere else
in October, this most forgiving of months.

Water and fire, earth and air, insist,
(we try to imagine other lovers) persist.
History, if it takes place at all,
is easily forgotten.

The hardy vegetables, leeks, turnips, cabbage
(is there comfort to be given or taken?)
grow in the cold brown earth. History
takes place only in the books on the shelves.

DAVID BLOSTEIN

Little Deaths

i. Michael and All Angels

Almost from the beginning and certainly at the end, Michael and Dan were close. They had met on the first day of grade one at King Edward School, two blond little boys who at first glance could have been brothers. But while both were very clever, temperamentally they were quite different. Dan, solidly built, energetic and bright-eyed, constantly outran and out-shouted the slighter, more thoughtful Michael (whom no one was tempted to call Mike). They fought, made up, in general carried on like the healthy boys they were, and without knowing it became each other's comfort in their natural isolation at the head of the class.

Their parents, though evangelical back in England, had moved into a part of the town that was strongly Anglican, so it was to churches of that denomination that the boys were taken regularly most Sundays during their childhood. Or rather, Michael was. Dan's physical exuberance frequently took the form of rebellion. It was not unusual for Michael, standing in the portal after a service and blinking to adjust his sight back to the dusty, glaring street, to make out the figure of his friend as he casually dribbled a soccer ball in full view of the departing congregation. Michael would be incensed. He was a serious boy and would undoubtedly be a serious young man; his parents, with three other children to look after, had gratefully concluded early on that he could be trusted to raise himself.

And so he did, and his parents never had cause to regret their confidence in him. Nevertheless, he had his private, inner life, which he cherished and protected. He knew, for instance, that though he had been told he was named after his paternal grandfather, it could not have been a complete coincidence that his birthday fell on September 26, only three days before Michaelmas Day, the feast of Michael and All Angels. He was certainly no idolator: the lore of angels was a legitimate interest for one whose faith was as strong as his. But even Dan was not to be trusted with his innermost hopes, not till many years had passed. After the report cards, the scout packs, the work on the student paper, the debacles and triumphs of dating, the matriculation exams (they took the top two college entrance scholarships in their school district), the freshman initiation, the college proms with nice girls, the University Students' Council, and, for Dan, the glory of the football field, the time at last came for such intimacy.

It was a summer morning after their second year at university. They were headed toward their summer jobs — Michael at his father's insurance office, Dan characteristically at a labouring project — when Dan jumped into Michael's path.

"I'll have to tell you sooner or later," he said, his eyes shining. "I've received a call."

Even as the joking reply passed his lips — "Oh? What's her name?" — Michael knew exactly what Dan meant. But it was shocking, it couldn't be true.

Dan frowned. "I'm going into theology. Going to be a priest, an Anglican priest."

Michael snorted. "Come on, Dan, you of *all* people."

"I know that's what everyone will say. 'Danny the rakehell gone and got religion.' But it's true, Michael, and I need your support. You can imagine what my folks thought, and nobody at the college will believe it — I can write off the football team."

They resumed walking.

"I'm with you," Michael said softly. "In fact, I guess I envy you. Dan, tell me . . ." Michael watched his friend intently, earnestly. "How did it come? Did you see something?"

"What do you mean?"

"See something, like — an angel?"

Dan exploded in laughter.

As if he had for years anticipated and feared this very moment but had determined to run right through it, Michael hurled himself into a kind of confession. They had reached Dan's bus stop but several buses went by while Michael's words tumbled out of their hiding place: he spoke of his sense of presences in early childhood, of feeling watched by invisible, loving watchers, of the seraphim who have wings covered in eyes, of the warrior angels who are clad in armour; he noted that three of the five times Michael is mentioned in the Bible are in the book of Daniel, that he himself might not have been a great fighter for the right but that he had done his best and Dan had been one that held with him in these things.

"But Dan," said Michael, growing calmer, "much as I expected as a child to see those visitants, much as I even constructed their likeness in my mind and imagined what it would be like to converse with them, I have been honest with myself. I have never succumbed to the sweet temptation to *imagine* that I have actually seen an angel, or to pretend that the voices that I and many people hear in half-sleep are their voices. Yet I confess to you that I still hope, because the Church teaches us that they exist, and therefore I believe."

Dan put his hand on Michael's shoulder. Evenly and kindly he said, "It doesn't happen like that any more." But Michael answered, "I don't see why not."

They saw less of each other for the remainder of their time at college. Dan switched his programme from science to arts, to be better prepared for theology. Michael began to specialize in biological sciences, with a view to entering medicine. They met from time to time at the Canterbury Club. On one such occasion, Michael introduced Dan to Margaret, his intended. Dan was as charming as in the old days; Marg was quite taken with him.

"And what about yourself?" she asked him. "I don't suppose you'll be single for long?"

He smiled. "I take my commitment to the priesthood very seriously, Marg. I don't think I'll be able to fit marriage in."

And on a much later occasion, when Marg and Michael (now an intern) had been married awhile, they found that he had become very high Anglican indeed, a great user of incense and ritual who let it be known that he preferred to be addressed by his parishioners as "Father". He told them this himself, and winked: "You can call me Father Dan."

"I can tell you a bit of news myself," Michael said. "I've decided to specialize in radiology. I was wavering between that and haematology but then I learned that the archangel Michael — bless him for a healer anyway — is the patron of roentgenologists. How could I resist!"

"Then you see what ordinary men cannot see?" said Dan; Michael met his eyes, and saw no mockery there.

"Not yet, but let's hope."

Marg was the presiding genius of the rented duplex in which the couple made their home during the time of Michael's medical studies; it was her open invitation that drew Father Dan once more into their circle. The two old friends could again provide each other with comfort — for the priest, his great vigour thrown as fully into his work as it had once been into youthful highjinks, was at times depressed by what he saw of human suffering and exhausted by the endless task of comforting others; he would then say that it was Michael who restored his faith.

As for Michael himself, he should have known better than to neglect his own paleness and weakness of limb, which he had dismissed at first as a bug, then as overwork. When it was confirmed, shortly after his thirty-first birthday, that he was suffering from leukemia, Margaret unhesitatingly called Father Dan. She called him again on the last day.

Marg met him at the door. She was tearful, but radiant.

"His faith has been such a blessing, such a blessing. I think he is quite composed, and ready."

They sat on either side of Michael. They were all silent, grateful that none of the usual words were necessary.

"Did you know," said Michael at last, putting as much strength as he could into a smile, "that the archangel Michael is the special protector of dying souls?"

"Yes," said Father Dan, "I did."

A little later, Michael spoke again. "Remember how I hoped to see him and his angels?"

"Yes, I do," said Father Dan, and he leaned forward tensely, expectantly. "And do you — now?"

"Oh, that would be too much to hope for."

"I'm not sure at all of that. I've thought about it, you know. I'm not the smug young convert who laughed at you once. You have lived a pure, blameless life. You have been honest in your dealings with others, with God, with yourself. Your faith is spoken of. Angels have been seen by such as you, dear friend."

In a moment Michael's grey, wasted face became animated, suffused with happiness. Even as the final, wrenching pains of death came upon him, he looked about him wildly, seeking, seeking everywhere. At the end, Margaret could not comprehend his wide open eyes. Nor, when she turned to the other watcher at the bed, whose eyes were still fixed upon those of his friend, could she account for why she found there that same mixture of hope, puzzlement, disappointment.

ii. Die Happy

Zenon Mihalchuk, once a partisan in the land of his birth, a hard worker and exacting husband and father in the country he had chosen when disillusioned with the cause for which he had fought as a young man, was now sixty-six years old and dying. While relatives and neighbours bustled in and out of his bedroom and prepared, in the kitchen and parlour, for the obsequies to come, Zenon's oldest daughter, Mrs Wozniak, sat with him and they talked. This is what they said.

"Don't worry, Tatu, we'll be okay. You're not the only one that knows what's what."

"You wouldn't talk to me like that when I was healthy."

"Sure not, you old bugger. I was scared of you all my life, who wasn't? Look, let's not talk rough now. Take it easy, you want a pill or anything?"

"No."

"You can die happy, like you always said. Remember? 'I don't care what they think of me, how bad it looks what I done, when I die I'll die happy cause I'll know I done right.' You remember? A hundred, maybe five hundred times I heard that in my life."

"You remember that, eh? Well it's true. And I got that bastard, lots of times."

"You sure did, Tatu. Remember that time with the election sign on the lawn? I must have been four then. Never forgot it."

"The time about the snow fence — boy what he looked like after that."

"The building permit, remember the building permit? He tried to add a back room onto his house and 'somebody' reported him."

"He had to pay fifty dollars for that one, he already poured the cement."

"Then when he tried to get the job with the city."

"Like hell. His kids had to go bare-assed."

"So did we."

"What are you talking!"

"Hey, remember the time he started the grocery store! That's when you really got him — you backed Shlemkevitch to open one next door. That must have been expensive."

"It was worth it. A sacrifice for a just cause is worth it. He had it coming. Maybe he got away with it *then*, but I never let him forget."

He was breathing with great difficulty now; she pushed him lightly on the shoulders, so that he lay back for a while and shut his eyes. She knew what he meant by "then". By now she could almost believe that she had been there herself, in the village of Rastopol, after the partisan raid that had killed the collaborator mayor and some German soldiers. One partisan had not been able to get out in time and was hidden in the larder of Vassil Kozin's house near the square. Someone betrayed him, and he was shot. It was near the end of the war; within days the Soviet troops passed through the village, and Zenon's partisan troop joined up with them on the way west. For a few seconds the two men had passed in the square: he looked hard at Vassil and saw the guilt written clearly in his eyes. Yet three years later, Zenon saw him on a Winnipeg street, free as a bird. That was the story. All their lives had been shaped by it.

Zenon opened his eyes.

"Lots of times I got him," he said. "Many, many times."

"So you're happy?"

"You're so rough — what kind of a woman."

"No, I'm really asking. I never understood why it was so important to die happy, anyhow. If you're dying, you're dying.

It's not as though you get fixed in plastic with a grin on your face — 'Look what a great life I had!' A believer I can understand, wanting to die in what they call it, a state of grace. But you, you old devil, you never believed that crap. Or did you? Hey, Tatu, have you been a secret believer all these years?"

"Shit, have respect. You know damn well I've always been an atheist. No. To die happy — ekh, you never think of it the way it's really going to be. I just meant — I always thought — whatever sacrifices, whatever. . . if you done the right thing . . .

"What I hate is, I go and get this happen to me, and he goes on living and now he can get a laugh out of it."

"He won't laugh, Tatu. He's a good ten or twelve years older than you. He's had a hard life. He won't laugh over you, absolutely he won't."

"How do you know so sure?"

"I know."

"What do you mean, you know?"

He tried to raise himself on one side as he stared at her. She looked back at him, but for a while kept silent. In the kitchen somebody was whistling softly.

"I know. I talked with him. Now take it easy."

"What are you talking! When?"

"Eight, nine years ago. I was about to have my first kid. I felt different about things. I was mad at the way our whole life was stuck to Vassil Kozin. So I walked up to his house and said I wanted to talk to him. He told me everything."

"Everything! What more could he tell you, the son of a bitch!"

"Plain and simple. I told him how you said he looked guilty that day, and he looked scared for a second and then he laughed. He cried too, right after. Said sure he felt guilty — he just came from Mrs Kuslak's bed. Been screwing her every day for the past month while her man was off in the army. Was hardly ever home, didn't even know the partisan was in the house, the Germans found him themselves. He always thought why you were against him was Kuslak. Couldn't figure it, thought you must be religious."

She adjusted his pillows and waited.

"You believed him?"

"Oh sure, of course. Makes sense."

"You knew this for nine years and never told me."

"I thought of telling you once or twice, but there was no point."

"Are you crazy? What do you mean 'no point'?"

"I thought about it. I figured, it gave a reason for your life, right? I mean, you already hated him like that almost thirty years."

"Thirty years. Now almost forty."

"It was important to you. I couldn't imagine you without it. What else could you have done with yourself?"

"I don't know."

"Sure." There was a smell of baking, and quiet talk in the parlour. "Maybe taken Mama for a holiday some time."

"Mama for a holiday. Yes, I could have done that. I could have gone to see my brother in Vancouver, couldn't spare the time or money.

"Could have taken you and the younger ones to City Park more, eh?

"Could have read more books. I never finished *Kobzar*.

"Could have done more singing. I had a good bass when I was young, did you know that?"

She shook her head faintly.

"I would like —" said Zenon Mihalchuk in the last minute of his life; then he wept. He wept and he wept.

iii. The Cemetery Club

That Morley Fineberg was Classics Tutor at St George's Academy for Boys was a constant source of perplexity for his relatives. He still had an uncle, after all, who was a chicken slaughterer down at the Market. The old question had now travelled from their tongues to their sad eyes and encamped there: how came a bright Jewish boy to be studying about Romans and Greeks? Morley had nevertheless studied them, had been devoted to them from an early age, ever since a zealous cousin had caught him eating a hot dog and pricked his curiosity by calling him an *apikoros*. To his delight he discovered the etymological justification for the similarity in sound between the name of the philosopher Epicurus and that Hebrew word for unbeliever. And after he had sought out whatever translations he could of the philosopher's works, what he found there persuaded him to learn more. So eventually he travelled on two continents to acquire advanced degrees in Classics, specializing in the Epicurean school of philosophy. And now he was teaching. But where? At St George's. A school for boys. When college classmates of far less ability were teaching at top universities in Canada and the States.

But St George's was special. One must ignore the wearing of gowns, the daily racing through Anglo-Catholic prayers, the throwing of buns in the refectory. What drew Morley to St George's — apart from the fact that good teaching posts in Classics were hard come by in rootless North America — was a combination of its setting and its teaching staff.

The school could easily remind one of Epicurus' own academy, the Garden. It lay in the city at the edge of settlement, at a point where the prairie unaccountably gives way to about three square miles of lightly rolling hills. Here, at the turn of the century, the city fathers had wisely made a public park; and where the last, great suburban houses came to a halt was erected, in a half dozen acres of delicately wooded valley, St George's Anglican Academy for Boys.

The place had style. The same Chicago architect who had designed several of the ornate office buildings at the city's centre had been induced, through Episcopalian friends, to sketch out the rambling frame-and-stone structure of the chapel, residence, and office-classroom buildings. Here, through hallways which had instantly taken on the creaking echoes and chalky odours of ancient colleges, now walked tall young men, bearing gowns, fair hair and acne with the natural dignity of those secure in their futures as bankers, grain brokers, ministers, lawyers.

Though he had grown up in the north end of the city, Morley had always known St George's boys, meeting them as a child in the piano competitions at the Music Festival, arguing with them on the Student Council at university. Eventually, he became friends with Rob McInerney, a St George's boy he met on the ship going over to Oxford. Each was astonished to discover that the other intended to read Greats there; if that were not enough coincidence (Rob made much more of it than Morley did), they were to be at neighbouring colleges. Both were given credit for one year of the four-year course, and they saw each other quite frequently during the three years of intellectual excitement and emotional depression, regularly battering out duets for piano and oboe and occasionally sharing a girl friend. It was a relief, Morley found, to be cut off from the intense feelings of his family circle; in exchange he now had the cool and easy tie with Rob and others like him. How right Epicurus had been to say that the possession of friends brings more happiness than any other gift. (Epicurus had received a bad press, of course; his was not a voluptuary's philosophy but a programme for serenity.)

Their tutors expected them both to do well, and they did. But the very afternoon that Morley was filling out his first application for admission to the doctoral programme at an American graduate school, Rob ambled into his room, scratched his sandy hair in slight embarrassment, and announced that he had received an invitation to join the faculty of St George's Academy. It helped, it seemed, to be an insider.

Three years later, during a summer visit home, Morley heard from Rob again, and they met for lunch. Rob told wonderful stories about the characters he worked with. Evidently this was no ordinary high school staff. Most of the teachers had Masters degrees, three or four had doctorates, some were naturals or eccentrics with no degrees at all. The students were occasionally snobbish but in the staff room there was a splendid atmosphere, friendly and sufficiently intellectual. Morley, who recently had reluctantly accepted an offer at a new university in the Ontario outback, listened with envy and decreasing attention until it registered on him that Rob was offering him a position at the school. He had never hesitated less in his life. Within a day he had gone through the once-over by an informal committee of Rob's colleagues, written an apologetic and somewhat disingenuous letter to his brief employer, and accepted the financially much less substantial offer from St George's.

This was in the summer of 1967, when the country was having

an extended birthday party. The occasion did not affect him much — why should he, imbued with the classics, "Oxford-trained," about to teach at a private school, care that his grandparents' refuge from pogroms had lasted out a hundred years of nationhood? But he felt good anyway, very, very good. There was nothing that he feared, much that pleased him, and nothing very much that he lacked. Even when his widowed father reminded him that he had been in school a long while and it was time to settle down — where was a son to be his *kaddish*? — he shrugged off the gloomy intrusion by labelling it his father's subcultural duty. Come to think of it, a spouse might be the one thing that his equilibrium still required; despite his discomfort with religious tradition, he considered the justice of the reminder. Betty Cramer, he noticed, still wasn't married and they had always liked each other. By the next spring they became man and wife. Rob, who was already married and the father of a two-year-old boy, came to the wedding even though he was still shaken by the sudden death of both his parents in a car accident.

Surrounded by the rustling of the crowd on the Cramers' large back lawn, Morley stood in the bower with his foot raised to smash the glass. He sensed to the right of him the haze of white satin and lace appliqué that was his bride, and before him the cantor clearing his throat and resting his strong, coarse lungs. Then something disturbing occurred: his mind was invaded by a thought, or rather a presentiment, or even a vision, which told him that this ritual, with which he had been familiar since childhood and to which he had agreed to submit because he held his disbelief less firmly than Betty's parents held their belief, had leapt up alive, out of its proper, mechanical rote form; that despite his indifference and the ignorance of most of those present of the very meaning of the words, an efficacy was about to come into force. In a place and time that seemed to be other than that moment in the bower on Mr. Cramer's lawn, he and Betty were about to become well and truly married, because some powerful truth resided within that ritual, as trembling with life as was the young woman (not quite a virgin) by his side.

The glass shattered under his heel, a whoop of approval went up all around them, and as he was swallowed into the universal gaiety, he quickly shook off the uncalled-for illusion, identifying it with those idols or *simulacra* that must often be cooked up on emotional occasions.

And as he hoped, life at the Garden was now even more pleasant than before. At home, Betty was a willing mate, a passable cook, and gratifyingly lacking in social ambition. She never lost her shyness with Rob and his impressive wife Elaine; though they sometimes went to the theatre or concerts as a foursome and spent the occasional evening playing chamber music, it was clear that they would never become very intimate. The McInerneys were active in Church affairs, so they had limited time for the Finebergs. At the school it was quite different. Morley found that his status as an Oxonian and a friend of Rob's, and of course, the tolerant atmosphere in general, assured him of a secure place in the community.

This situation was to alter at the beginning of the third school year. That autumn, St George's replaced several members of the staff, recently retired or departed. Among the new recruits were two likeable young men who soon joined up with Morley and Rob. Gerald Oatley was a tall, shambling Englishman, red of hair and face, with a hearty manner and rough humour. At Cambridge he had studied languages, and he had come here to teach Italian and Spanish. The new music tutor was to be Paul Sowerby, a gentle, pudding-faced, dark-haired little man whose wit was more restrained. The four of them usually ate their meals together, watched each other play chess in the faculty room, said many witty things and laughed at them, were looked upon by faculty and students alike as good acquisitions.

During an unavoidable family gathering during the Christmas vacation, Morley regaled his relatives with stories about his companions. Much of it went over their heads, but it was the reaction of his wife and his father that interested him most. Betty had heard much of it before, but it seemed from the way she exchanged glances with her father-in-law that he too knew the anecdotes, and that they must have been talking together about Morley and the school. His father waited out the performance, then said drily, "Do you really think you're a part of that place? You think they really accept you?"

Furious, Morley blurted out something about disgusting paranoia and left the room.

When, during the new term, evidence began to grow that his father might be right, Morley became depressed. It seemed to him that among equals he was becoming the least equal. Rob, Paul, and Gerald appeared to have something that drew them together. When he went to the refectory for lunch, they were often already there, well into a conversation that at times would be cut off as he approached. Sometimes he would see the three of them walking away from the campus together after classes, clearly with a place to go to; they had not told him about it. And finally, on a Friday afternoon in March he overheard Gerald asking Rob, "Where is it this Sunday?" and then the answer, "St Timothy's". Ah well, thought Morley, at least it's not the race thing, I knew it wasn't. He said that to Betty, but she replied, "I thought Gerald was an atheist." She was right. But perhaps it wasn't a religious activity, perhaps it was a social service; or they could be in the choir. Yet why couldn't they just mention it to him once? His peace of mind was not, he observed, what it had been.

He therefore let his curiosity draw him after the clue that Paul inadvertently let fall within earshot. "St Michael's it is, then," the pudgy musician was saying, as Morley overtook the trio on the path leading to the classroom wing. It was reasonable to assume that the reference was not to the Catholic cathedral but to Michael and All Angels near the river. It was now April, the thaw had come, and after checking the time for the first Sunday service, Morley found an excuse to take the car out for a drive alone. He parked a block from the church, within sight of the entrance, and waited. There were members of the St George's staff and some students in the arriving congregation but, as far as he could tell, none of the three friends. He waited for the end of the service to be sure of it, then for the beginning of the second. Finally, somewhat disgusted with himself, he went in and stood at the back for a few minutes, long enough to be oppressed by the music and the darkness, and left. As he crossed the church grounds, he looked back towards the old graveyard, and stopped. There were Rob, Gerald, and Paul, walking in and out among the grave-stones, pointing at times, calling to one another. Then Paul saw him, waited a moment, and waved. Morley moved towards them.

"I guess you ought to get an explanation," said Rob.

"Well, yes," said Morley.

"Oh dear," said Paul.

They stood about in various postures. Gerald and Paul watched Rob as he spoke.

"It's a sort of club," he said. "You know about my parents, how they died."

"Yes, in a car accident."

"Well, it's sort of funny, but the fact is that both Paul and Gerald lost their folks in the same way. Car accidents. Both parents at once. Weird, isn't it?"

"And we're all only sons," added Gerald, and guffawed, then nodded to Rob to continue.

"So we started this club, or whatever. And we visit cemeteries once a month. It started as a sort of gruesome joke — no need to ask whose idea."

Gerald guffawed again.

"Needless to say, we didn't advertise for members," said Paul. "For one thing, we didn't want to jinx anyone."

"My mother's dead already," said Morley. They asked him to stay and share their bag lunch — a picnic was part of the observance — but he told them he was already late.

It was all rather disappointing. Morley found the immaturity of these men in their morbid game an affront to the whole purpose of a civilized academy, and a more thorough rejection of himself than any mere social snub could be. He was alone again, surrounded by the irrational in friends and family.

But there were compensations. Betty was pregnant. His father would see him with his *kaddish* after all. They prepared the nursery room, they planned the education; they went for walks and rides together.

On a Sunday in July, when Betty was in her eighth month, and they were driving along a country road, Morley saw far off to the left four figures seated at the side of a crossroad, apparently having a picnic. He turned at the crossing and saw that his friends were sitting on a row of tombstones that had been salvaged from a former graveyard and set into a length of concrete. He stopped, got out, and exchanged hearty greetings.

"Who was with you just now?" he asked.

"What do you mean? Nobody."

"Oh, of course, I must have been distracted, I thought I counted four."

And after a minute or two he rejoined Betty in the car, and headed homeward.

The afternoon was rapidly turning to dusk, the red glow over the city was coming into sight, and one light shone in the sky ahead of them. Then in an instant it grew to an immeasurable size. It became limbs and head and armour. It was clothed in linen, and girded with gold; it stood shining between heaven and earth with a gem-like body of radiant green, with arms and legs of molten copper, with lightning where the face must be, and eyes of flaming torches; it engulfed Morley in heat and sound, sound that shook through him, through and through, so that his senses told him and his protesting reason that this was indeed the Malach-ha-Movis, for below those feet were headlights crossing the median, and as the Angel of Death came and came and the thundering was within him and without Morley looked at his pointing wife and knew she must be screaming, and he cried out:

"This is wrong, this is wrong! I will not accept it!"

"You are given no choice," said the Angel of Death, and lifted his sword.

"But my son isn't born, I'll have no *kaddish!*"

"This was foreseen," said the Angel of Death.

"But it fits no pattern. IT MAKES NO SENSE!"

"Who said it must?" said the Angel of Death.

iv. Little Deaths

It was a handful of clichés. The honeymoon was lovely. It had been worth it, after all, not insisting before.

To be frank, that was why she had been so attractive to him anyway. After the life he had led, the women he had known.

His friends would never be told. Who would believe him? Who would believe that his wife was a virgin on her wedding night, and for several days thereafter?

She had been grateful.

She was so vulnerable.

When she thanked him for being gentle, for being understanding, he felt guilty, for he didn't want to be understanding. Her passive, defenceless beauty drove him mad; well, it stirred him up prodigiously. It was all he could do to hold back from forcing her, both before the wedding and now.

By the time the second month had gone by, when they had indeed become husband and wife, he realized too that he would have to teach her everything. Everything. She was too shy to initiate anything, to touch him where he wanted to be touched.

It was a bother, really.

But the process fascinated him somewhat. It was different. He was beginning to be entertained by the excruciating prolongation: she had obviously never climaxed in her life.

So, giving himself a ration of two or three nights a week, usually on days when he had had a fairly easy time of it at work, he would lead her by the hand to bed, hardly daring to heed the signals his nerves received that told him how fragile her fingers were, how cool her skin. He would ignore and then pounce upon the minute events that calibrated her growing sensuality.

You could compare it, in a way, with watching an infant during the first years of its life. He remembered that from his first marriage. The comparison made him uncomfortable, and he dismissed it.

They went for their first holiday to Mexico. There they saw a bull-fight. It was a bore, but she liked it. After the second kill, she turned to him and said, "It's the ultimate reality, isn't it!" She must have read it somewhere. That night, on their hotel bed, she had her first orgasm.

Probably a connection, he thought. But how lovely it had been. Such a tiny trepidation. Not like Noreen, who would grunt, holler, and kick like a peasant; self-advertising, most of it. Or like the blonde girl at Nick's — Shelley somebody. He smiled to himself. That was the real thing — as if she had a spring knife in her waist, boing, boing.

Or the professionals in Europe — fakery better than the real thing, to tell the truth.

Or, to be fair, good old Marjory, that week in the Bahamas. Had to put his hand over her mouth a couple of times.

But she, this little one, his lovely wife. What a sweet, almost silent tremor of warmth underneath his enfolding limbs. All her vulnerability offered to him as to a sacrifice, as to the matador's *estoque*. At last he knew why the French sometimes referred to it as *la petite mort*. Or was it *morte*. Anyhow the French were right about it.

She did seem to go through a little death, that night in Mexico, and at times afterwards at home. She was becoming — he was reluctant to think that she had now become — a woman. She was putting her fragility, her mortality, in his hands. In his hands were her infinitesimally pulsing veins, the tiny bones of her throat, the beat below the moist hollow between her breasts.

On March 8, at 12:15 at night — it was on a Tuesday, he remembered it exactly — a thought entered his head. He remembered it so well because he had never had such a thought before, and he considered that it might change his life utterly. He was lying beside his sleeping wife, remembering Mexico and the cliché she had uttered at the bull-fight. The ultimate reality was the moment of truth, when you faced mortality, yours or another's, when you had the courage to follow through. It would be, he knew, a sweet, quiet little death. What a silly idea, he thought, shook himself, and went to sleep.

The next day, he went for a walk at lunchtime. What a silly idea, he thought again. I don't even want to. Who gets ideas like that? Is it because of who I am? Is it my age and experience? Is it what I do for a living? Is it the exact level of my intelligence? Fascinating, though; I could easily get very interested.

He walked on. He hoped something that he saw on his walk would illuminate his problem. Nothing seemed to. I don't like this at all, he thought. I would like to but do I really want to?

That night, in bed, they made love. That blessed girl, that woman, gave her soul up to pleasure, him, death itself, it seemed — for a few seconds; and as she did she said, "Oh, how lovely!"

It was nothing to enshrine in gilt letters, but he saw that it might suffice. The thought would be thought no more. Life is lovely. Death's a metaphor. Ultimate reality will come soon enough.

DAVID KNIGHT

Cardiac Event

The shapes are these:

The man that was;
The threat that stood there,
Altering landscapes;
The fact that stopped.

Love, and my wife;
Hospital-time;
The weather homewards.

Lastly, the man
Who, under everything,
Always perhaps was —
Had he been known.

      * * *

I have no high best world. I have
What I have: that only. I have as much
Of a life as I have. For the time being
I have myself. My time's measured,
But I haven't got the clock to it.

I have the sweep-second on my wrist,
And if I stand too long, one shoe
Pains a small toe (but there's no blister).
I make love every second day
If the time's right. I do it well,

And am well-used, and set the clock
Ritually, at the same bed's function.
I still have no high world. I have
The niggling mortal nagging itch.
(And it's such a little thing!) The radiance
Of all Eternity provokes me;
Heroism offends desire.
(I want these.)

                What I have, I have.
The bed-spring whimpers, keeping time.

I have what I want, I guess. The time.

        * * *

What's given attention lets it go:
Black railings, a museum garden
Patched grey with snow. Mourners, beasts, guard
A tomb-heap of black burnished shit.
Tires sizzle on the pavement: taxi,
Sucked towards wet traffic-green. Stopped feet
Wrap rags of asbestos-and-lead air. Heads are
Impertinently occupied
With unbelief. Morningstar sunburst
(Cotton-wool vacuous, bloating pain
Like a pedantry of nerves) shouts, shouts,
As if something ought to wonder at it.

What's breathed is sacked in membranes of pearl-hard,
Lustering, diffuse, alarmed, bright, breathless,
Piston-rammed pain. Elbows, wrist-bones,
Long forearm-bones, whited with ice-light,
Hurt, hurt, hurt. Cramped close ribs wall
An electric-light photon-Montgolfier
Bellying wind-lurched, heavy to the galoshed feet.

As if something ought to wonder at it
Like a pedantry of nerves (shouts, shouts,
Cotton-wool vacuous, bloating pain

With unbelief), morningstar sunburst,
Impertinently occupied,
Wraps rags of asbestos-and-lead air. Heads are
Sucked towards wet traffic-green, stopped feet;
Tires sizzle on the pavement (taxi:
A tomb-heap of black burnished shit
Patched grey with snow). Mourners, beasts, guard
Black railings, a museum garden...
What's given attention lets it go...

* * *

Scummed under the moon,
Endless black water, stagnant,
Stirs, heaves, drags star-points.

The sea-bed stretches.
Drum-shock! Ice-floes, a mile up,
Jump, crack, tilt, teeter.

Faint waves shift. The moon,
Through a disturbed ceiling, bathes
Blind, sleepless fishes.

* * *

...And I see you
Walking through corridors
Blank with blank tile
On walls, on floors,
Corridors with no doors
(But here); I see you
Stumping decisively
Regardless of which way
Floors dip; I see you
Firm in your coat
(With no hat),
Your cane imperial
As your softness...
And so I know you
Have been, will be,

Swinging in your decision
Through such tiled halls
Whether I sleep, wake,
Am well, sick,
Headached, panicked,
Or soft in child's sweating
Sleeping off death
That didn't happen —
And know one fact then,
Certain as life,
That in all my corridors
You walk, are waiting,
Are my heart's heart . . .

* * *

A steel vomit-dish
Curves like the button's smiling:
I'm crying in it.

Forgettable, all,
Faces, family, kind friends
Materialize.

My hand, awake, warm,
Gathers for shelter into
My wife's ice-cold one.

Face longs for face, mine
Crustily unshaven, hers
Bright-boned, and frightened.

Oh my, she's active!
Dredging things out of a sack:
Cards, pen, love, toothpaste . . .

She's like a small fire
Busy about heat; my eyes
Sting if they watch her.

No introductions.
We're as we are, both lovers,
Strained, strange, scared, staring.

Time's up; she's near: one
Feather-kiss touch on my face.
She's gone; she's here still.

Light's off, bed's cold; life
Wallops like a pegged balloon:
Me! in a banged wind!

   * * *

Clouds, clouds, wind-bellying upwards!
Gold-silver contrails higher still;
Highest, the tympanum of air
And the wind jousting where it will . . .

   * * *

"Your body-image?"
Sun in clouds, winds skittering,
Rain bright as ice-cubes.

I can't explain it:
The road flickers under heat,
Flicks to the next bend.

"But are you threatened?"
Whole mountains slide; wonderful
Shocks shape rivers, cliffs.

I wouldn't change it:
Blue vistas, sunwarmed ruins,
Green hills and valleys . . .

There's nothing new here.
Simply, the picture's open.
Light flows, sweeps wide, cuts

(Crystal bulldozer)
Tough as the earth-bones it moulds.
It dances, *I* dance.

"Mere euphoria!
Venetian palaces slump
On their reflections;

Fresh twirled glass shatters."
Heaped rainbow garbage clutters
Bone-bright swept back-streets.

My body-image?
Venice when the rain strikes it,
All cheapjack glamour

Ready to dissolve,
Brick bones and swamp, peeled stucco —
All exultation.

Nothing can defeat
What the next sun-glint fixes,
So superficial:

Jumpy reflections,
Shimmering interference
Of stain and vista,

Jewel and grit, slime,
The most incandescent slum,
Glory at a whim . . .

As water rises,
Exultant black slash on stone
Proclaims, *"This high once!"*

Suns singe the hems of
Mountains in rising past them,
Burn tracks on water;

All clouds dismantle;
Winds, belting storms, peter to
Translucent stillness;

Freight-cars burning in
Gold sunset, rainbow, gemmed rain,
Burn out, stink, smoulder —

But in what light! as
Tangible as any quick
Animal pride: look!

What body-image?
Clearly what it has to be:
Thinned, wakened, heart-swept,

Buoyed on its own bones,
Mortal for the fun of it:
This body, standing,

Brain, glass, light, landscape,
Lover for the chance, dying . . .
Quick now, quick later.

Petrarch's "Sonnet CXL," Done Bare.

("The long love that in my thought doth harbour . . .")

All right, I want her so much I can pretend her into my head
And put us both to bed, with my chest so tight I'd stutter
And my blood going where you'd think — and she's in the real room,
And if the rest of me isn't stripped, well, you can think my face is.

That's what it's all about now — and I got it from her
(So if it's come over me now that I want to come over her,
She started it) — but what she wants is what the magazines say,
And it's got to be lovely, and we aren't supposed to be animals . . .

It feels like being scared, and it doesn't: somebody's unzipped a zipper
And there you all are, only it's as if you don't feel that either;
You're just sticking out, sort of dead — and then you put it all away.

What the hell am I supposed to do? be a nice cool limp love and no bother
And worship her? or pretend myself into feeling warm again
Because at least *that's* real? It's no bad thing, being real.

JIM CHRISTY

To Hell with This Cockeyed World

The last time I was with Charlie he said, "Remember these three — Pres, Charlie Parker and Billie Holiday. And the greatest of these was Pres."* And he ran off down the Boardwalk and I never saw him again.

Well I did see him again although at the time it certainly didn't seem very likely; it was possible, I thought, about as possible as,

---

*"Pres" is Lester Young, the tenor sax player. Billie Holliday gave him the name "Pres" because "he was the greatest."

say, God coming into the 500 Club. But, then again, according to Charlie, He did come into the 500 Club, " . . . when I was playing there but I didn't get a chance to talk to him. He went into the backroom to talk to Skinny and Jack Lescoulie."

Hell, the 500 Club isn't even there anymore; neither is the goddamn Marlborough-Blenheim and neither, for that matter, is Charlie.

Now this is going back a ways but there I was on a bus with my girl Sue passing through Downingtown, Pennsylvania. We had just met, it was spring, we were in love. Earlier that afternoon we had purchased a record album by tenor man Bud Shank and were going back to my place to listen to it and do nasty things to each other. We were talking about jazz and all we had in common and how great that was. She said, "Maybe you would be interested in reading these . . ."

She took some sheets of paper from her handbag. I read a couple and thought, Jesus Christ! Well, Jesus Christ . . . what the hell is *this*?

> I pledge allegiance to my flag . . .
> Let them have their Mott Streets in July
> their endless fields of wheat, and corn and
> East side west side. All around the Mulberry Bush.
> What is it — Chicago — Killer of hogs . . .?
> Carl Sandburg — Teller of Lies —
> Screw Chicago, I'm hungry
> Come here, Baby

My first thought was "Stop the Bus!" My second was to ask her, "Who *is* this guy and what does it all mean?"

"They're written by a guy named Charlie Leeds, a friend of my sister in Atlantic City and he plays jazz and draws pictures and takes a lot of dope but he's not mean and he's extremely weird from all I've heard. That's all I know about him."

It was like jazz alright. Not so much poetry as riffs, like bebop haikus, choruses on a theme.

> All right lovely one, let it go . . .
> I never *really* counted on it anyway

It would have been too beautiful and right
and made too much sense to ever happen
in this neighborhood

Well, I said to her, let's go to Atlantic City.

That next evening, Friday, we were in Atlantic City, in Nancy's apartment waiting for Charlie to show. He never did but while we sat there working on wine, Nancy told us that Charlie would come over at any hour, day or night, and always brought a gift of some sort, a poem, a picture he had cut out of a magazine and framed, a book or one of the roses he was forever making from coat hangers and bits of paper and plastic. It was Charlie who taught her about music, who had shown her how to listen and not just to hear. His great great something-or-other, name of Jeremiah, was the first resident of the peninsula that came to be known as Atlantic City and his great great something else, name of Chalkey, was the burg's first mayor. "But like Charlie himself would say, 'See if that will keep you out of jail for one day.'"

It never did, she continued, "And as proof, one day Charlie nodded out in the little park down the Avenue and in that park there is a statue of Chalkey but the cops picked him up and took him in irregardless of his relative staring down at him."

He didn't show up all the next day so at night we went looking. He was supposed to be playing at a place called Cody's Bar but he hadn't made that either. We went all around the town and nobody knew *where* he was but everyone knew *who* he was and each had a story to tell, usually concerning some impossibly ridiculous situation he had gotten into or involved them in and they all sort of shook their heads knowingly although in a kindly manner, as if to say, "That Charlie, land sakes . . ."

Sunday afternoon, sitting around Nancy's living room again, Sue and I had just about decided to head back to Pennsylvania when the door opened and in walked a man in a trenchcoat and cloth cap carrying an attaché case that appeared to be so heavy that it caused the man to lean forward and to one side. He was quite nattily turned out, sharp, with a pencil thin moustache. My first impression was that he must have run the backroom gambling at one of the clubs or else he was in charge of fixing the races at Garden State; like, he just reeked of shady deals. He looked around the room, mumbled something and headed for the kitchen. "That's him," said Nancy.

"Who?"

"Charlie."

"*Him*?"

I looked toward the kitchen and saw him open the case, reach in, start throwing papers around and finally sit and attack one with a mechanical pencil. He scribbled frantically, crossed out, erased and all the time was bent over the kitchen table, over his work, making guttural sounds, "Hmmm, ummm, hummm," just like certain musicians as you see them, eyes closed over the piano; just as I would later see him, Charlie Leeds, hunkered over his bass oblivious to everything but his music.

I took a deep breath, stood, walked into the kitchen, sat across the table and said something like, "See here, now what is the meaning of all this and what the hell do you think you're doing?"

He stared at me and I stared back and then I giggled and he smiled and said, "You want to hear me beat out some rebop on the table top?"

"All reet, I'm hep, dad."

We both fell out and he said, "Yeah, babe. . . ."

We began to talk and talked for five hours, the only interruptions occurring when one of us had to go to the bathroom. Only he stayed in there longer than I did.

And I can see it like it was yesterday. We came marching right down Old Broadway and there were millions of people screaming and carrying on and all that paper and stuff was flying around and the band was playing "Slap a Dirty Little Jap" and it was hot as a son of a bitch and I remember I looked up into the air and I saw that sign with those smoke rings coming out of it and all of a sudden I started to cry and I said to a friend of mine: I can't *make* it anymore, man.

At last we got to 52nd and Broadway where I made a Squads Right — all by myself — until I got to Sixth Avenue where the White Rose Bar used to be and I sat down on the curb right in front of it and I took off my helmet and gasmask and I laid my rifle down next to me and I picked up a 26¼ inch hypodermic needle and stuck it right in my goddamn arm. Just like that. It was as easy as pie. Because that was the first day I saw what was happening and it was too awful. I knew that day that it didn't mean anything.

I left with plays, stories and poems and I read them and they knocked me out. We wrote letters and I went down to Atlantic City whenever I could and we hung around together. He was inseparable from his writing or from his playing for that matter. He had it all, Charlie Leeds did, all except what was needed to get along in the world; that was something he could and would never possess, something he fought all his life and what got him eventually.

He had no defenses. When I met him I had just finished reading Dostoevski's *The Idiot* and that was Charlie. Only a hip, funny Mishkin. He couldn't handle the world, the cheating and hypocrisy, the general all-around awfulness of the world. All of it hurt him personally. What's more, none of it made sense. Yes, I know; we all realize these things to different degrees, but to many of us it doesn't matter that much, or, if it does, we Can't Let It Get Us Down or we turn our back on it, or build up an arsenal of defenses. But, like I say, he had none, except dope and you know where that leads.

Come to think of it, Charlie had offenses, not defenses. Besides dope, he figured, in the beginning, music and love would see him through. And it was probably because the last two didn't work that he turned to the first.

> I suppose in my childish mind, I figured that if I could just play music like Lester Young, and have somebody beautiful to do awful things to all the time, and *then* if I went to Heaven when I died — everything would be all right.

At the time I met Charlie I was struggling with a great undirected appetite. I wanted to know things, to listen to music — jazz — and to understand it, and even more I wanted to know the world. I had knocked about myself, travelled in rough company and was acquainted with a few jails in various parts of the country. I knew the criminal life and life on the bum. I read anything I could lay my hands on, indiscriminately, drugged on printer's ink, and would spend hours in the public libraries of towns I was passing through. I had met intellectuals, professors, people whose views of the world I respected and whom I knew could serve as teachers. I also hung around with jazz musicians. But every one of these disparate worlds proved lacking somehow. There were the rounders, the scholars and the hip. I had never met anyone who combined within themselves all of these worlds and I had begun to believe that perhaps it was not possible and that I would have to narrow my vision.

Charlie Leeds was the man of all these parts, and each enhanced the other. Of course, he *had* to come out of Atlantic City. He was a product of a century of Boardwalk vaudeville, from earliest childhood his landscape was peopled by hustlers, hookers and carnies and his landmarks were Young's Million Dollar Pier and the Jockey Club. To other kids "adults" meant the butcher and the baker but to Charlie they were Joe Penner walking down the Boardwalk with his duck and W.C. Fields shooting pool at the corner saloon. Like the other kids he also spent every spare minute in the movie house. But he saw all of it, the Hollywood interpretation of the world, from his own perspective, the same one as the original founders of the town and the industry, the old time vaudeville hustler perspective. To him it meant Darryl Zanuck and Fatty Arbuckle. Charlie Chaplin waddling away. It was no homesteader's cabin at the bend in the river by the cottonwood trees. If Hollywood was nuts so was the world; it was cockeyed, and Charlie looked at everything going on around him and became his own director. I mean, he certainly had the actors and the props.

For this was back in a time and a place long since dead and gone. A time that will never come again. It was those Goodbye Broadway, Hello Riker's Island years — when a man could get roaring drunk for 3½ cents, get down on his knees to pray and STAY there . . . a time to be happy and a time to be sad — a time that saw Herman Goering, an irrepressible Kid in dirty knickers, sell newspapers out in front of the old Sodomy Bathhouse with ALWAYS a smile on his freckled, never to be forgotten pan, and a look in his dancing Irish eyes that ALREADY said: Look out world here I come! — when some rum crazed fool down at Tennessee Avenue and the Beach looked down at the sand, up into the sun, screamed GOLD! and all HELL broke loose — when

Adolf Hitler crossed the border into Austerlitz and got caught
in the broom closet with the Kaiser's favorite police dog —
when some glorious nut named right way Corrigan did the
wrong thing and didn't crack up but flew directly into the
hearts of all America alREADY full to bursting with Shirley
Temple, Fatty Arbuckle, Capt. Benjamin Anderson, Will
Rogers, Dickie Loeb, Nathan Leopold, and the 3 Ritz
Brothers (count em) while Van E. Johnson was continually
flying straight to Hell in a ruptured mother fucking duck of a
P-34½, with one engine afire, a picture of Carole Landis over
the cockpit and his hand on the knee of a guy named Joe,
some poor son-of-a-bitch who never had a chance. . . .

Charlie Leeds had been there, been part of everything, had
seen the lowest and the worst, and he had passed through it; he
was not defeated by it but emerged with his soul intact. He was a
frail, bent shadow but he had survived things that would have
killed most other people, bludgeonings, not only of the heart and
the spirit but of the body. He had been in the bad prisons, the
Rahways and Forida State peniteniaries; the hospitals where they
filled you with Prolixin and threw you in the hole for two months,
where they strapped you down and administered the elec-
troshock treatments day after day after day. A frail, bent shadow . . .

But none of this hurt him as badly as his affairs of the heart. He
would crack up and fall out at the flutter of an eyelash or the coy
tilt of a head. He wrote me letters about someone he had just met
who "is so *impossible*, the end all and be all. . . ."

> You're crazy anyway just as you are,
> standing all by yourself and being
>
> more beautiful than anyone ——
> in the corner
>
> of the attic
> (of my memory)

And he'd insist that I make it on down to A.C. and check her
out and I would and the beauty he had on a pedestal would, like
as not, be a hard-eyed Club Harlem hooker or a gum chewing fast

fading beautician and what they had in common was they were going to take him, take him for love or money. If he had either he gave of it. He never held back and they took him. You couldn't *tell* him though. A week or a month later would come the letter, usually from a hospital somewhere, and he would describe, in detail, how she had done him wrong and how he had flipped out.

Yet, in other things he could not be fooled. He could spot a hypocrite or a phoney from around the corner as long as he wasn't in love with her. Music, art, writing — you couldn't put anything past him. Especially music. He always told me, particularly when I was encouraging him about his writing, "Yes, but I'm a musician; first, last and always . . ."

Man, he could write; but God could he ever play.

When he made that squads right out of the Victory parade on Broadway and stuck the needle in his arm he assumed his only salvation was to play. He picked up an instrument for the first time right after the War and a year later was playing bass in Charlie Spivak's big band. He moved over to Woody Herman, Buddy Rich and then Stan Getz. Ira Gitler, the critic, called him the best white bass player in jazz. But he couldn't make that big time scene either. He cared too much. He walked into the recording studio in New York one time and saw his fellow musicians sitting around reading comic books and he walked back out, right out of that scene.

He played with more esoteric figures, the underground legends of jazz, of bebop, the small combos of Tadd Dameron, Brew Moore, Tony Fruscella, George Wallington. He played all over the country. With Wardell Gray in Los Angeles and Philly to Jones in Miami. Always playing. He even formed a combo with the artist Larry Rivers playing baritone and once toured the South in the western swing band of Cowboy Copas.

When that scene died a part of him died, although it took me years to understand that. The music changed and all the people who had mattered just dropped by the wayside. Gene Quill was living in a skid row hotel in Atlantic City. Joe Albany disappeared. Brew Moore went to Europe and died alone, in Copenhagen. But Charlie continued to play, in honky tonks, in strip joints, in fancy restaurants where he might sneak in a little bebop while the diners were slurping up the gravy, maybe a little "How High the

Moon" smack dab in the middle of "Moon River" and they'd never know.

I would go to hear him play in some back alley bar and he'd be bent over his bass, eyes closed, talking to himself, laying something down that was just outside of everything, beyond all of it, and while he was there doing that he had transcended. He was finally out there in the wild blue crazy yonder and if it never would have ended he would have been alright.

It was 1968 when he ran off down the Boardwalk and straight (back) into the long arms of the law and I went up to Canada. October it was, and if there were any trees in Atlantic City they would have been radiant with autumn's palette and even Baltic Avenue would have been all in chirascuro, but as it was fog enshrouded the Steel Pier and an icy wind came off the ocean as we leaned on the Boardwalk rail and Charlie told me the story of his arrest, the latest, and the fact that in two days he went for sentencing and knew what was coming down; thirteen years as an habitual. It was a very funny story at least until he mentioned the thirteen.

Charlie had been hanging around a drugstore as he was wont to do; in fact he had a meeting with the druggist who was going to give him some pills and some paregoric. Charlie was waiting in the little hallway just beyond where they fill the prescriptions, right outside the stockroom. Keeping in the back so as not to call undue attention to himself and thus, the druggist, an upstanding citizen, Rotarian, etc. who filled script for Charlie nevertheless, in exchange for free meals at Zaberer's or drinks at Cody's or wherever, Charlie was playing.

Charlie got tired of leaning against the shelves with all the Ace bandages and little statuettes in trusses, so he went into the stockroom and sat down and every ten minutes he'd go out to the counter and say, "Is it time?" And the answer would be, "Not yet."

Finally Charlie lay down in the laundry hamper to rest, pulled an old uniform over his eyes and fell asleep. When he woke it was very late, the drugstore closed at ten, there were several uniforms on top of him now. The employees must have just tossed them on never knowing he was under there. Now he had to get out of the place without setting off any alarms but then he wouldn't have his medicine and would have to come back the next day and start all over again, so, he reasoned, he might as well take it with him.

There he was, a forty-four-year-old man, crawling on his belly across the polished linoleum floor of a drugstore headed for the shelf where they kept the paregoric. He felt like he was in a John Wayne movie sneaking through no-man's-land, and the reason he was down like that was because of the magic eye that would set off the alarm at the police station. He stopped first when he came to the cough medicine, genuine codeine, and snatched a bottle, took a drink. Just before he got to the paregoic he paused to reach up and feel around in the cash register drawer. The alarm went off. Charlie ran to the back door and couldn't get it open. He jumped into the laundry hamper and burrowed down deep. A few minutes later the cops arrived, flashed their lights around, looked here and there but not in the hamper. They mumbled about some kind of mistake and left.

Charlie began again but his mistake this time was the ice cream. He grabbed a quart out of the cooler and scooped some up with his fingers. It was very soft, almost melted, a mess actually. He got the paregoric but in his greed and against his better judgement he reached to a shelf he *knew* was above the four foot level, for a handful of Christmas trees (Tuinals), and the alarm caught him in the act. There was nothing for it but to dive again into the laundry.

And it was there they found him. He sensed it growing lighter and lighter as one by one they removed the uniforms from atop his face and finally he was staring into the eyes of two cops on the beat.

"Hi, Chaz."

"How'd you find me?"

"You left a trail."

To me he recalled, "It was the goddamned ice cream. *Bing* cherry."

We laughed at that leaning on the cold rail looking out at the steel gray ocean and the cobalt sky, and out on the horizon where the two met we would have expected the sun to be sinking if there had been a sun or at least the MGM lion to be aroaring. But nothing happened. We stopped laughing and Charlie told me about those thirteen years he was looking at and he wasn't bitter. After all, as he liked to say, he had been in every prison and hospital east of the Mississippi and many of the ones west, and, if indeed he was exaggerating — just a little — he had made up for it in repeats. He gave me a package that contained a couple hundred pages of his writings and then he said that about Pres and Bird and Billie and walked away.

After I arrived in Canada I began sending his writings out to journals and little magazines. I had no idea what to expect. He had never been published in the States and his writing just seemed so American. But nearly every place took something and one editor, Jake Zilber of *Prism* in Vancouver, wrote that he believed Charlie was as important a writer as anyone in North America and, further, he vowed to do whatever was possible to get a book published. Zilber collaborated with November House, run by Cherie Smith, and the result was a book of plays, stories and poems called *Tillie's Punctured Romance*. Naturally Charlie was overwhelmed. The reviews appeared and they were all favorable. He was playing alto sax in the prison band and receiving visitors from Canada as well as the local press. All of this attention served him well when he came up before the parole board. It convinced the authorities that he had a purpose in life, something to go out to.

Charlie made parole and got married. And this wife, number three or four, was someone to whom I had shown his book. She wrote to him while he was in the joint and they fell in love by mail. He came up to see me in Toronto and he looked better than he ever had, his hair long and curled at the back like Wild Bill Hickok. He was happy and he had Martha and plenty of dope and he almost looked healthy. Sure, he was a junkie, no getting around that but, well, he was an old fashioned junkie which is all the difference in the world. We made a tour of Toronto, went to all the Shoppers Drug Marts, took turns going into to buy Benzedrex nasal inhalants which were illegal in the U.S. due to the contents. Benzedrine and Dexedrine.

We listened to music as always. Charlie had long ago steered me, gently, from Ornette Coleman to Lester Young, from Miles Davis to Nick Scott.

But, alas, Charlie went home to A.C.; they discovered he had violated his parole and back he went to Rahway. He was released in six months but everything had changed. I went to see him a year later when he was in Narconon, a drug rehab place, just like I

had visited him in Lexington, Kentucky ten years earlier. In 1974
he had a heart attack and this time when I went down he was old,
not like an old man but rather a very weird, overaged kid. Martha
had left him. He was going with a college girl. It was a pattern
over the next few years. One young girl and one hospital after
another.

He had started to drink. It was a necessity. He got beat on the
dope deals and he had to have *something*. The girls took him for
bread. Everything was coming apart. One of the last times I saw
him, he had just gotten out of the hospital two days before. He
had been pronounced dead. His heart had stopped. He said,
"Man, I was lying on the table and it was beautiful, I had this
dream about you and Lana Turner and the twelve apostles."

We went to Nicholson's Bar and Charlie was feeding his
quarters into the jukebox, playing Boz Scaggs' "Get Down" over
and over, snapping his fingers and dancing alone on the little
floor. Later we went back to his place and watched the Young-
Foreman fight on television. Charlie, my friend Mif and I, and
some character who hung around Charlie trying to impress the
legend with how hip he was. One of those people who tries so
hard they can't *ever* make it. Charlie very subtly began to play off
his pose. We had been talking of old fighters, the guy was
signifying and Charlie said to me, "Remember Red Norvo?"

"Great fighter."

"Yeah," said Charlie, "fast hands."

"Say, Chaz" I inquired, "You recall the Red Norvo-Kid Ory
fight?"

He nodded, "Saw it live, the Gardens and I sat with the *Tribune*
scribe, that revered old sage of pugilism, Stan Levey."

And to the guy he said, "What'd you think of Kid Ory?"

"Uh, yeah. Pound for pound, he was, uh, one of the best."

We eventually dropped Charlie at some bar way in the pine
forest, three in the morning, where he hoped his latest young
thing might appear.

I was staying in Florida and he started writing me about how
bad things had become. In and out of the hospital. Drinking a
quart and a half of Five Star a day plus taking whatever came his
way. The letters became telegrams. "*Please* come and see me."

I did but he hardly knew I was there. He was drunk sick and
raving. We took him to the hospital. Me and him and another

junkie in one car. Friends in a second. He was passed out, woke every few miles to say, "You really came to see me, Babe."

It was another hospital and another doctor. In the Fifties he had written about how all his life doctors with bad breath and crew cuts had been telling him that he had to "straighten up" and here was another one, while he was dying, doing the same thing, only the haircut was different. It was a state mental hospital, Ancora, thirty miles from A.C. "You have to let him in. If you don't he's going to buy it."

This bastard actually was smoking a pipe and looking at me very seriously in his little room and he had a copy of *Psychology Today* on his desk and he said, "Why is he like this?"

In twenty-five words or less. I wanted to smash him, which is a difference between Charlie and me, but I didn't, instead, I said what Charlie would have said, "Like *what*?"

He told me it was against all rules to let him in. He had already checked the file. Charlie had been a patient twelve times. "Then what's one more time?"

"He's only permitted in twice a year. It's the rules. I don't make them . . . blah blah blah. . . etc."

"Should I take him back to the Boardwalk, lay him down there, near the Diving Horse? Let him expire right there with your name pinned to his chest?"

Finally they admitted him. He was coming around by then and started telling the doctor about Cezanne. "Just sign the papers Charlie . . ."

They called a nurse and put him in a wheel chair and began to take him away. They pushed him across the lobby to the heavy swinging doors and just as they were going through he said to her, a big fat chocolate colored nurse, "Do you know what Lester Young was?"

And then he looked back over his shoulder at me just before the doors closed.

And I never saw him again.

I loved him and he died.

("And you can play that on your mother-fuckin' piano sometime")

PETER STEVENS

The Bix Poems

1   His Music

I taste the whipped marshmallow puffs
Of Rachmaninoff, then swig the beer
Of Chopin, Liszt's chocolate soda
Syrups my mouth — the easy sweetness
Of a body dreamed around me. . . .

Then they melt, these insubstantial menus,
Appetite unslaked; it's then I grab reality
In whiskey, fierce and acrid, palpable
In my throat, the very breath for making song.

2

These furnishings within the rooms of music —
gilt-edged mirrors, ponderous ottomans of velvet
with clawless pads sliding through plush pile.

The bedrooms give no rest, no love, no dreams
within their grip of clinical chrome, strapped
plastic stiff against a body's slump.

He searches for sounds that offer him welcome,

*These poems are based on ideas and incidents from the life of Bix
Beiderbecke, a cornet player of genius in the early days of jazz.*

colour splashed on walls, surprises round each corner,
a sudden blaze of sunlight through an atrium.

Chairs and tables higgle-piggle in his head,
clutter his need for space, precision, open doors.
He breaks his shins lumbering through fat-stuffed deafness.

He fingers valves in silent, mocking fanfares,
then placing his sweet cornet by his bottle,
he starts to fist the hotel room to splinters.

3

Snow in thin sheets scattered in lavender
Under the moony mist of Indiana. . . .

A Model T lurches and bounces over winter fields
And flutters crusted soil whitely from the wheels.

It stops mid-field — two men inside the car
Reach down and lift their trumpets to the stars

To tumble walls of darkness, one's cracked dribble,
The other's spark ignites the dried out-stubble

To grow through snow, breaking through ice to swell
To full, sound cobs, seen green and tasselled.

When morning straddles the horizon he fills
The sky with a cornet's golden bell.

4

His lips are wiped to dryness
when he blows his song

with chaste kisses into melody.

He took a detour on a journey
just to place his sweet dry mouth
on a woman's opening lips.

Through this passionate aridity
a woman softly breathes her yes —
her virgin body breaks in music.

5   *Vision*

Balled in a corner, bawl-
ing agonies, head banged
on his knees, and his hand
shapes the fingering's grip
at notes that shift to hot
slivers knuckled, slavers:
No, they'll not murder me,
those fierce desperados
under the bed, plunder
my heart with knives. Oh why
can't I close my eyes, hunt
dreamless sleep, for they frame
these nights with violence, seize
songs my horn waits to sing?

Dark — and murderers stalk:
incessant assassins
climb staff lines after him.

6

At his graveside
a simple bouquet

a name on the card
but not herself.

No one has traced her
after he dropped from life —
she walked down the dark
marrying her silence to his.

DOUGLAS BEARDSLEY

Two Prose Poems

Talcum

Only when he got her back to his room did he
remember the baby powder. The last time he'd seen his brother
naked, shaving in the bathroom one morning before work, he'd
barely been able to see his genitals they were so encrusted in
white powder like a paste that would harden him to a statue
admired by all. He'd always felt that way about his brother's
body. But now hers was offered to him, she had removed
everything and it was obvious he was expected to do the same.

As he took off his jeans he saw that his jockey-blue
underwear had turned white. It's only fear he thought, but
when he pulled them down a great cloud of powder was the
only thing that rose from his private parts. 'Powder', he
coughed, 'it's only powder to keep fresh.' 'Powder my ass', she
said as she left by the back door: 'it's dust', she laughed, 'god
damn dust!'

Celebration

A jazz quartet has invaded my apartment. The piano player is in my study, assembling 88 books in a row. The drummer is emptying out the kitchen shelves, setting up my pots and pans. The bass player has disappeared into the bedroom, tossing my mattress to side one, he tilts my cot on end, limbering up his fingers on the springs. And, when last heard from, the tenor saxophonist, disguised as a plumber, had entered the bathroom and was busy disconnecting the pipe beneath my wash-basin.

All of this, for only $5.95.

GREG HOLLINGSHEAD

IGA Days

In the early days fate had my wife in the role of the old friend with a knapsack who is on the road. This was before our marriage. Vancouver 1967, and you know how things were out there in those days, with a new age dawning. It was not my own personal renaissance, however. I would say that in some ways I am easily more in the dark now than I ever was. All the ingredients were there in 1967 but either they just sat around and screamed at their palms or they left. To take one example that also contains the seeds for my present state of mind, I was living with Clare then, the most beautiful woman that I have ever seen. You could hang a brick from the erections I got just from her ankles alone. Once around that time I was in conversation with a psychiatrist who later got himself jailed for demonstrating when they killed the Winter Works Program. This was when the Liberals were having one of their hundred-dollar-a-plate fund-raising dinners, and we were standing around in the heat abusing guests as they slowed down for the turn into the parking lot. I was complaining to this psychiatrist about wanting a woman with a great mind, when we saw Clare herself come swinging through the crowd towards us. The psychiatrist said, "Isn't that your girlfriend there?"

And I said, "Yes."

And he said, "I sure as hell wouldn't complain," and then he turned from me, shouting, "If you're so hungry, eat this!" and tossed a hotdog with the works through the open window of a Mercedes-Benz.

Actually, Clare did have an interesting mind, but it was crazy and mixed up, and I'm not thinking of her taste for the one-handed magazines. She moved out after five or six months to work on a fishing boat. A lot of young women out there work on boats, and a lot of the young men log. Everybody else is either retired or a junkie or an artist for the government, drawing unemployment. It was me and Mandrax that drove her out, I am ashamed to admit, but a few months later I had my spinal column back. You could say that I was afraid of her. She loved me so much that I'd get scared and then she'd get scared and go rigid for two or three hours, etc. It wasn't much of a life for her.

So Clare moved out and I went cold turkey — my whole life before me a plate of leftovers — and then Susan, with the knap-sack, was visiting, and she was an old friend from adolescence in Etobicoke, which is part of Toronto, and she dove in and dragged me out of the sere fussiness thickets I was wandering strange in by that time from trying to live the straight life from the outside, which never works. And who arrives a week later back on surprise leave from the fishing boat? Also, I had been evicted from my apartment over Kosiak's IGA. That was Friday, and I was due out at Sunday midnight.

Susan was upstairs in the kitchen packing a crate of my books while I was down below, hanging around the stinking back door of the store for cardboard boxes. Every once in a while Finn, the store manager, would back open the door and throw out another one, saying, "*Nok da?*" which translates approximately out of Norwegian as "Enough, eh?" and I would reply, "Nope," as large tenderness vibrations welled outwards from my heart for him in his grudgeless forgiving toil. Susceptible to emotion composed equally of departure nostalgia and guilt for causing Finn this extra trouble, it was his poor ruined arches I dwelt on, his horrible shiny red IGA blazer, his expressive baffled wince, similar to that of a man who has just received an arrow in the back, when a customer would say, "My husband bought ice cream, so's I guess we don't really need this," and hold out to him across the checkout counter a pie in a box, the box ripped open, the top of the pie — one of those red chemical structures designed and built out of all-new materials by chemist maniacs — smeared, the whole pie in a state of real dubious congelation, against the top of the box, and Finn would gaze into the box anxiously, with sadness — the way I have seen him gaze at the corpse of a rat — and tape it up (masking tape) and give the woman her refund with a small laugh. "Thanks, Finn!" I shouted into the rotting vegetable storeroom, but he must have been called away back up front.

The entrance to my apartment was from off the street, so I didn't see Clare arrive. She was drinking tea in the kitchen with Susan when I started tossing and booming boxes up the stairs. All ignorant then, I wandered into the kitchen, and though Susan still had on that special humorous defiance look that when a man walks in will enter the faces of any two or three women who are gathered together, I never dreamt. "Let's eat," I said, and Clare stepping out of the broom closet, I added, "Hi, Clare," going reflex casual when my selves are in collision.

"Hi, Blasé," said Clare, uncharacteristically, and kissed me.

"Our new broom," I told Susan, who replied,

"Touché!" her wit running, even in those days, to gnomic, and nuttily inserted.

"You said it," I moaned, countering under a whole new emotion complex settling in on me.

We sat down and had tea. I grilled a sandwich while Clare and Susan watched. Clare said, "How's Finn?"

"I think it broke his heart to have to do it, but he doesn't own the building. Kosiak found our Northwest Passage." And I told them the story, highlighting comic facets of the behaviour of Allen G. Kosiak. It wasn't easy. Even in those days he wanted to be an MP, and had the vulgar hard mouth for it. He almost fired poor Finn, and it was not Finn's fault at all.

Later Clare showed around a colour magazine she'd got from one of the fishermen. She told us that the other girl on the boat had an orgasm while just standing there on the deck looking through it. I don't think there was any other girl on the boat. In the first picture three people are sitting on a sofa toasting each other. The guy promises to be a regular stallion, while in real life I would say the girls are filing clerks from Odense. In the second picture all hell has broken loose, and the guy fulfills his promise. Flip the pages and everybody's a contortionist. But it's not until the inside back cover that the cat's pajamas are sprawled all over the table, and this one almost actually offends me. I nearly had an orgasm myself. As for Susan, she giggled in a frank happy shocking way, observing, "All's well that ends well, Booboo!" Clare laughed once, then looked at her strangely, and went out suddenly for cigarettes, so that Susan and I were left remarkably alone at the kitchen table wearing matching helpless embarrassment expressions, with the magazine alongside our respective hands, and I don't know what we were thinking of, until Susan jumped up and returned to packing. When Clare got back she whispered that she wanted to go to bed with Susan and me together.

"What did Susan say?" I asked, the question of a paranoid,

"I haven't said anything. You ask her."

So I went to Susan and I said, "Ha ha. Hey Susie. Clare wants the three of us to go to bed. What do you think?" And Susan lifted her head up from inside the crate she was packing, and drawing the back of her wrist across her forehead, she replied, "Love is no potato!"

Uncertain of her meaning, I nodded thoughtfully. She smiled.

We were starving. We got in my van and drove to a Chinese restaurant, and the sleek streets and the buildings lolled and basked in the warm dusk sunshine of our foreknowledge. What a secret we had! The Chinese half of the menu, the expression on the face of our waiter... such routine enigmas had nothing on us, who were magic. I understood fraternity. I understood homosexuals, and I heard the fall of their hatpins. I understood the Masons and all secret societies from the beginning of history. On the way home I wrapped the van around a large dead elm. In a dream it seemed we were standing as we stood and watched the tow-truck winch and tear my mangled friend out of its terrible final embrace. Scatheless, shaken, we walked the rest of the way home, wits tremulous at first — I know my own brain was working in a foam of contrition to clear out some permanent (this time) road allowance for heaven's next showstopper — and then we were all talking at once, and everybody's point of view was interesting: the long driftpast of house, streetlight, hedge, that Clare was witness to; the rocker panel bulging in like grey tinfoil at Susan, and my notice of the calm way the windshield sent out, as in a spirit of exploration, from where the fist of a stump of elm nosed through, a network of tentative crackings, and the way, slowly, that great handfuls of niblets began to fall from around that widening hole and others, until Clare and I held the windshield's complete weight heavy and comforting in our laps. After discussing these things, we didn't say anything until we were safe home and had drunk a mickey of brandy.

My bathtub in that apartment over the IGA was heavy and deep, and had feet the size of softballs. When water splashed down the overflow it sooner or later passed through the acoustic ceiling tiles over the section of the fruit and vegetable display counter variously lettuce and cucumbers, and dripped. It must also have soaked through the years along the floorboards, because towards my bathtub from every direction they sagged. A marble dropped anywhere in that cavernous hall that Kosiak declared a bathroom, nosed clicking in with all the other once free-rolling objects under the tub. So when three of us got in, with a grim half-smile I thought of heaven's encore: Tub Plunges Orgiasts to Vegetable Death. As it happened, in our distraction, we splashed, probably, and the lettuce or the cukes got anointed, but the floor itself held strong, and before long there was no water left at all — a toe must've brushed out the plug — and so twined and passionate were we that we never noticed it, and believe me I am the world's last person to be able normally to sit in a tub while all the water drains.

What had not occurred to me was how thoroughly the women

would hit it off. Later, on the bed, they kept saying how it was just like reaching into the mirror. I pointed out that surely they were saying the thing that was not, since few women could be less alike in point of build or anatomical feature. They had to agree, and Susan in an unforgettable moment of gruff lucidity suggested they were not used to a woman up close, that's all. Of course, they did know their way around, by analogy, and I was only indulging myself.— the kid in the candy store with ten bucks in his back pocket — when, for example, the five senses of each I introduced to the nether-leaping locus of the other. Sure our amours were *outré*. In spirit, however, they were wholesome and issued only eventually in a kind of sickening in the heart's pit, pure quotidian sorrow for gone joys. If there were sense-of-sin bubbles, they might've clung to that insularity dream I mentioned, the one we were all caught up in dreaming, but knowing that the world would soon enough come rasping at our door, as it always does, was enough to pot those qualms, fast.

Our sleep that night was an infant rest. Susan chose a pallet of foam alongside the bed. Before I turned out the light, she knelt and looked on watching over the edge. Afterwards — "Woof! Woof!" — she indicated she had felt like the dog. At dawn's first sigh Saturday we floated out into the city, to the flea market, and were luminous. But the whole morning really was prelude to bed, and we were back in by 10 A.M., and that's where you could have found us until dusk, except for breathers on the sun-mottled fire escape, radiating our secret out into the back lane. That night we went to a party given by somebody that Clare and I knew, and those cool people all seemed so booshwah. And then in the cab on the way home Clare lobbed a casual brick through our minds by mentioning she'd decided to sleep with both of us together because she didn't want to miss the beginning of my next love affair, and exactly as the cabby's eyes hit the rearview, Susan and I as one cried, "What!?" because both of us had already started dropping such wholehearted asides as, all the three of us need now is an island and we can die happy, and only then did we realize the awful truth. Together we struggled to demonstrate to Clare the palpable folly of her approach, and I have never heard Susan speak with such passionate if cryptic eloquence; but Clare went vague on us, her face turned to the smeary glass, and we knew that beautiful woman had the demon of our joy's undoing slouched and lurking in the secret shadows of her anxious, stubborn heart. Heaven's encore, I thought to myself, has arrived small and ordinary, like a worm in the night. But either I was wrong or else heaven's blows, like everything else heaven bundles off earthwards, she bundles off in threes, because later as I lowered myself for the sake of a few bananas by way of a rope ladder into the downstairs storeroom (having gone crafty and handed over to Kosiak only one of a whole slew of keys to the Northwest Passage), there cam a blinding glare, and out of it a voice that said, "Freeze, hippie." I dropped to the floor, rehearsing: *I heard a noise down here, and so, slipping on my jeans, I jimmied* . . .

We made a sort of deal, though really it was all Kosiak's idea, his pet, and I could not have dissuaded him. He would not call the police if I agreed to work, starting Monday, one hundred hours on his election campaign. He explained that this would be my chance to change the system from the inside, and I realized he was not such a bad guy after all; he was a real idiot. He made me climb the rope and pull it up after me and padlock the trap door, then meet him at the bottom of the front stairs to my apartment and there hand over the second key. He was very moved by this enlightened, recountable punishment, and I thought he was going to try to hug me. We shook hands, and efforts were made by him to lock my eyes significantly with his. Later, on the sidewalk, as he pressed his card ("Back Kosiak") into my other palm, compassion came leaking out from around my heart for him and his doomed — if I could help it — lurch towards the legislature. A few minutes still later, demoralized, I lowered myself again into the storeroom for bananas while watching one of those mental landscapes with a sunset into which Good Times, in white convertible, is accelerating.

The women hadn't missed me. At times like that you wonder why they bother with us as much as they do. They enjoyed the bananas, and soon thereafter, day breaking, we sank into poignant sleep, poignant because we'd all noticed by then the indestructible new Bulova that Eros was wearing. Sunday early we got immediately down to rampant carnality, being all around twenty years old in those days, with one foot still in the cradle and that

Bulova echoing tick tick tick tick all around us: now Susan and I working side by side like sweaty volunteer sandbaggers to bank up Clare's rapture; now both women bent over me, surgeons saving a life; now the whole quivering configuration collapsing to limb and mouth. There wasn't much talk, only giggles, though once I remember Susan while somewhere in the middle of being transported by her along a certain high-voltage wire, cried, "You're so beautiful, Clare!" from the heart, and of course she was. A woman could see it as well as I could. Better.

I don't know where, aside from ecstasy, that day got to. Reason dictates we must occasionally heave eaten and napped. Rain, I remember, kept us off the fire escape. Otherwise the fragrant smooth skin of the beloveds of one hell of a lucky yours truly is all that comes to mind. At 8:30 A.M. Monday we were all still engaged in the sleep of novice voluptuaries when something woke me up, and there was Finn's face staring in at the door, the door swiftly closing, then a knock, a pause, and this croaky despairing whisper, in English: "You must be moved out last night!"

"Noon! Noon today!" I bluffed, and the yell at her ear caused doe-like Clare to bolt up. Vanless, however, and renting a truck, it took, even with Finn generously helping us during lulls in the store, until five o'clock, and all the while the new, speedfreak tenants were whipping promiscuously their stuff in amidst mine, which Clare let me store in the basement of her parents, who were on their silver wedding anniversary Hawaiian second honeymoon, and would be only nominally surprised she said, to find *it* — not me, she meant — there when they got back. Susan called some people she knew vaguely, and in the cool dark of Clare's parents' basement hugged us soberly goodbye, kissing Clare's cheek as Clare hugged her sadly. When Clare invited me upstairs for a glass of water, I sat her down in her parents' startling, neo-Green Girl living room and begged her without shame to go away with Susan and me to an island paradise. She, however, said outright and without scorn that kind of scene was not where her destiny lay, and even as I watched gathered up her stuff, told me to lock the door when I left, kissed me, and went back to the fishing boat.

So there I was, unaccommodated, the happy guy who twenty-four hours earlier was elect, was Riley, sitting now in a clear-plastic-covered living room in fading dusklight, thinking only of the look on Finn's flattened face as he opened the bedroom door, the look of a man with an arrow fresh in his back: startled, anxious, offended; of Clare stepping out from that kitchen broom closet as eager as a flame; of Susan giggling up from the inside back cover depravity of Clare's magazine; of the weight of half my van's windshield, heavier in my lap than any napkin. It was like the end of a movie, those highlight snippets, each one going into a heart-tugging freeze, a very sentimental experience for me, and I crawled into Clare's narrow teenage bed and there, with no apology to the massively hung and glossy wedge of beefcake reclined with his hand on it and a simper on the wall I'd turned my face to, cried for all that we had so scarcely had.

Next morning I returned the rented truck and reported, one day — but to the minute — late, to Kosiak's campaign headquarters. There his staff were unimpressed to see me. Later I caught a few whispers, though not their substance, just the eyes, and they and no doubt others served to render me the kind of Stepin Fetchit who nobody trusts. Not once in the eight twelve-hour days that followed were tools for significant sabotage placed either absently or amidst the heat of crisis in my hands. Kosiak waved once from across the room, his eyes already shifting away. For putting a sheen on people, or taking it off, for putting a glaze on their gaze and leaving it there, human cunning has never come up with any gimmick so slick as hierarchy. Here Kosiak was Kingfish, and I was a walking instance of his creative yet somehow courageous if at times unorthodox solutions to very real, very immediate social problems of vital concern to all of us blah blah.

One night late I went to visit Susan at her friends', and she had fallen sick. It looked like a bad case of sorrow to me. One thing opened out into another as, failing to comprehend her replies, I ravelled on until I was standing in a kind of corner and there I confessed I didn't feel I understood her well enough to be her constant lover all on my own. The tears flowed immediately, like wine, and in the days ahead we came to know each other better. Clare was back in town, and sometimes we would talk about how to seduce her. We never succeeded. One of us would have dinner or go to a movie with her and come back and admit defeat. Clare had moved on. Today it is Bio-energetics. Tomorrow — ? As for Susan and me, we got, as I let slip earlier, married. With the occasional exception, I still haven't the faintest idea what she is talking about, not so much as my ten-speed. But her heart, her beautiful heart, is comprehensible to me, and in dark times like these, when the spirit of Allen G. Kosiak is writ gigantic, like some vast noxious growth that drags its shadow through the minds of a dispirited citizenry, believe me, love is no potato.

SUSAN MUSGRAVE

I Took a Wire Cage into the Woods

I took a wire cage into the woods
in which to sit and watch the animals.
They gathered round me as I'd hoped they would
and sat, expressionless, with closed eyes,
warming themselves in the sun.

Their bodies were beautiful, unlike mine;
their bodies were solitary, never lonely.
They must have sat for hours in one place
as if to reassure me all was understood.

Their patience was exhausting. All night
I watched till dark and light were
blotted out and whole seasons passed.

I did not leave that cage again but lay
under the cool influence of the stars,
awake and dreaming.

My dreams were always the same.
Always in my own image those animals rose
out of the dust, animals with human faces
whose eyes were open, sorrowful.

Their bodies were broken.
No longer content to sit and stare
at one such as this, confined by choice
within the shadows of a spectral cage,
they paced as those condemned, and wept,
while I, the guilty one, was saved.

Second Sight

The flies were thick in the bush
and we had nothing but trouble.

Our clothes were uncomfortable;
like sleep-walkers we stripped
and spread wide our arms

it was misty and cool

our eyes could not focus on
details

and everywhere the smell of the
wild, wild roses
assaulted our senses.

We found a clearing and built a
fire.
We were two little sisters
and life together was awesome.

Being born into that wide, cool,
misty, wild rose morning

we touched each other and a
bear came.
A bear came running with a crowd
after him,
a black bear with a secret black hole
in his heart.

We wanted to help.
Two sisters we believed in sharing
and called him to our human fire,
content with caring.

He was an ugly bear, unused to
kindness.
He did not forgive us
but embraced us.

Two old gaping women we
still remember that touch

and try to recall the vision
in words:

an old bear echoes
enough, enough!

A Feat of Arms

I slept with war
all night I slept with war once.
I did not sleep peacefully
but killed without guilt whatever it was
I needed.

There are wounds you never wake from,
wounds that lie silent under an enemy
of skin.
There are desperate wounds
that keep you alive for hours.
They stick to you for days.
You can't heal them.

There are costly tombs on the
perfect grass
and lonely flights through drunken spaces
with nothing to pray for and
no one to listen.

It's a rut.
It's drab.
I'd like to go somewhere.

I'd like to find something worth being
wounded about
and sleep without comfort forever again.

GARY MICHAEL DAULT

Poem Before Sleeping

I am sealed.

I am perfect for
What covers me.

I go to the eggshell.

A Thought About Thought

A knot is a kind of root,
Lozenge or diamond on a line,
A node but no object yet.

And so a thought to boot,
An ancient present tense of mine,
A priestly clockwork mirror to get.

False Poem of Among-Between

    One flattery out of four:
Sailing into blindness
    One foot from the door.

    One foolishness out of two;
Folding paper in the cold
    A compliment to you.

    One rebellion out of three,
Permitting me to tell the truth
    When the truth is free.

    One cancellation in the five:
The bad way, come this way,
    Into my participial alive.

    One composing of the one:
Let us pretend the mysticism's done.
    Help us to be unmindful of the fun.

MARILYN POWELL

A Psychological Story

At the top of the house Agnes is in a brown study. It's a study in hysteria. She's middle-aged and raw-boned, lean from constantly running ahead of her past — nothing if not crazed — or so those who know her would think if they could look into her head. She'd better get to a psychiatrist who can cure what pain and traffic, what illogical, inconclusive affairs with the opposite sex have caused. Or so she imagines. Anyway, she's going directly to the horse's mouth.

The light filters through the window, out from under the sharp edges of the blind in dull, grey winter shafts. Past the fireplace with its heavy Victorian varnish and shelves for knick-knacks, over the hole in the floor where the gas jet was once, finally illuminating the couch where I'm lying, a crochet throw over my knees and two needlepoint pillows under my head. I've tacked up an oriental carpet, a facsimile anyway, six by nine, on the wall (I've worked out the dimensions in my head as best I could from the photographs); exactly as he had it behind his couch, with the chair, fat and upholstered, anchored in position, to the side and behind, waiting for him. Of course I know Sigmund Freud is dead.

If he weren't, at three o'clock on an afternoon like this he'd be seeing patients. Vienna at the turn of the century. City of Dreams and steamy awakenings. And Dora at eighteen. A torte with Oedipal icing, she admits: "I yearn for my father. My father covets his neighbour's wife, but his neighbour lusts after me." Recalling that he treated Dora's father for syphilis four years earlier, Freud

110

nods. A little domestic intrigue holds his attention. Dora con-
cedes: "I'm a portrait in symptoms." Migraine, depression, loss of
voice, nervous cough, aggression followed by bouts of with-
drawal and preoccupation with suicide, all to punish her father
for his lack of — uh — paternal caring. Freud, "Professor" to his
intimates but not to Dora, smiles and fingers the edge of his
beard, drawing the contour around his chin and emphasizing the
mask of his neutrality.

Then ushers in the forty-year old. Frau Emmy von N., stammering and clacking, making a ticking sound that ends with a pop
and a hiss, able to express herself flat on her back without the
benefit of hypnosis. In my upstairs room, reeling with the significance of metaphor, I can hear her call out as she extends her arm,
spreading and crooking the fingers of her hand like hooks: "Keep
still! — Don't say anything! — Don't touch me!" But do. Again
the same formula — (Frau Emmy doesn't like to be interrupted in
the flow of her narrative), while Freud in the wings of his chair
takes notes and wonders why case histories resemble short
stories. In fantasy they do.

Agnes is surrounded by paperback books, an inexpensive set of
the works in print, Ernest Jones' biography of the little doctor.
She's dog-eared several pages. What she doesn't remember she
can always look up. Her world is captivated by fading concepts
and inhabited by shadows. There's an old Viennese saying: "If
you wish it, it's no fairy tale"; so Agnes is on her way to a
showdown with penis envy.

Three o'clock it is, then, in the afternoon; the door, the double
door for soundproofing, opens — (he's always punctual) — and
I'm invited in. Freud's voice is sharp, high and thin as a reed,
adroit at inducing and controlling panic. He's a consulting room
Pan on his pipes. And I, as I settle into his couch, establish
kinship with those daffy women he stroked, massaged, kneaded,
analyzed and immortalized, whose articulator he became. I am
descended from that line of stammering, clacking heroines who
assisted in the invention of a plot for the unconscious. If I wish, I
can get up tomorrow morning with a cough, partial paralysis of
an arm or maybe anorexia nervosa. I know how to heave and

push a ghost through my body and give birth to a nine pound hysteria. It's simply psychosomatic — the imagination connives with the uterus, and I have a ghost-writer.

Her chin is tilted to the ceiling because of the angle of the headrest on the couch, and the lines on her neck, like spidery bands on an oak, are exposed. Agnes struggles to keep the mood of grand romance without devolving to Grand Guignol. *"Was will das Weib?"* — she hears Freud's voice chirping in her ear — "what does a woman want?" She croons, "I'm taking a night course in psychology to find out, and having my consciousness raised." "You are a dark continent," he teases, "we will attempt to penetrate." Pong! The springs of his chair contract, and there is the scratch of fabric as one leg crosses the other and the crack of a match as a cigar is lit. One of twenty cigars in a therapeutic day.

Oh, I know I'm not the first. First came Anna O., rising and falling, inflated with her fake pregnancy. Then the English governess, Miss Lucy R., who was obsessed with the smell of burnt pastry. And Fräulein Elizabeth von R., palpitating from pains in her legs, the first to free associate and connect them with love for her sister's husband. They were troopers, giving their all— "Eureka," he cried, "there's an association between syndrome and sex! — Who would have thought that behind the former the latter could be so raw! How ungenteel neurosis is, but how feminine!" — then wrote up their saucy scandals and circulated them in the world at large. He presses my forehead with his palm and urges: "Tell me everything; censor nothing, even if it is unpleasant or impolite." Freud is a conquistador in his prime, familiar with both the raptures of cocaine and the lows of depression, without a hint of grey at his temples, with a sign at his entry announcing his specialty in nervous diseases; I abandon myself to his devices. I confess I have these exquisite pains in my thighs, that I experience a voluptuous tickling sensation when he pinches my skin and the heat makes my face flush. I throw back my head; my body bends, spastic, obedient and on cue. Item in the *Neues Wiener Tageblatt*: "Seduction has taken place in a doctor's office — doctor denies patient's charges." *"Gott im Himmel!"* Freud is adamant, "the fact that you're spread out here like a picnic has nothing to do with me. Don't make me call in my wife, Martha, from the family apartment across the hall. She's a good woman. Every night she lays toothpaste out on my toothbrush and my pajamas out on the bed. She knows nothing of my work. Calm yourself, *bitte, bitte!*"

How do you make your analyses of women, Doctor, when you haven't been involved with one for years? The smell of his cigar smoke is a perfume that curls around my nose and almost causes me to faint with disappointed ecstasy. He says, "Don't blame me for your early troubles with your dada." In the background an unseen orchestra strikes up a Strauss waltz, abandoned and sweet, "Tales from the Vienna Woods."

From under closed eyes, Agnes listens and watches as the walls of the room fall away, and there is Freud in a dance hall, dressed in black tie and tails, clicking the heels of his shiny, patent leather boots and swaying in three-quarter time. He extends a white-gloved hand, and as he presents a rose, there is a flash of silver cufflink. "Does your lover resemble your father?" he is beaming. "Does he resemble the man you would have liked to have been, your missing part rather than your other half, your totem as opposed to your taboo?" Observation from a German visitor to the dance-halls of Vienna: " . . . no censorship can have anything to do with waltzes . . . music stimulates our emotions directly . . . lust is let loose." Everywhere couples are waving champagne glasses, while Johann Strauss, his very self, dances wildly with his fiddle bow, and a man called Fliess waltzes by.

Freud extracts traumas like nuggets from my soul and burnishes them. His body brushes against mine, and there is fire. He whispers: "It's merely transference you feel, my dove," as we glide smoothly across the floor. This passion, since it does not begin in understanding, cannot end in indifference—"*Nein, nein, nein,* it will not do! I can't take part in this hallucination! I really don't like music!" So he's back in his chair again, hunkering down, contracting six feet of the perfect hero into a mere five feet seven, and drumming his fingers on the knee of his salt-and-pepper suit.

Doctor, oh Doctor, I've had this recurrent dream of some kind of wordless communication between us that makes symbols transparent and allows our spirits to touch—"Are there any sticks, umbrellas, trees, pistols or revolvers in your dream?" Doctor, Doctor, I am plagued by reminiscences. I am a web of interlacing incidents. Interpret, interpret. I don't know what I am intend- ing — and he says: "Nothing more than the age-old repressed sexual desire, half-forgotten, half-articulated in infancy, maybe articulated never, insufficiently abreacted, that is, discharged in your present state." Not only do I dream of boxes, trunks, chests, cupboards and stoves, when I wake I am locked inside an enclosure of skin that is beginning to sag and wrinkle, betraying me. Brightness falls from the hair. How can a man differ from me in that event?

His heart is thumping wildly (I can hear it), but not from desire. Freud suffers from heart palpitations and digestive upsets. He has anxiety attacks on trains, and his breathing is slightly nasal because of constant infections in the nose. "I must remind you this is not a Wiener Schnitzler play about sexual hedonism" — there is a certain urgency in his tone—"this is not *Ring Around the Rosey* any more than it is the dance of death. What is wanted cannot be had, and what can be had isn't wanted — this is life. But, oh, *timor mortis conturbat me!*" The music of Mahler has replaced that of Strauss, his third symphony, in which drumbeats keep tempo with Freud's finger-tapping. There's saliva dribbling down the side of his polished spittoon. As he opens his mouth to aim again, a cone of blood emerges instead of a concentration of spit.

On each side of her, in her mind's eye, lodge the cabinets with their storehouse of antiquities, funerary objects. His collection. Roman, Egyptian, Assyrian and Etruscan. Heads and headless figures as streamlined as timeless rocket ships, preserved because they were buried, as the unconscious, according to Freud, is buried. Across from her, Agnes sees the small, almost secret door covered with the room's wallpaper open to reveal a tomb-like inner chamber. And there he is, sitting in a wrought-iron chair under a naked bulb beside a tray of surgical instruments. His head is propped against a leather support. His right cheek has fallen away. Quotation from the composer who is lugubriously wielding the baton: "The realm of music starts where the dark, shadowy feelings assume full sway... at the threshold of that other world where things are no longer bounded by time and space." She wants to get up and go to him. But from behind her ear, she hears him inquire: "What are you looking at?" "The future, your future," she says, and tells him.

Gustav Mahler will be one of Freud's cures, cured of his impotence but not of the loneliness beyond the tongue's reach. Not of incompleteness. One day a prosthesis will be fitted to the roof of Freud's mouth, and he will be examined by his doctor, probing with surgical instruments, in that inner torture chamber daily until he dies of cancer of the jaw. And there will be a Greek urn waiting for his ashes, the gift of a woman. Then the peace will shatter. There will be rival, multiple therapies, where groups battle each other with rubber clubs, roll on mattresses, float suspended in water, suck on pacifiers and spiral, primaling back to the womb, craving relationship. Civilization will be discontented. Psychology will be sectarian. And Jung will be revered. There will be male chauvinism, bisexuality, radical lesbianism and worship of the goddess. There will be fewer and fewer of the old true hysterics when obsessive compulsives appear in number, like zombies, and belief in the vaginal orgasm explodes. And there will be rage. Doctor, dear Doctor, the riddle of the sphinx is female as well as male. Couldn't you have done something more than theory, deeper than words, to unite the sexes, renew the bond — restore the trust, was it there in your time? On your own way to a lonely, painful end, what tied you to Martha? The soul is gratified in images, when it feels love. How can we tell the dancer from the dance?

There is a dry sound like atmospheric electricity; Freud is chuckling while under him the music dies. He is still at the head of the couch. "A bridegroom comes to a marriage broker to complain about his bartered bride," he says; "he whispers that she's old and ugly, with tooth decay and bleary eyes. But the broker replies that he needn't lower his voice because she's deaf as well." The air is charged. "You may not find the joke funny because your sense of humour is less well developed than a man's. You may not even see it as a distillation of the wisdom of the ages. I have never been responsible for what is, only for my version of it, my *Weltanschauung*. Listen to me. You are more prone to neurosis than a man. You have contributed little to the art and science of society in the past. Because of envy of the phallus, you lack the male social instinct as well as the male sense of justice. That is all I have to say about femininity except to warn you that you can't escape your patrimony. You are my daughter and throughout this century you have been shrunk!"

Agnes reaches for the cigarette he customarily provides his patients at the end of an hour, though she hasn't been given a full fifty-five minutes (the psychoanalytic definition of an hour). But even the cigarette doesn't materialize. She just has a moment to cry out: "You know what you can do with your male member!" before Freud vanishes with all his paraphernalia. His collection of antique statues, mummy covers and reliefs on every table-top and sideboard, his spittoon, his pain, his images of myth, explanations and confabulations disappear with him because it's her fiction. Her story after all, but she allows him one final observation. "Remember," disembodied, his pronouncement reaches her and imprints itself on her biography, "only when a woman holds back and denies her complete sexuality, does a man's love for her grow in the extreme. It's not reciprocity or equality we're dreaming of. What brings us together frequently, finally drives us apart. The right moves are a matter of choreography. Death is real, and life is not immortal."

"I feel so much better," Agnes confides, opening both her eyes now and stretching. "Anna O., the first and most celebrated hysteric, became a champion of female rights in her old age. The new woman, I feel confident, will rise from the ashes of the old. And I am cleared of symptoms.

> *Wir gehen in chambre séparée,*
> *Ach, zu dem süssen tête-à-tête . . .*

She's singing to herself. The attic room has resumed its former prosaic dimensions. Sorting through the pile of paperback books and thinking ahead to her night class at eight o'clock — and the subject for discussion, the feminist attack on Sigmund Freud — she reflects: "Sex could be romantic as well as dangerous in old Vienna. Coffee with whipped cream at the Café Central, promenades down the tree-lined Ringstrasse, evenings at the Theater an der Wien, and assignations in the afternoon with Herr Professor at Berggasse 19." Her expression is sentimental. "He wasn't such a bad sort really. Just a little old-fashioned when it came to interpreting a woman."

M. L. KNIGHT

A Talk with the Psychiatrist About Anniversaries

How now my gentleman of heart's ease?
Not-lost pleasantries,
Lobotomies fly by.
He says with a seatedness,
A nerve:
"I'd know immediately
You were a neurotic,
You observe
So many conscientiously peculiar
Odd anniversaries."

Well, he's hit the nail,
Blows his mauve nose.
Real books,
Real furniture
Have gone since last time; unwell groups
Sit on the amortized chairs,
Spill cups of instant soups.
I hang the year on anniversaries
As though on hooks.

There's a geometry,
Almost a slant,
To mornings, afternoons,
When I jump to old phones, old screams,

117

Again fail at Greek,
Re-swallow the turquoise tranquies,
Recall but do not speak
Of accurately awful messes,
As bound to come back as moons.

One sure thing, an anniversary
Is NOT the original day,
But references daily rise
Through memory's drinking straws
(Image). It's morning,
Time for another commemorative pause.
Will someone in mercy
Take these our anniversaries away?

Yet by some unexplained play
Of atmosphere, sun and shade,
Now what else CAN it be
But the year's own geometry,
Palpable, accurate, persistent,
That so recalls to me:
Just about ten years
And fifteen minutes ago,
I was afraid.

Life of a Clergyman's Daughter on Both Sides of the Border

I was Canadian-O till the age of ten.
Fair-domain sun rose over cheap-brick street,
Where thirty-five children in Scotch-wool home-done knit
Each crisp October ate early Thanksgiving pies.
My grandmother crocheted Englishy afghan blocks.
Poor mother pioneered beans through the rocked backyard.

Suddenly U.S.A.! A driveway, not backyard.
Where were the children? Couldn't find even ten.
They were all on bikes, spread over twenty blocks,
Or driving with their mothers down the street.
The pious drove hard, entering churches with pies,
Where at rich tables Brotherhood was knit.

How confusing. Not everyone was a nit.
Yet there we were in a Fourth-of-July backyard,
Holding our loneliness high above the pies.
The flags were very bright. I was only ten.
I was a little happy with the leafy street,
The sleepy car-ride home through the sleepy blocks.

Years passed Americanly. No memory blocks
The fact that into the Republic we were knit
With every ripple cone. Each piddling street
Was self-important. Farewell, childhood's backyard.
We had rich schoolmates, with coloured cashmeres times ten.
We rode round our lake and ate little lemon pies.

The day we moved back! a *Dies Irae* to despise.
"Canada's ruled by the King!" we screamed for blocks
To make our father mad. And the first (say) ten
Miles over the border seemed empty, shacky, unknit,
Under lonely light, with time turning back by the yard,
And fewer ice cream flavours on every street.

Dark night: the London Hotel, which impressed from the street,
I must honestly say. What a coffee shop and pies,
After snowy roads, and Canada's sad backyard.
From the seventh floor (I think) we looked out at blocks
Of what-father-said-was-native. I'm sorry we nit-
wits repeated the joke *re* the King too cruelly often.

I'm grown. Tens of years have passed since each border street.
O, Nationalism's all knit up with those lemon pies,
Fortuitous mental blocks, pure chance, a foetal backyard.

Trying to Get Comfortable at a Toronto Symphony Orchestra Concert

The back!
The affront!
Slide forward!
Slide backwards!
God-damned subscription sugar-scoop!
God now I know how infants feel in sit-up stands
                Which aren't even as adjustable as
                Proppable shorthand pads.

What shall I *do*?
Sometimes I fancy I'm Mahler
Thinking of the Ninth for the first.

The lazy orchestra works to another loud loud orgasm.
Everybody but me and the players has one.
Christ they are living proof you can
                Progress by unenergetic means to orgasm.

But not before a clump of the clumsy-footed
(Does anyone with *good* coordination ever leave early?)
                Has clumped out,
Slink slink while the Junior Women's Committee sells
Pink roses kept from water by the former belles.

FRANCIS SPARSHOTT

The Vowels

To a chorus of ahs and ohs
the vowels ride by.
In a world without vowels
you would have to stay at the Y.
Where would I be without them?
Where would you?
How could we take our ease?

If it wasn't for vowels,
Trudeau would be tired and Carter his Creator —
he would trade his pants for peanuts.
But for the vowels,
no one could tell his arse from a rose;
only the vowels keep pantyhose from Penthouse.

Let's hear it then for the vowels:
without them, a writer succumbs to wear and tear
and finds his reader ruder.

Ode:
A Quiet Morning on Campus

Strophe:

On heaven's holiest hill
the Shepherd of Being smokes his pipe —
ut hoy!
he of his pipe has so much joy.
Anthems of anthers rise
into the incense-bearing wind
and bees remembering the dance
are lured to distant sweetness,
all unashamed to wear
the dirt of flowers on their fur.
In the soft valley of his paradise
pass and repass
the Bearers of Becoming, cute coeds,
serious persons learning law,
parading ignorance of the proud skin
that fills with more than pedantry
their tattered denim and the Shepherd's eye.

The Shepherd's pipe is out. Ants crawl
bewildered over his sandal strap,
their freeway lost on an unsigned flyover —
call this a cloverleaf?
The girls are to their classes gone.
They are opening notes behind screened windows.
A rich career drones in the pierced ears.
He is alone with birds and bees.

Antistrophe:

Now from his shading bush
a fly with crisp wings and a sharp suit
holding below the threshold of his vision
watch-chain and walky-talky, emblems of insect power,

investigates the Shepherd's arm.
Shall this be bitten?
No. Let the warning of his blank regard
suffice. Adjusting his subfusc presence
more squarely, he withdraws
to the shattered undergrowth of empties
that are unreturnable in his wilderness.

Light wears away. The Shepherd tilts his head
to the plane of the ecliptic. At once he sees
the Galilean dance, a ponderous pirouetting
of earth teetering round where the sun stands.
Planets behind the multiple grey veils
perform unseen their solitary reels —
not as the Graces linked in a naked ring,
nor face to face, crazed by screaming Stones
like kids in the disco night, but each in her own time
draws far, draws near, stoops swiftly round
the unmoved reactor. And at the other centre
to each her own, her solitary sun,
weightless, invisible. All this the Shepherd sees
in his canted almucantar.

Epode:

He is the Shepherd of the Truth of Being.
Lunchtime. Leaving the bright girls
germinating under the gentle rain
he shambles slowly home,
scattering spiders out of their damp webs,
his pocketed pipe nested in ashy fluff.
He holds the world poised on his clumsy love.

SUZANNE SANDOR-LOFFT

Victim

Alan works slowly. It takes him half an hour to set up a shot. But I don't mind because there's nothing I enjoy so much as having him take my picture. He gives such detailed instructions for my every gesture that I have no decisions to make. No responsibilities except to stay alive. Sometimes for a whole afternoon.

Alan, my husband is only a spare-time photographer, so we don't have a proper studio. We don't even live in a loft. Nevertheless, he's a good photographer. Each time, he takes all the furniture in the livingroom and carries it carefully to one side, and then he's left with a long, narrow empty space, one length all northern light. I just sit expectant on a white Bentwood chair, in my floor-length polka dot T-shirt, like Whistler's mother's daughter.

Alan had just bought this new Japanese tripod, the kind where you can't pinch your fingers. He might anyways, though. He's very accident prone. He's always pinching his fingers, or stubbing his toes. Not me. I'm always watchful; I have never had the slightest accident. Alan even got hit by a car last November, but nothing happened. Although our lawyer said you can't get hit by a car and have "nothing happen." I can still see the two policemen standing in the doorway telling me. They were very nice, and pretended not to hear me screaming. I had been frying chicken (beer batter) and thinking I'd been deserted. I'd only asked him to go down and get some broccoli at Mac's. Anyway, as I said, nothing happened. But I've been worrying more ever since.

We were taking pictures because my mother's birthday was

coming up soon. Every year we present her with a new picture of me, like a baby. That's all she ever wants. She hangs them all in her bedroom. Not in any chronological order, either; just at random. It's strange, because she bears me a lot of resentment, so it's a wonder she gets any sleep in that room at all.

Whenever I know my picture is being taken, I fall into my sad Madonna look. There's nothing I can do about it. I'm too self-conscious to smile with my mouth, and I never learnt the trick of putting a smile into my eyes. This time, Alan and I were determined to get some light-hearted shots. Perhaps even devil-may-care. To prove to her that I'm as happy as I claim I am. My mother thinks everyone is as unhappy as she is, but that other people (me) won't admit it. She is embittered by this hypocrisy.

Finally Alan finds an angle he likes. "Look over at the Manulife Building." I solemnly stare at it. All of a sudden I realize I'm really looking at the building on top of the Charles Promenade. I quickly try to realign my stare, but just then Alan was allowing light through his shutter, so the first shot is spoiled. A bad omen. We laugh. Alan comes from a small town in Ontario and never heard people using words like "omen" except as related to the weather. He still thinks it's exotic when he hears me darkly putting a curse on someone who's wronged me. I once tried to teach him some Hungarian, but had to give it up it made me laugh so hard. You rarely get to hear someone speaking Hungarian with an English accent.

Alan's taking a lot of profile shots of me, now I've located the Manulife Building. My profiles, both of them, are terrible. I don't even know which is worse. It's because I have no cheekbones. I have a broad Slavic face. God only knows why, when any linguist knows Hungarians are not Slavs. My mother keeps telling me I have fabulous cheekbones — that they grow more prominent with every passing year. But she says she'll pay for it if I want to go to a plastic surgeon. Alan says he loves my chubby cheeks. Anyways, I don't know what a plastic surgeon could do. Can they build up bones like that?

It would be easier for us to get cheery shots if it weren't raining outside. All this rain reminds me of Zurich. My mother and I were there last week and it rained every day. Something about the clouds hitting the Alps. My mother kept losing her umbrella. I'd rather get wet than carry one, but she minds about her hair. Somehow she kept leaving them behind. Everywhere. In the cigar store in the lobby where she buys the *Herald Tribune*; on the Biedermeier chairs in the Baur-au-lac where we run in to have an outrageously expensive cup of Ovomaltine; she even put one in the waste basket, mistaking it for an umbrella stand. Because it rained so much, she'd always have to buy a new one. By the time we left, though, they'd all turned up again. You know the Swiss — they only keep your money. I thought it was stupid to lug all four of them back on the plane, so she left them in lieu of a tip for the chamber maid.

I hated every minute in Zurich. I only went with her because she was so depressed. All day long we ran up and down Bahnhof Strasse spending money. That makes her feel secure. I bought Alan a pair of Italian driving gloves, you know, with the holes at the knuckles. But $50 did seem a bit much. The lady said it was because it was pigskin. But if pork is so cheap, how come pigskin is so dear? Oh, and then I didn't know what size he would be. "He has very small hands . . . for a man." I enunciated very clearly in case the lady didn't speak English too well. My mother speaks a sort of Burgenland German, but I didn't like to fall back on that. "Our smallest men's size is an eight." "Oh, could I see them?" I tried them on myself, but they were barely large enough, so they wouldn't do for Alan. His hands are a little larger than mine — I know because we measured once by pressing our palms together, and then examining how much finger was left on his side after mine ended. "Have you an eight and a half?" She looked through the stack and pulled one out. But it wasn't the same colour. I mean, it was a natural shade too, but somehow grayer. My mother said she couldn't see any difference. The lady said that she only had a nine in the shade I liked. It was more a nutty colour. I tried them on. There seemed like quite a bit of overlap on them. "Here, let me try them on," my mother said. "What good would that do?" I snapped. After all, she hadn't done the palm-pressing test. I could see she was hurt. "OK, see what you think," She carefully turned her rings backwards, and slid them on. She loves being useful to me. "They'll be perfect", she said, "look, they're just larger than what I need, and his hands must be bigger than mine." I wasn't so sure, but I bought them anyway. They turned out to be perfect. I hope he doesn't lose them now.

"Why don't you try putting some make-up on — that sometimes makes you feel better," Alan suggested. I have enough make-up to open a cosmetic counter, but I hardly ever wear any. Only if we go out, and we hardly ever go out. We're so content together, just the two of us. My mother can't understand this — she says, "what are you going to do when you're in your fifties?" More of the same.

I went and put on lots of eye make-up, and some blush, and that new lipstick I bought at Grieder's but I still couldn't get into my ra-ta-ta mood. "Maybe if you put on one of your Sonia Rykiel sweaters," Alan said. He's learnt the names of the French designers, just as I've picked up a lot of his hi-fi jargon. I even know what an anti-skating device is. Alan and I are turning into one person. Which is how we like it, but it does sort of leave my mother out in the cold.

She's been very lonely ever since my father died ten years ago. It wasn't such a wonderful marriage, but at least she wasn't alone so much. My father was a reclusive man who taught Classics at the University of Toronto and he always hoped I would go into Classics too. He started teaching me the Greek alphabet when I was six. But I wasn't interested — not till well after his death.

Because it was a gray day, Alan had to keep checking to see if there was enough available light. He walked forwards, then backwards between me and the tripod, peering down at his light metre. I love the way his eyes can fall on my face for whole minutes, and know he's not seeing a person but an object that reflects lights in varying degrees. It's more relaxing being an object than a person. After he lowers the tripod he moves back and forth again, swaying, not moving his feet. I don't know what he's seeing, but I'm content just to watch him. He's very graceful. He used to be a dancer. Well, not really. He was an actor, but in musical comedy, so there was a lot of singing and dancing going on. I didn't know him in those days. I would have loved to. I would have gone to the theatre every single night and clapped my heart out at his curtain calls. But by the time I met him, he was reading the eleven o'clock news on TV, which is nothing to cheer about. I'm sorry I missed out on being the star's wife, but I like the photographer's-model role a lot, too.

I also like the rich North American tourist role. I play that one in Hungary. You can't play it in Switzerland because they're richer, and tend to think Americans are trash. They haven't even bothered to think up a separate category for Canadians. In Hungary though, you can still tart it up. I went there to see my brother who lives in Budapest. Actually, he's my stepbrother. He's only a year younger than my mother. Whenever I'm in Europe, I go over to visit him, but it's a very unsatisfactory relationship we have. I'm not so much interested in him, as I am in finding traces of my father in him. I can't tell him this, because he's so flattered that I've started taking an interest in him. We always walk from his apartment to the Hungaria coffeehouse. There, he asks me questions about myself. Like "what kind of music do you like?" My first impulse is to say "none" — it's true; I have no ear. But this would only strengthen his conviction that there is no culture in America. So I try and recall the names of the albums Alan has recently bought. "I like the Bach partitas." "Yes," he nods slowly, "I thought you would like only such heavy music." Actually, now I think about it, the only music I ever loved was in my teen-age years, pre-Beatles, stuff like "Tell Laura I Love Her" and "Walk like a Man." But I can't admit this to anyone because they'd just assume I was perversely espousing an anti-intellectual stance. When Elvis Presley died, I mourned for a week.

I can't find any traces of my father in my brother. He's just a sad, old man with no charm at all. My father was very big on charm. Actually, I didn't inherit any of it, either. My mother says I can be, when I want to be, but I don't think that's quite the same thing. My father used to make me laugh a lot. Mostly during fights with my mother. She used to yell at him a lot when I was growing up. I think she was quite unhappy living in the New World. Plus, my father wasn't very kind to her — he did sort of treat her like a servant, which is what got her into her froths in the first place. She would accuse him of being deluded — "the days of Socrates are over, you know." "Why?" he innocently asked, "when Xanthippe is so well and blooming?" At the time I found this sally hilariously to the point, and had to pinch my nostrils together with my fingers to keep my giggling silent. My mother never forgave me for those long bouts of uncontrollable mirth.

These thoughts of my father were making me smile. Alan was elated. "That's great — that's great," he exulted. His directions came thick and fast now. "Tilt your chin up more — a little to the left — follow my hand — OK — that's great." Maybe, if the pictures turned out, I would even send one to my brother. He keeps asking for one. He gave me one of himself, though I didn't ask for it. Every visit I ask him for old pictures of my father. He was so handsome.

"OK — now we're cooking," Alan was excited. "why don't you put on your black Liliane Burty?" That was my one "party dress," and it made me look very vulnerable, which is a favourite look of mine. "OK — now stand leaning against the wall." He was changing from his portrait lens to a wide-angle. "OK — now go back to whatever you were just thinking about." My father.

My father often used to quote lines of Greek to us, but declined to translate them. That's why I started to take Greek classes two years ago at the University. I spend hours laboriously translating Socratic dialogues in search of him. The other day in class, I almost laughed aloud when we came to a line of the Apology that goes: "οὐδὲν δὲ δεινὸν μὴ ἐν ἐμοὶ στῇ." It was a line he had often cited, shaking his head in mock desperation, when he got exasperated with all my mother's harassments. It means: "there is no prospect that I shall be the last victim."

TOM WAYMAN

Iron

I am ironing. I still use the steam iron
I was given when I first left home.
How many miles has it travelled since,
pressing heavily back and forth on cloth
and being packed and uncrated
in how many different rooms.

The clothes underneath it
have been replaced several times,
but it continues to slide
across ironing boards
or towels placed over tables.
Women have come and gone around it;
the music in the air as it hisses and spits
has also altered how often.

But the iron's expression never varies.
Whatever happens, wherever we are,
when I want to iron it is ready to iron.
It's like the guy you meet on almost any job
who does the work, period.
He's not particularly good at it,
he doesn't particularly like it,
but he's competent; he never complains
or becomes excited.

When anyone else gets talking
about Sunday's football game,
or a TV program, or a lottery draw
or an election
he has nothing to say. As far as anybody knows
he doesn't do anything after work either:
has an apartment, no family that we've heard of,
and if he goes anywhere interesting on his holidays
he never mentions it.

If you end up having to spend a whole morning
off in a strange corner of the plant
on some special job with only him
you might discover he was married once
but he doesn't hear from his ex-wife
or he used to collect police force shoulder badges.
Nothing more. He just works with you,
and when you go he'll work with someone else
until he retires.

                So with my iron:
as long as he can work, he'll work.
It's the same to it
if it presses jeans
or my snappy new dress pants,
if we're moving to Calgary tomorrow
or remain in this house.
It irons. That's all.

J. D. CARPENTER

The Sebright Dances

The night we spun out
on the road to Uphill
was any good summer night
    the spruces perfuming the air
    the air our heavy sweaters
    as we ran among hedges with cottage girls

Some of us swam in the back lake
in the silver wake of the moon
the island a black confusion
beyond rafts, voices of loons
Others, drawn by the store lights
drank Pure Spring, played the juke
flirted up against fenders
warm in the mothy air

Under the steps of the store dock
we smoked our first cigarette
The farmboy Alva Hackett
provided Phillip Morrises
(his father will die
  fifteen years from now
  in a Barrie five-and-ten
  his mother one day later
  at her mailbox, in her weeds)

Oh the Sebright dances
Old Hackett drove the wagon

up the Dalrymple road
Johnny B stuffed straw
down the necks of neckers
mickeys made the rounds
We lolled our legs and kissed our faces
bunted the big farm tires

Farmwomen danced with daughters
while the men drank out in the yard
Cottagers promenaded
and summer boys, made brave
reeled in drunken marriage
gallant and profane

And outside among crickets
trysts were finished, bottles
passed, splintered on cinders
or flung at the nameless dark

The night we spun out
on the road to Uphill
was any good August night
    the kids out running the starlight
    launching lawnchairs into the lake
    while parents played euchre on porches
    poured themselves their gin

We followed the oiled point road
out past the graveyard turn
where Gary May loved his sister
where Burns threw pillows on Hallowe'en
under the wheels of cars
(he will be dead seven years ahead, fireworks
 in a shed)

We flew the Cold Creek bridge
floorboards rattling down
and pelted into the fragrant dark
each farmhouse winking us on
We knew a place we could spend the night

up a mile from Coboconk, and we sang
in the undersea light of the dash
and thumped the roof with our hands
and missed a turn
and dove
down
into a ditch
came up and out squealing
like a foundered horse, spun
and stopped, body rocking on the carriage
our headlights lighting a hayfield
and all the nightlife there

The night we spun out
on the road to Uphill
was any good motel night
    the radio played a slow one
    fireflies danced in air
    I knelt in the dirt with all the dead birds
    you covered your eyes with your hands

JOHN REIBETANZ

Thomas Warrener, Beekeeper

This poem is part of *Ashbourn Changes*, a
sequence of monologues exploring the search
for personal and social fulfillment as
experienced by the people of a small Suffolk
community. (Warrener runs the local apple
orchard and tends a thriving apiary in one
corner of it, but is not a native of the village.
He piloted an R.A.F. bomber during World
War II, and when it was over he came to
Ashbourn to keep bees and grow fruit,
buying the property and equipment that a
distant relative -- Mrs. Leila Jarmin — had
put up for sale.)

That this too was a fraud took time to learn:
   The heart of the honey, crystals
Like needles. At first, it was all sweet difference,
Where the air was laced with lavender forage scent —
   Calling me in, the way
Winking flowers flag down bees to hug and gorge.

The bees poured over this hedge — a waterfall,
   And like its splash their pollen load
Flashed the field's colours: jewel thieves, and yet
But for their take, there'd never an apple ripen.
   Stealing away, their flights
Shot life through the harvest; mine had sprayed death broadcast.

You wipe the bloody sights like wounds: the sudden
   Nothings, holes that gut

Flight lists, the circle at the pub, a smudged sky,
Or ooze from the red night you left behind you;
   You wipe, and still they burn
Your eyes — bees' eyes, the pain of a thousand scorched lenses.

She sat here throned in wicker, queen of the bees,
   Serene, old Leila Jarmin, under
Her broad straw hat, hub of a world at peace.
A dozen hives hummed round her: I thought them petals
   Beaming from a daisy's eye,
Not minded to find trap lines spun from the clot at a net's core.

Her fault? Her world was shaped by the warp of need.
   With turns as innocent as a spider's,
She took herself in: "I like to think each hive
A hollow tree, pure source." Or "All I do
   Is tuck them in with love." Or "Listen:
Harmony's in the rounds the bees play on their combs."

Summer and autumn taught me otherwise.
   July, one of her hollow trees
Turned Nazi oven, spitting shrivelled corpses
Onto the grass. Like milkmen every morning
   Before the dew burnt off, guard-bees
Set out the cold white pupae sucked dry by the hive.

My fault, to think that love would flow like honey
   To tide them between runs of nectar.
Yet, who's to blame for the hives' October purge?
With honey stacked like decks on ocean liners,
   Riding the flood, they chucked their drones
Overboard, fat and kicking — live bait for the killer frost.

What can they know of love — or hate? They move
   In circles as mechanical as clocks.
When our world's warm curves freeze to sharpened steel,
We turn to this world of bees and trees for comfort;
   But the green machine ticks on,
Too wound up in the race to embrace a solitary need.

This was the sharpest sting — not roaring hives
  That echoed engines gunned before a run,
Or hives dead quiet in the wake of robber bees —
But to find them all indifferently deaf, to screams
  Or music — incurables, gorged on honey
Yet blind to sweetness, immune to the bite of salt.

To be one with nature is to share an isolation —
  Two sides of a stone wall.
The bees mindlessly barb the crossing-points
In stinging coils, or suffer our touch as a rock
  Endures its moss — cool patience
Awaiting the storm, the swarming that sloughs off
    needless attachments.

While bees prick blossoms and thread boughs like streamers,
  Hands alone plant or pick.
But when love looks at apple trees, it sees
Only its banner — the ripe blush stirring; hate
  Rakes the ground but finds no more
Than its flag — stiff arms, stiff legs, the spider at the core.

We run the standards up or down. Peace
  Never drops from trees with windfalls.
Yet, honey schools our tongues in peace, and we learn
To see its promise ripen in the fruit.
  The bees keep me here: if I meet
Their needs, they meet the needs I cannot share with them.

GUY VANDERHAEGHE

The Expatriates' Party, or Je Me Souviens

Joe was dreaming and in his dream his wife and he were having an argument. She had chosen a bad time to start this one. There Joe was, rubbers buckled, overcoat buttoned to his chin, gloves pulled on — all ready to set out for school. He stood with his hand impatiently gripping the doorknob, prickly with heat and wool and anger, feeling the sweat begin to crawl down his sides, waiting for her to finish with her damn nonsense. He suspected she was going to make him late for class and at this thought he felt very anxious indeed. In thirty-five years of teaching he had never been late more than once or twice that he could remember.

"Of course I'm pregnant," she said. "And you're the dirty old man who slipped the bun in my oven. At your age. Imagine."

"Don't be silly," he replied, doing his best to disguise his exasperation with her. "You're fifty-seven years old and women fifty-seven years old *don't* have babies."

"Well if I don't have a bun in the oven, what do I have?" she inquired with a schoolgirlish petulance that made him feel slightly queasy, a trifle faint with disgust. This wasn't at all like Marie. And why did she keep using that idiotic euphemism?

"You know what you have," he said, angry with her for having it, and angry too that she refused to admit it. "You have a tumour on your uterus, and it's no good pretending it's a baby. Old women don't have babies. It's a goddamn law of nature. It's a *fact*."

It was the steep descent of the plane that woke him. The sense

138

of imbalance, of disorientation, of falling snapped him abruptly out of the dream. Almost immediately he was conscious of where he was, of his surroundings. He seldom stumbled and groped his way out of sleep any more, but was often jarred out of his dreams in this way, catapulted into reality.

He sat absolutely still and upright, acknowledging the insistent pressure of the seatbelt on his bladder, uncomfortably aware of his damp, sticky shirt rucked up his back.

I never think of her when I'm awake, he thought. Is that why I dream? Is there a law of psychological compensation which I must pay?

The woman sitting beside him, realizing he was no longer asleep, said: "We're beginning our landing approach now."

Joe smiled and nodded to her while he took final stock of how she had fared on the flight. She had certainly boarded pert and powdered enough, but in the course of eight hours her makeup had been ravaged and she had undergone some changes for the worse. Everyone over forty had. At that age the body forgets how to forgive, thought Joe. Here we sit, swollen with gas, eyes raw from lack of sleep, legs cramped and toes afire with pins and needles, smiling cheerfully and socking back the charter flight booze, prepared to cheerfully suffer the consequences and pay the penalties.

Joe turned and looked out his window. Rags of vapour tore past, luminous with a feeble, watery sunshine. He couldn't see land below, only a thick, undulating surface of cloud. Nor could he make out what the pilot was saying. His ears had blocked with the change in altitude.

"What's that? What's he saying?" he inquired of the woman beside him. He cocked his head to indicate deafness.

"The temperature is 54 degrees," she said, mouthing the words carefully. "Sweater weather."

"Good," he replied, acting as if it genuinely mattered to him.

"We'll be there in minutes," she commented, smoothing a plaid skirt down on her heavy thighs. "I can hardly wait to take a bath and crawl between clean sheets." The woman laughed uncomfortably and inexplicably. Was it the word sheets? "I'm staying at the Penta." she paused. "What about you? Where are you staying?"

Good God woman, Joe thought.

"I'm staying with my son and daughter-in-law," he lied.

"In London?"

"Yes."

"Well, that's lovely isn't it? You'll have a full schedule with them taking you around to see the sights, won't you?"

"Sure will." Hungry, hunting widow. At least she had said her husband was dead, explaining her ring. But how did you know? Nowadays women were liable to lie about that sort of thing.

The plane suddenly dropped out of the bank of clouds. They were much lower than Joe had suspected. Below him he saw a rush of hummocked, rank turf of such a startling green, a green so unprecedented in his experience that it struck him as false, a tourist's hopeful, unrealistic vision. A tiny man toiled in his garden allotment, unconcerned as the plane bellied over him, sweeping him in its dark shadow, surrounding him in a shimmering bath of sound waves.

Joe's ears popped, clearing, and simultaneously he heard the pilot announce, seconds before the tires touched the tarmac — a fine display of a sense of the dramatic: "Ladies and gentlemen, welcome to England in Jubilee year."

There was a ragged cheer of approval and a smattering of hand clapping. Relief at journey's end, at escaping this aluminium tube, at being safe.

Joe smacked his hands together too. And old English teacher, out of harness though he was, muttered a line of Blake's that ran through his mind as swiftly and verdantly as had the ground, only seconds before, sped beneath him.

"In England's green and pleasant land."

He was wasn't he? In England's green and pleasant land?

His son Mark was waiting to meet him at Gatwick as he had promised, but Joe had difficulty in recognizing him at first. It had been two years since he had seen his son. Now he appeared sporting a fine fan of feathery beard, wearing a flat tweed cap and carrying a furled umbrella under his arm.

Like a bloody convert to Catholicism, Joe thought, more Catholic than the Pope. It appeared the boy had gone ersatz English on him. Joe felt a little embarrassed for his son, particularly when they hesitantly and clumsily shook hands. There was a first time for everything, Joe mused, even shaking hands with your father. You had to acquire the method.

Mark was obviously on edge. He kept fidgeting with his umbrella, stabbing the point at the toe of his shoe and saying, "You look great, Dad. Really fit. Just fine." His stay in England had clipped his speech and truncated his vowels.

"Fit for an old duffer, you mean," his father said, pinching up a roll of fat above his waistband and putting it on display.

They collected Joe's baggage and then, luggage banging their legs, sidled up to a wicket and bought tickets for Victoria Station from a man so black he shone with the iridescent purplish hue of an overripe plum. After boarding a third class coach they stowed Joe's bags and seated themselves just as the train pulled out. It slid away so quietly and serenely from the platform that Joe wondered for a minute if he were hallucinating. Where were the jerks, bangs and metallic clangs he remembered from the CNR milkruns of his boyhood?

The train gathered speed, and through a window pane smudged with nose grease Joe watched, without apparent interest, the row houses and villas shudder past, waiting for Mark to have his say. To get all that off his chest. It wasn't long in coming. After pointing out a few sights and architectural oddities Mark said: "I'm sorry we didn't make it, Dad. It wasn't right that you had to go through that yourself. But we were broke and it was a hell of a long way to go. I hope you see our point."

The train swayed past a school. A group of boys were huddling bleakly on a playing field. What was it that Wellington had claimed? The battle of Waterloo was won in the playing fields of Eton. Joe pitied those kids their grey flannel shorts and muddy knees. It must be damn cold standing there. On the platform he had felt a raw, wet wind that had cut to the bone.

He turned away from the window to his son. "I didn't expect you and Joan to come, Mark," he said softly. "I told you that on the phone. I don't want you to worry about that any longer. You know I never set much store in the formalities." Having said that, he reached inside his jacket and took out an envelope which he passed to his son. "I brought these pictures for you," he said. "I don't know if that was wise or not. I took them with the Polaroid and they didn't turn out all the best."

Joe wasn't sure why he had taken the snapshots. Funeral photographs had never been a family tradition, although some of the old country Germans, Marie's people, had always taken coffin portraits. Perhaps that was where he had got the idea. Still, it wasn't like him. But then lately he had been acting in surprising ways that he could hardly credit. The world had changed since his wife had died.

Mark was tearing open the flap when Joe warned him. "I wouldn't look at those now," he said quietly. "Not here. Wait until you get home. She's in the coffin and I'll warn you — she doesn't look herself."

That was an understatement. The mortician's creation, that's what she was. A frenzy of grey Little Orphan Annie curls, hectic blotches of rouge on the cheeks, a pathetic, vain attempt at lending colour to a corpse. So thin. So thin. Eaten hollow by cancer, a fragile husk consumed by the worm within.

"What?"

"They are pictures of your mother in the coffin, of your mother's funeral," said Joe deliberately.

"Jesus Christ," Mark said, stuffing the envelope in his pocket and giving his father a strange, searching look. Or was it only his imagination? Joe had trouble reading his boy's bearded face. The strong regular planes had been lost in the thick, curling hair, and only the mild eyes were familiar.

"And you're really making out all right on your own?" his son asked a little doubtfully. "Tell me the truth, Dad."

"Fine," said Joe.

"And the pension? It's okay, no problems there?"

"Full pension," said Joe.

"And the charges were dropped?"

"Yes."

"Jesus," said Mark, "you're a real tiger. What the hell got into you?"

Joe looked at his hand. What had gotten into him? He had broken that kid's jaw as easily as if he were snapping kindling.

"Too long in the trenches," he said, trying to smile. "Shell shock."

"On to other topics," said Mark with feigned heartiness. "That's the past. It's dead isn't it? Forgotten. And you're in England. You made it, Pop. After thirty years of talking about it you made it."

"I made it," said Joe. He reflected that Mark would see this trip in a different light. He would remember the brochures read at the breakfast table, the magazines and travel books piled on the end table that slithered down in a cascade of shiny, slick paper at the slightest touch. All of them illustrated with quaint prospects, thatched cottages, the dark mellow interior of old pubs with great adze-hewn beams.

But that wasn't what he had necessarily come looking for. Joe had never explained to anyone what this place meant to him. If he had had to, he would have said: water mostly, tame rivers, soft rain, mist, coolness, greenery and arbours, shady oaks. Things of refreshment and ease. Poetry too. Yes. Things that cut the deepest thirst. Peace.

Of course, these notions had grown slowly over the years. They began in his first school in a small country place in southwestern Saskatchewan in 1937. He started in May as a replacement for a Scot who had shot himself in the teacherage. Nobody knew exactly why.

It wasn't a happy place he had come to. The kids sat hunched in their desks and bit their dried lips and cast anxious glances out the window at dust devils that spun tortuously across the fields. They all looked tired and old and worried. The ceaseless wind rattled grit against the windows. Dust seeped in under the doors, crept under the sills, powdered them all with greyness and desperation. Their pinched faces and smudged eyes, irritated and bleary, watched him closely.

It was an accident his giving them what country folk wanted: a vision of water, of fecundity, of transparent plenty. He would never have planned it; he would have considered the idea cruel.

How still they had gone when he had read:

> On either side the river lie,
> Long fields of barley and of rye,
> That clothe the wold and meet the sky;
> And thro' the field the road runs by
> To many-towered Camelot.

Even the littlest ones had seemed momentarily transported. Towers, sweet water, heavy crops. He had begun to comb his anthologies of British poetry and mark certain passages with little slips of paper. When they became restless or edgy as the wind scored the siding of the school or the stove pipes began to hum and vibrate, Joe would read to them. He was a good reader. He knew that.

> How pleasant thy banks and green valleys below,
> Where wild in the woodlands the primroses blow;
> There oft as mild evening weeps over the lea,
> The sweet-scented birk shades my Mary and me.

Looking back he considered it a miracle. But then you tempt people with the impossible. What did ad men give a society with its belly full? The dream of perfect sex: blissful friction. There? Water, meadows, honeysuckle, fat fields.

> O sound to rout the brood of cares,
> The sweep of scythe in morning dew,
> The gust that round the garden flew,
> And tumbled half the mellowing pears!

Those kids were lucky to get a goddamn orange in their stockings at Christmas. Few ever did. Tumbling pears.

> And brushing ankle-deep in flowers,
> We heard behind the woodbine veil
> The milk that bubbled in the pail,
> And buzzings of the honeyed hours.

And gradually, with each of the succeeding thirty odd years of small towns and stifling classrooms these visions of refreshment sustained *him*, although the poetry stopped working for the students. He came to the conclusion that they no longer needed it or wanted it. With prosperity their dreams became more elaborate, more opulent, less dictated by peculiar circumstances. Their desires were the conventional lusts of that society that stretches from the Gulf of Mexico to the upper limits of urban settlement in the north.

But Joe needed those old visions during those sweltering June days as he prepared class after class, row after row, face after face for the Department of Education final examinations. Every year his head pounded and ached from the stunning sunlight, the smell of hot paper and dirty hair.

"I heard the water lapping on the crag/And the long ripple

washing in the reeds." It had always helped to imagine the cool sinuousness of moving water, the liquid coiling between green lavish banks, the silken run so silent and so deep.

Perhaps, Joe thought, that is why I have come. For the healing waters. Like a nineteenth century gentleman in search of a cure for what ails him, I have come to take the waters. I have come to be made whole.

Mark was speaking to him. "I made a reservation at the Bloomsbury Centre," he said. "We'll go there now so you can catch up on missed sleep. That jet lag is a killer. I was a zombie for a week."

Joe nodded. It was a good idea. Already jet lag was making it difficult for him to concentrate. He felt stretched on the rack of two continents. Physically *here:* in time located some place back *there*.

"It's a good location," his son said. "It's within walking distance of the University of London and the British Museum so we'll be able to meet easily. I can slip out of the Reading Room at noon and we can have lunch together in a pub or at your hotel."

"That's fine," said Joe equably. "I don't want to take you away from your work. Just go about your usual business." He was proud to have a son a scholar.

"You know," Mark said, shrugging apologetically, "we only have a bedsitter. Not even our own bathroom. We'd put you up if we could, but there's no room. Joan's mortified. She's afraid you'll think she doesn't want you."

"Christ," said Joe, hurrying to interrupt him, "as if I didn't know? The shack your mother and I lived in when we were first married — a crackerbox. . . ." He trailed off, uncertain if the boy had flinched at mention of his mother. The beard was a mask he couldn't penetrate, the face couldn't be read.

"Look at that!" said Mark suddenly fierce, diverting the conversation. "Bastards! The National Front thugs are at it again."

The train was slowing for a station. Brakes binding it slid by a carious warehouse with skirts of broken-brick rubble, windows painted blind. A message several feet high was painted on the building in white letters. "No Wogs Here."

"It seems," said Joe, "that the sun has finally set on the British Empire."

"No," said Mark, his face intent, "the Empire's come home to roost."

Joe woke to hunger and the sound of voices speaking German in the hall outside his doorway. The glowing numerals of the clock on the dresser announced that it was two o'clock in the morning, but his belly informed him that if he were back in North America he would be sitting down to a meal. What meal — breakfast, dinner, supper — he couldn't say. He wasn't sure how to compute the time change.

The woman outside his door was drunk. There was an alcoholic, forced gaiety to her voice that couldn't be mistaken. And although Joe barely knew three words of German, he could guess that the man's guttural purr was directed towards convincing her to go to bed with him.

Joe got out of bed and flicked on the TV. The screen was empty. He ran quickly through the channel selections. BBC one and two, ITV, all blank. Bathed in the aquatic, wavering blue light and kept company by the hum of the box, he sat on the foot of the bed and lit a cigarette.

Odd the often simple source of our most complex imaginings, our most disturbing dreams. The sounds of an attempted seduction heard in indistinct German and he had dreamed that his wife and her mother (dead these twenty years past) had been sitting talking the Deutsch in his livingroom, just as they had in the first years of his marriage when the old girl was still alive.

He had always resented that. He had felt left out not being able to follow the conversation. He was suspicious that his mother-in-law asked questions and pried into their private life. He hadn't liked her much. Frieda was what his own father would have called a creeping Christer. A woman of a narrow, fundamental piety and sour views who hadn't liked her daughter marrying outside the charmed circle of the Kirche.

But a dream has its own rules and logic and Joe had understood *this* conversation perfectly well. He knew that Frieda was trying to take Marie away with her. She was trying to persuade her to leave Joe and go away someplace with her. Silly old bitch. The only thing was that Marie seemed half-inclined to follow her mother's suggestions.

And while all this had been going on Joe had found himself unable to move out of his chair. He was paralyzed, and no matter how he struggled to unlock his rigid limbs he could not do it. He was unable to stir a muscle, not even to speak.

He saw at last that they were in agreement. Marie got up and put on her coat. She went around the house turning out the lights as if he weren't there. Then she followed her mother out the door. But she forgot to close the door. That was strange.

And there Joe sat in an empty house rooted in a chair, blinded with tears. Not even a decent goodbye.

The sounds outside intruded. Joe was sure that the man's voice seemed to be growing more insistent and demanding, and the woman's more encouraging in a sad, passive sort of way. The bargains struck, the diplomacy and language of love.

Joe made the rounds. He began as a proper tourist. He wound through the Jubilee-jammed streets of London on a tour bus. The banners were out, the buildings were being cleansed of a century of dirt and grime. The workmen exposed clean stone in patches, it shone through like white bone on an incinerated corpse. The windows in Oxford street were stuffed with regal souvenirs; the crowds surged on the sidewalks.

Everything was done with haste. They disembarked for a thirty minute gawk at St. Paul's, a stampede through the Tower, a whirl around Picadilly Circus. Their female guide was disconcertingly brazen. She browbeat outlandishly large tips out of them. She claimed intimacy with famous people. Described a night out on the town with Lord Snowden. She drove her charges relentlessly through the sacred places, hectoring, scolding, full of dire warnings not to be late, not to dawdle. Joe put up with the woman and the company he was thrown in with for two days; then he gave it up as a bad business, likely only to get worse.

It didn't take him long to realize that something was wrong. He was filled with anxiety. The long English faces filled with bad teeth made him shift his shoulders uneasily when he looked at them. The streets were too full. The lure of royalty and the weak pound was a powerful attraction.

Joe was surprised to find that nothing much pleased him. Most things he saw made him feel sad, or lost, or lonely, or guilty. He was sorry to see the English look like the landlords of boarding houses, possessors of a testy dignity, forced by straitened circumstances into a touchy hospitality.

Where were the healing waters? He might have said that he never expected to find them in London. They were in the Cotswolds. Or Kent. Or Norfok. Or Yorkshire. But he knew that wasn't true. He knew that now. The great trees in Hyde Park should have been enough, but weren't.

He left off sight-seeing and began to aimlessly wander the streets. Following his nose, he found himself drawn down narrow alleys daubed with graffiti and slogans. The messages disturbed him. He could see nothing suggestive of the vigour with which they were executed in the tired people he saw in the streets. NO BOKS HERE! they said. CFC RULE OK! DAVID ESSEX IS KING! MICK IS KING! ARSENAL RULE! He was not sure why they made him angry, why they upset him. Most of them he couldn't even understand. Later he had to ask Mark to explain to him what they signified.

At first Joe had imagined them the work of senile, angry old men — they gave off the crazy intensity he associated with an old man's rage. But in time he came to believe them the handiwork of the bizarre creatures he sometimes came across lounging in subway stations like lizards, bathing themselves in the noise, smells and smuts. Horrible, self-mutilated young people. They blandished safety pins driven through their bottom lips, ear lobes, nostrils. Bristling porcupine haircuts quivered on their heads radiating electric rage and venom. They were clad in intricately torn tee shirts and dresses made of shiny green garbage bags. Joe felt like the discoverer of a whole subterranean culture down in the tube, a whole crazed tribe intent on festooning itself with refuse and offal.

Staring bewildered at them for the first time in the harsh light of the station he had been frightened, suspected they might attack him. And then he found himself laughing when he thought of Dryden's lines:

These Adam-wits, too fortunately free,
Began to dream they wanted liberty;
And when no rule, no precedent was found,

Of men by laws less circumscrib'd and bound
They led their wild desires to woods and caves,
And thought that all but savages were slaves.

His edginess grew. He seemed drawn to the train stations with
their dirt and noise and pigeons and stink and movement. He
wandered the Embankment and stared at the sullen Thames filled
with commerce. It seemed that this stretch of river bank was
dotted with old men and old women bundled in unravelling
sweaters and shapeless coats, some drunk, some crazy.

Joe began to drink. He sought out pubs seldom frequented by
tourists. This was resented. But nevertheless he sat stubbornly in
the midst of strangers who talked past him at the bar, who even
occasionally made jokes about him while he drank his whiskies
and got falling-down drunk. At afternoon closing the proprietors
turned him out and he took to the streets again. He walked mile
after mile, often losing himself entirely in the city. He tramped
past the British Museum and its imposing portico with barely a
glance. Inside his son was reading documents. He ignored the
blandishments of Madame Tussaud's, of the Victoria and Albert,
of the National Gallery.

He felt he was on the verge of losing control as he had back
home. When he was jostled and elbowed and pushed outside
Harrod's he had sworn viciously and even taken a kick at a man
who had stepped on his foot. Yet his behaviour didn't particularly
worry him. He decided that he didn't give a damn.

In the first week of his visit Joe spent two evenings at his son's.
He climbed three flights of stairs past strange sounds and Asiatic
smells to a bedsitter you couldn't swing a cat in. His daughter-in-
law cooked them pork pies in a tiny range and they drank whisky
that Joe brought with him. Mark and Joe sat at the table on the
only chairs and Joan, his daughter-in-law, sat on the couch with
her plate on her knee. Conversation never ran the way it should
have. Mark kept asking questions Joe didn't consider any of his
goddamn business and that he tried to avoid answering.

"So that thing with the kid is finished now, all cleared up?"

Joe splashed some whisky in his glass. "Yes," he said. "It's
finished and I prefer to leave it that way."

"Why did they decide to drop the charges?"

Joan coughed and gave Mark a warning look. It was funny, she seemed able to read him better than his own son could.

"They settled out of court for a thousand bucks. They said they felt sorry for me, my wife having just died. They talked about the poor kid walking around with wire cutters in his back pocket, living on soup and milk shakes."

Mark's eyes had that squinty, harried look they got when he was worried. He had had that look even as a child. He hated trouble. "I don't know," he said. "I can't imagine you doing that."

"Maybe you don't know me as well as you think you do," said Joe.

He *had* surprised a lot of people: his principal, himself, the kid most of all. A lot was forgiven because it happened two weeks after the funeral. Everybody thought he had come back to work too soon. But Joe wasn't sure that he hadn't understood that would be the reaction before he did what he did. Maybe he had calculated the consequences. He couldn't remember now.

That particular kid, Wesjik, had been giving him trouble all year. Not that he was especially bad. He was representative of a type becoming more and more common. He did the usual insolent, stupid things: farting noises out of the side of his mouth while Joe read a poem; backchat; bothering people; arriving late for class; destruction of books and school property.

That day Joe had had to tell him at the beginning of class (as he had every day for the past four months) to get in his desk and get his text out. The boy had given him a witheringly contemptuous smile and slouching to his place, said: "You got it. Sure thing."

Joe had ignored him. "Open your books to page 130, grade twelve," he said, "and we'll begin the class with Tennyson's "The Splendor Falls." After the books had all thumped open and the banging and foot shuffling had subsided, Joe gave a little hitch to his voice and read, "The splendor falls — "

And there he was interrupted by a voice from the back of the room, brazen and sullen, " — on shit house walls." There was laughter. Most of it nervous. Some encouraging.

Joe looked up from his book. He knew who had said that. "Mr. Wesjik," he said, "get your carcass out of this room."

"I didn't say anything," the kid announced, his face set in a mockery of innocence. "How could you know who said anything? You were reading." A classroom lawyer.

Joe closed the book and carefully put it down. "You come along with me, Wesjik," he said. There were titters when the kid followed him grinning out of the room. A trip to the office. It didn't mean anything any more.

And that was where Joe had intended to take him when they set out. But there was something about the way the kid slouched along, lazily and indifferently swivelling his hips, that grated. Joe changed his mind on the way. He led Wesjik into the vestibule where the student union soft-drink machine was kept, and pulled the doors closed behind him.

"What's this?" said Wesjik. "How come I'm not going to the office?"

"You like talking to Mr. Cooper, don't you?" asked Joe, adopting an artificially pleasant tone. Cooper was a smooth-cheeked character with a master's degree in educational administration. Joe thought he was a dink, although he never mouthed off about Cooper in the staffroom the way some others did.

"Sure," said Wesjik sarcastically, "he's one honey of a guy. He *understands* me."

"Is that right?" said Joe.

"Hey," the kid said, "give me the Dutch Uncle treatment and let's get out of here. There's a draft. I'm getting cold."

"I'm sorry, Mr. Wesjik," said Joe. "What is it? Is it your hands that are cold?"

"Yeah," said the kid smiling, "my hands are *terribly* cold. I think I got chillblains maybe."

"Put them in your pockets."

"What?"

"Put your goddamn hands in your pockets if they're cold," said Joe calmly. To himself he said, I don't give a shit anymore. About anything. Let it ride.

"You swore," said Wesjik surprised. "You swore at me."

"Put your goddamn hands in your pockets, Wesjik," said Joe. Get them in there Wesjik, he thought. I'm an old man. Get them in there.

He could see he was beginning to scare the kid. He didn't mind. Maybe the kid thought he was crazy. Wesjik put his hands slowly into his pockets, licked his lips and tried to freeze his smart-ass smile on his lips.

"How old are you, Wesjik?" he asked.

"What?"

"How *fucking old* are you, Wesjik? And the word is pardon."

"Eighteen."

"Is that right? Eighteen? Is that your correct age, eighteen?"

"Yes." Joe could barely hear his answer.

"I didn't hear that, Wesjik. How old?"

Wesjik cleared his throat, "Eighteen," he said a little more loudly.

"My brother was dead at your age," said Joe. "He died in Italy during the Second World War. Ever hear of the Second World War, Wesjik? Any knowledge of that little incident?"

"Yes." A whisper.

"Do you want to know something, Wesjik?" said Joe, his voice rising dangerously. "I'm so tired. I'm so goddamn tired. I wish I had had that fucking chance," he said. "I wish I could have died when I was eighteen." He looked around the vestibule, surprised by what he had said, as if searching for the source of that idea. But it was true. His saying it had made it true. "That's what I wish now, looking back. You know why?"

"Let me out of here," the kid said whining. "You've got no business keeping me here, swearing at me!"

"Because I didn't know life was shit," said Joe, ignoring him. "I didn't know it was taking shit, year after year. I didn't know it was putting up with punks who crap on everything they can't under-stand, who piss on everything they can't eat or fuck — just to ruin it for someone else. To make it unusable."

"I'm sorry," said Wesjik. But Joe knew he wasn't. He was just afraid. Most of these kids thought they were the same thing. You were never sorry unless you were scared. Only when it paid.

"I want you to say this after me," said Joe. "So listen carefully, Wesjik. Here goes."

> The splendor falls on castle walls,
> And snowy summits old in story;
> The long light shakes across the lakes,
> And the wild cataract leaps in glory.

"Now you say it, Mr. Wesjik — with feeling. Like I did."

"I can't," said Wesjik. "I don't remember. Let me out of here."

"You can't," said Joe. "Why? Because you don't choose to, or because you're stupid?"

"I ain't stupid," said Wesjik sullenly. "You guys aren't allowed to call us stupid."

"Yes, you are," said Joe doubling his hand behind his back into a fist. "You're stupid, Wesjik. Otherwise you wouldn't stand around somebody who is as pissed off at you as I am with your hands in your pockets." And that said, Joe hit the kid before he could drag his hands out of his pockets and cover up.

Of course he had been forced to resign. But that was no hardship. He was eligible for a pension. There was talk of a court case and that frightened him, but his lawyer smoothed it out. In a meeting with the parents and their lawyer Joe had calmly said he had hit the kid because the kid had spat on him. He could see that Mr. and Mrs. Wesjik weren't sure how far they could trust their kid, and that was an advantage. Their lawyer quite correctly pointed out that being spat on didn't justify a broken jaw. Joe was glad to see they had swallowed the lie. He consoled himself by convincing himself it was metaphorically true.

The Wesjik's backed away from the expense and trouble. They were pleased with the offer of a thousand dollars and no hard feelings.

Joe didn't bother filling Mark in on any of the details. He could see his son didn't know what to make of the way he was acting. And the boy was particularly disturbed by the way he went at the bottle. He had never really seen his father drunk before and it set his teeth on edge.

"Jesus," he said, noting the level of liquid in the bottle of Scotch, "there isn't a prize at the bottom of that, Dad. It isn't Crackerjack. Slow down."

"That's where you're wrong my boy," said Joe. "There's a prize. Oh yes, there certainly is." He poured himself another tumbler.

"Well, just remember you have to find your way home tonight," Mark said, trying to maintain a light tone and avoid sounding preachy..

"If worse comes to worst," said Joe, "I shall rely on the good offices of London's finest."

"Maybe you should just ease up a bit. Joan'll make some coffee."

"Joan is English," said Joe, suddenly belligerent. "What the hell does she know about making coffee?"

"And who the hell taught me my manners?" said Mark sharply.

The party held in Joe's honour was Mark's way of asking to be forgiven for the quarrel that had resulted. Joe's way of apologizing was to arrive in a taxi laden with gifts: several bottles of booze, roses for Joan, a canned ham, cheeses, pickles. He was also careful to arrive sober.

The two tiny rooms were filled with Mark's and Joan's student friends. They were expatriates. There was an American couple, an Aussie studying to be an engineer and the rest were Canadian graduate students mining the English libraries.

The atmosphere was a happy one. They greeted the arrival of the extra bottles with cheers. It was obvious they were all a little hard-up and that this wealth of liquor was unexpected and entirely appreciated.

But Joe knew it was a place where he didn't belong. They were polite. They asked his impressions of England. Gave him names of inexpensive restaurants. Made suggestions for day excursions outside of London. Reviewed the latest stage offerings. But he had really nothing in common with these young people. They were full of their work and anxious to regale friends with tales of the idiosyncracies of thesis advisors or the smarminess of English students. More than ever before Joe felt as if he were disconnected and out of touch with his surroundings. After introductions he willingly disengaged himself from their conversations and leaned against a wall with a drink in his hand, watching.

There was something that bothered him about his son and his friends. They didn't much like England. But they could leave it at that. Home was what bothered them, seemed to nag at them like a sore tooth. It seemed that as expatriates they were afraid the country they left behind was going to embarrass them, pull down its pants on the world stage. The American was the most afraid of this.

"Ford," he said. "Gerald Ford. I mean there's a limit to it. Nixon was an unshaved weasel — but Ford. He hit somebody with a golf ball again the other day."

The girl from Edmonton who was studying at the Royal Academy said, "I heard it was a tennis ball. The BBC announcer said tennis ball. And then he gave that little knowing smile — the one that means 'only in America folks.'"

They were allies here apparently.

"I don't know why the English press can't leave Margaret Trudeau alone," said a blocky girl who had a settled air of grievance about her. "They certainly kept their mouth shut about Mrs. Simpson and Edward didn't they? A fine sense of honour there. When it comes to their own precious royal family."

"Jesus, Anne," said the doctoral candidate in eighteenth century English history, "show a little perspective. That was forty years ago. They don't let Charles off the hook, do they? Lots of speculation about this Prince of Wales."

"This Jubilee business is getting under my skin," said the wife of the American. It's *medieval*."

"Interesting word, medieval," said Mark. "That dismisses it all neatly. The Queen of England is worth millions upon millions of tourist dollars a year. The republicans come from all over the world to hunger."

"You wouldn't think it was so goddamn funny," she said, "if you came with me on my rounds." She was a volunteer social worker. "West Indian families I visit have spent milk money to buy commemorative teacups and saucers. Those ghastly bloody things with the Queen's *image* painted on them. Those black kids meanwhile don't know anything about *their* heritage, do they? I mean what the hell does the Queen of England mean to them? The great White Mother?"

A fellow with dirty blond hair said laughing: "The House of Windsor is the opiate of the working class."

"Even back home," said the young man standing beside him. "My mother will actually cry if you say anything against the Queen. I don't know what the hell it is. A different generation I guess."

"Ah bullshit," said a tall, thin man who had been introduced to Joe as Daniel. Joe had thought he had been told Daniel came from Trois Rivières but decided he must have got it wrong. His English was unaccented and perfectly idiomatic. "All Anglo-Saxons are monarchists. You just have to scratch deep enough." He laughed to show it was all a joke. That he was only being charmingly provocative.

He's French all right, thought Joe. He's got one of those goddamn aristocratic noses that looks like it could slice butter. The kind that makes mine look like a peasant's potato.

"Well they're trying to do their best to turn the niggers in Deptford into honest liegemen," said the American sourly.

"What the hell do you want?" said Joe, suddenly angry. "Those niggers in Deptford are English aren't they? They were born in this country weren't they? It's their damn queen isn't it?"

The American girl looked at him steadily. She took a sip out of her glass and casually tucked her hair behind her ears. "They're *black*," she said calmly. "There is a *difference*. I can see the same thing happening here that happened back home. They'll grow up without a base, without their *own* values and traditions."

"They're Englishmen," said Joe stubbornly. He knew that in a way that wasn't quite right, but he knew it wasn't quite wrong either. And he felt better for saying it.

The room was quiet. No one agreed with him but they weren't about to contradict him. He realized that they thought arguing with him would be a waste of time. That he was too out of touch with things. Well, he supposed he was.

"I understand that a little better than some people," said the American girl. "My family came to Maine from Quebec ninety years ago. We were wiped out. I can't speak French. I don't know where I'm from. It's like we never were."

Jesus Christ, thought Joe. What he said was, "That guy who wrote that book *Roots* ought to be held personally responsible for filling people's heads with this bullshit."

"It may be bullshit to you," said the girl. "But it hurts, you know?" She pressed the heel of her hand under her ribcage. Joe realized that she was very drunk, even though her speech didn't show a trace of slurring. "Hey, Daniel," she said. "You'll teach me to speak French won't you?"

He smiled and nodded. "Sure."

"Daniel," said the girl earnestly, "knows who the hell he is. Nobody else here does. But Daniel does. He's a *Québécois*."

"Daniel our *péquiste*," said Mark affectionately. "But I shouldn't say that around Dad or he'll have a bone to pick with you."

"I don't have a bone to pick with anyone," said Joe.

"*Vive Québec libre*," said the bearded boy from Chatham drunkenly.

Daniel smiled. Joe saw that he was embarrassed for the rest of them. But they couldn't see it. They continued.

"To what do you owe your success?" said the Chathamite. "Why are you, as Rose suggests, so together? So *Québécois*?"

It isn't funny, Joe thought. They think it is, but it isn't. He is serious. It seemed to Joe that Daniel was speaking directly to him.

"What is the secret of our success?" said Daniel. "We're like the Irish, or the Jews, or the south of the confederacy. We don't forget. Anything. The good or the bad." He laughed. "You can see it in our faces." He pointed to Joe. "We all have mouths like that."

"And that's the secret?"

"Yeah," said Daniel, suddenly becoming irritable with the game, "that's it. *Je me souviens*. It's the motto of Quebec. I remember. *Je me souviens*."

"Well, that seems simple enough," said the bearded boy. "That's easy."

No it isn't, thought Joe. He felt a little panicky. It isn't easy at all. He finished his drink, picked up his coat and spoke to Mark.

"I think I'll be going now," he said. He felt he had to get out of there.

Mark was alarmed. "Jesus, Dad," he said, "is there something the matter? Are you feeling okay?"

"Fine," said Joe. "I feel fine. I'm just tired. I'm too old for this party." He smiled. "Everybody here is too quick for me. I'm out of step."

"No you're not," said Mark holding on to his coat sleeve. "Don't go."

"I'd better."

He left Mark at the doorway. In the hall Joe pushed the timed light switch that would illuminate the stairwell for a minute so that he could get down to street level. After that time it would automatically shut off. One of those ingenious energy savers never found in North America.

Joe started down, moving through the thick smells of curry and cabbage. Something caught his eye. On the wall of the stairwell, scribbled in felt pen, was written, PUNK RULE O.K.!

What a long way I came for this, Joe thought.

He took a pen out of his breast pocket and, directly beneath the slogan, wrote in his neat, schoolmasterish script Blake's line: "Albion's coast is sick, silent; the American meadows faint!"

The light in the stairwell clicked off and he was left in darkness.

The penalty for tardiness and vandalism. But at last, hidden in the dusty narrow tomb of the hallway, hidden in utter night, he found himself whispering it. I remember. I remember. Now I do.

She was a long time dying. Two years. But neither of them had admitted the possibility. That was foolish. In the early days after she had been diagnosed they would load the car and drive down to the ferry to fish for goldeye. They would drive their rods into the soft sand strewn with flood refuse and sit huddled together watching the bright floats riding the oily dark water. That might have been the time to say something. But the sun polished the heavy water, sluggish with silt, and the breeze tugged at their pant legs and they were full of expectation, certain of a strike, eager to mark a plunging float. The magpies dragged their tailfeathers along the beach and the earliest geese rode far out in the river along the flank of a sandbar. Nothing could touch them and they pressed their shoulders together hard as they leaned into a sharp breeze that came off the face of the water.

At the end, of course, it was different. He spent every night in the armchair in her hospital room. Instead of watching a bright float, he stared at the intravenous bottle slowly drain, and when it emptied he called the little blonde nurse who wore too much makeup.

By then Marie was out of her head, wingy as hell. The things she said, accused him of. Poisoning her food, stealing her slippers, lying to her, sleeping with her friends now that she was sick — even of sleeping with her sister.

The doctor explained it by saying that the cancer had spread to her brain. That was true. But why did she think of him in that way? Had she drawn on some silent, subterranean stream of ill will he had never sensed for those crazy notions? How had she really seen him all those years they had spent together? Had she read in his smoothly shaved face some malignancy?

And that of course was his difficulty. Who was he? Everything had changed since her death. His son didn't recognize him. He hardly recognized himself. Had he been lost for thirty years, an expatriate wandering? Had all those hot classrooms been exile? Was he a harder man than anyone had imagined? And had his wife known that? Was he a breaker of jaws? A drunkard who kicked at strangers in the streets, a man who punished his son by giving him pictures of his dead mother?

Or was he the man who had dreamed of water, who had sat quietly on a stretch of ashy-grey sand and watched a gently tugging line, huddled with his wife?

He began to cry in that dark passage, his first tears. He felt his way down the walls with shaking hands. Why had the light been so brief? And why was the trick so hard, the trick every expatriate and every conquered people had to learn to survive.

Je me souviens, he said. *Je me souviens*.

TERRANCE COX

Blocks of the Faithful

(for the Gush Emunim)

Deserts bloom now
where olive groves once grew.
A *Gush* settlement siphons water & name
from the remains of a nearby village;
bulldozers square off crescented hills
& eradicate all evidence of houses & groves,
of vineyards & centuries-old stone terraces
to clear bleak space & hard time
for their pre-fabs & mobile homes.

A perimeter of coiled barbed wire & weeds,
chain-link rusted fences, guards in towers
from which the *Magen David* flies,
a cement blockhouse elevates the *menorah*;
all these conjure nothing so clearly

as a concentration camp, perversely altered
& filled with volunteers.

The straight rows of shabby boxes
shape & shelter the latest zealots,
people known to consider a machine pistol
a welcome wedding gift.
Naked next to an emptied field they squat,
architectural covenants of a tribe
with an abvious need to build ghettos
& act out the longing for deserts
that dwell, like Masada, in their vision.

Nebi Saleh, West Bank, October 1978

STEPHEN SCOBIE

A Death in the Family

The clock on her sideboard still
shows summer time: she died
a week before winter.
                    Here we sit
nephew and grand-daughter
sifting through
                    photographs, papers
a death in the family.
                    Young

and handsome in uniform, direct eyes
disguising the trenches, this
was a man she loved. On the back
in her scrawly hand, with
no further comment: "Died in France,
1917."

      Here is the man she married,
trim moustache pointed: her cousin
over from Canada to fight
the war to end all wars. And here
is a postcard showing the bride-ship
which sailed war-brides to Canada, cargo
of peacetime promises.

                 She left her home
early in summer: by the end of the year
her mother had died of cancer.
Letters describing the death:
"she went to sleep like a tired child"
reminding her husband of a hymn
at sunset. Also my father wrote
formally signing himself
"Your loving brother." 1922.

                  The years
on farms in Alberta: Whitecourt,
Athabasca. No letters survive.
A photograph shows her in snow
holding the skin of what may be
a wolf. More formal poses taken
at studios in Edmonton. Her children
toddling through gumbo. Farming
Alberta in the 30s. No letters,
no diaries survive.

         1937:
my father writes again. A death
in the family. Their father died
in January, harsh New Year.
"I sat with him several nights,
He did not speak, I think he knew me,"

Why did she keep *these* letters?
Oh, there are also
wedding announcements, photographs
of brides and babies, clippings
of public events and celebrations —
                    but the letters,
the letters she kept are all
about death. Forty years later preserving
my father's last letter before *he* died:
the generations, a continuity.

They abandoned Alberta in '38:
her husband swore he'd leave
if Aberhart got in, and he did.
Then lied about his age in 1940
to join the Reserves: she wrote
a poem in his honour. "Off
to fight the Hun."
                    (In France:
1917.) Old soldiers fade:
in 1949. I never heard her
speak about him.
                    The photographs
show children, a visit home to Scotland,
grandchildren. Years in the wind,
years in the rain.
                    She began to write
an autobiography, recalling
she was born at 8.20 p.m.
on a Saturday evening, a most
inconvenient time in a manse
remembers her father muttering
under his breath, rehearsing his sermons;
a cryptic note on the Boxer Rebellion;
how as a child she had longed
for a middle initial:
five lucid, beautiful pages
then stopped.
                    In 1972

my father died; and their only
sister in '77. Oldest of three
and the last alive
she gathered her photographs;
wrote out family trees in a now
much shakier hand; neatly
labelled the letters; picked up the phone
to talk to a friend one morning
and died.
               A week before winter,
the North Vancouver rains, the long
sweep of the wind on Athabasca,
Stirring her fine white hair.
Closing her hooded eyes.

YVETTE NAUBERT

Première Saison: Le Printemps (1900)

Lorsqu'elle quitta la maison d'Ubald et de Blanche Pierrefendre où l'on n'aurait jamais plus besoin d'elle, la sage-femme Claudia Regimbald se rendit tout droit chez leur fils aîné, Joseph-Télesphore, qu'elle mit à la porte en disant:

From the novel in progress, *Les Pierrefendre, Tome V*. This excerpt is from the book entitled "Sonate en quatre saisons."

— Disparais. Ça doit se passer entre nous autres, créatures. Je t'appellerai quand ce sera le temps.

Joseph-Télesphore alla se réfugier dans la remise derrière la maison en souhaitant que sa femme crie plus fort que toutes les autres accouchées afin de détruire le silence qui venait de s'abattre sur la maison de son père et le plongeait lui-même dans une telle stupeur qu'il perdait l'équilibre dans cette journée qui faisait de lui à la fois un père et un orphelin. Avec une force qui anéantissait tout le reste, le rejetait comme inutile, le faisait apparaître comme irréel même, les deux événements presque simultanés éclataient, se répercutaient dans tout l'être de Joseph-Télesphore: la mort de sa mère à son dix-huitième accouchement et la naissance de son premier enfant. Incapable de se départager entre la joie et le chagrin, Joseph-Télesphore contemplait des objets qui n'avaient plus de nom, dont il ne connaissait plus l'usage. Hébété, il ne comprenait pas pourquoi cette journée ne se déroulait pas dans le sens prévu, pour quelle raison elle avait bifurqué de telle sorte que même le soleil printanier qui éclatait dans toute son intensité retrouvée ne l'éclairait plus.

Il chercha alors à occuper cette attente qui pouvait être longue. Personne ne savait encore comment Ida s'en tirerait puisqu'elle accouchait pour la première fois. D'ailleurs, la vie de la femme et de l'enfant tenait souvent à un fil bien ténu en cette circonstance. Le destin ne venait-il pas de mettre un terme aux accouchements de Blanche Pierrefendre en lui prenant la vie? Après tout, cette fin que personne n'avait prévue d'une femme qui mettait au monde son dix-huitième enfant pouvait atteindre celle qui donnait en ce moment naissance à son premier. Un spasme secoua Joseph-Télesphore et pour sortir de l'angoisse où il s'enlisait, il commença à mettre de l'ordre dans la remise. Mais chaque geste lui demandait un tel effort, chaque mouvement exigeait une telle tension qu'il transpirait et soufflait comme lorsqu'il abattait les arbres dans le chantier de l'Outaouais où il avait travaillé comme bûcheron tout l'hiver. Renonçant alors à bouger, il s'assit sur une bûche en face de la porte ouverte d'où il pouvait observer la maison barricadée de silence et attendit l'appel de la sage-femme comme le condamné attend l'énoncé de sa sentence. Tout autour de lui, le printemps déferlait dans une explosion de sons, d'odeurs, de rayons de lumière. La nature se dépêtrait de l'hiver avec une hâte inaccoutumée comme pour saluer le plus tôt possible le premier printemps du vingtième siècle. La neige se résorbait d'heure en heure, les taches sombres de la terre grandissaient presque à vue d'oeil et se paraient de verdure tandis que dans les arbres enfin libérés du gel, les bourgeons s'ouvraient sous la poussée irrésistible de la sève. Un croassement de corneille fit tressaillir Joseph-Télesphore comme s'il entendait, non pas le cri d'un oiseau annonçant la fin de l'hiver mais un chant de mort. Son coeur battit au rythme des glaçons accrochés au toit que la chaleur du soleil distillait en gouttes rapides et sonores. Il eut pendant un moment la perception si aiguë du printemps qu'il crut entendre monter la sève dans les arbres, sourdre du sol les pousses encore timides. Le printemps tout entier lui entrait par les yeux, les narines, la bouche, coulait dans ses veines avec son sang, charriant une tension qui lui faisait serrer et desserrer les doigts, comme s'il essayait d'en saisir toute la substance. Chassé de sa maison, il avait été confiné dans cette remise alors qu'il désirait tant être auprès d'Ida afin de l'aider dans son labeur, d'intervenir, ne serait-ce qu'en lui tenant la main ou en lui épongeant le front. Mais puisque sa présence aux côtés de sa femme n'était pas souhaitée, il aurait voulu être sur la rivière avec les hommes qui taillaient la glace en gros blocs qu'ils allaient ensuite enterrer dans le bran de scie des glacières jusqu'à l'été. Depuis son retour des chantiers, Joseph-Télesphore s'était joint à ceux qui découpaient la rivière gelée. Mais ils devaient se hâter car depuis quelques jours, la rivière était agitée de remous qui présageaient la grande débâcle. Bientôt, sur les eaux gonflées apparaîtraient les billots que les draveurs acheminaient depuis les chantiers jusqu'aux scieries de la ville encore silencieuses. Assis sur la bûche, devant la porte de la remise qui l'encerclait, tissait autour de lui un réseau de fils invisibles mais solides, élevait devant lui les barreaux de l'interdiction qui lui avait été faite de s'approcher de sa maison avant de recevoir un appel précis, Joseph-Télesphore sentait le grignotement du temps sur lui comme des milliers de fourmis. Aucun bruit, aucun son, aucun souffle ne pouvait briser le fil tendu entre la maison où Ida Pierrefendre accouchait de son premier enfant et la remise où son mari comptait les minutes de cette journée qui ressemblait tant à un cauchemar. Cependant, ce n'était pas dans un rêve que

Joseph-Télesphore se débattait mais dans la terrible réalité de deux événements irréversibles qui créaient dans son esprit une confusion insoutenable, lui infligeaient une souffrance aiguë, incisive. Son impuissance devant la vie et la mort qui se croisaient sur son chemin lui insufflait une colère qui s'adressait à tout et à rien, un désir de se mesurer avec un obstacle formidable et de l'abattre afin de mettre un terme à cette infernale immobilité à laquelle on le condamnait. Jamais encore Joseph-Télesphore n'avait vécu dans une telle angoisse, même le jour où croyant s'être perdu dans la forêt, il ne voyait pas, aveuglé par la poudrerie, la "cambuse" du chantier toute proche alors qu'il entendait hurler les loups. La maison qu'il ne quittait pas des yeux lui apparaissait aussi lointaine et inaccessible que s'il en avait été séparé par une chute ou un torrent infranchissable, des rapides dangereux. Et bien qu'une partie de son être fût restée dans l'autre maison où sa mère ne se relèverait pas de cet acte que sa femme accomplissait en ce moment, son regard restait rivé à cette porte fermée pour lui, à cette maison dont l'accès lui était pour l'instant interdit. Il voulut mettre fin coûte que coûte à cette angoisse qui lui déchirait la poitrine mais il ne put que contempler avec haine ses mains qui n'avaient pu empêcher sa mère de mourir et qui ne servaient à rien dans l'acte de donner la vie que sa femme devait accomplir sans lui.

Incapable de rester immobile plus longtemps, de supporter ce silence qui se prolongeait, cette attente qui n'en finissait pas, Joseph-Télesphore se releva, empoigna une hache, redressa une bûche énorme, leva les bras, puis les abattit avec une telle vigueur que la bûche se fendit en deux, sans un copeau. De la chair vive du bois se répandit dans l'air déjà saturé une forte odeur de résine. Secoué par les sanglots dont il n'avait même pas conscience, aveuglé par les larmes qu'il ne sentait pas couler, Joseph-Télesphore fendait les bûches avec rage, comme si chacune était un ennemi à abattre, un adversaire à exterminer. Chaque coup se répercutait en lui comme lorsqu'il ébranlait à coups de hache l'arbre condamné qui allait bientôt s'écraser dans un formidable craquement dont frémirait la forêt tout entière. Mais ni les coups de hache, ni la clameur de la souffrance et de l'angoisse qui débordaient de son être ne parvenaient à détruire le silence que Joseph-Télesphore ne crut pas pouvoir supporter plus longtemps lorsqu'un hurlement le fit basculer dans la terreur. Les bras levés, la hache menaçante, il attendit il ne savait plus quoi, peut-être une preuve plus tangible, irréfutable, que le cri n'était pas sorti de sa propre poitrine, que ce n'était pas ses propres entrailles qui avaient hurlé de la sorte. De tout son corps tendu à se briser, il voulut l'entendre une fois encore, ne fût-ce qu'en écho. Mais, dévorant l'espace, le silence s'étendit jusqu'aux limites de l'endurance de cet homme qui, la hache levée, prêt à frapper, n'entendit qu'au troisième appel son nom crié par la sage-femme. Alors, rejetant l'outil, il bondit vers la maison.

— Regarde ce que t'as fait, mon garçon. Il pèse bien neuf livres et demie. C'est un vrai beau rejeton d'une bonne branche de Pierrefendre.

Au silence succéda la clameur de la vie. Une présence envahissante remplaça la solitude insupportable de la dernière heure. Eberlué, Joseph-Télesphore promenait son regard de la sage-femme qu'il avait si souvent aperçue auprès de sa mère dans une circonstance identique à cette nouvelle accouchée qui lui offrait son sourire épuisé. Aîné de dix-huit enfants dont onze vivants (le dernier venait de coûter la vie à sa mère), il avait l'habitude de ce désordre que provoque l'arrivée d'un nouveau-né. Mais cette fois, entre le passé et le présent, une ligne se traçait car ce n'était pas un frère que la sage-femme emmaillotait en ce moment mais son propre fils. Il était à son tour le père de cette chose hurlante que les mains expertes déposaient auprès d'une Ida que Joseph-Télesphore reconnaissait à peine.

— Tiens, ma belle. C'est ton premier mais pas ton dernier. On se fait la main avec le premier. C'est après que la famille commence pour de vrai.

— Comment est-ce que tu le trouves, Joseph-Télesphore?

— Ben beau.

Cette naissance éloignait pour le moment la pensée de la mort. Ce bébé dont il n'était ni le frère ni le cousin mais le père, lui faisait oublier pour l'instant son chagrin. Une existence commune à presque tous les hommes de la ville s'ouvrait pour lui. Joseph-Télesphore ne se dérobait pas puisque telle était la loi de l'espèce. Mais au moment où se formait le noyau de sa famille, sa mère désertait la sienne. Celle qui n'avait jamais failli à aucune tâche, renoncé à aucun devoir, abandonnait à d'autres le soin de recevoir et d'élever son dernier enfant. Joseph-Télesphore chercha un réconfort sur le visage transfiguré de sa femme. Il perçut alors cette lumière qui éclaire du dedans les nouvelles accouchées et qu'il avait si souvent observée dans les yeux de sa mère. A son tour, Ida habitait une certitude qui l'excluait à demi parce qu'il était un homme. Sa femme ne lui appartenait plus tout entière: le fruit détaché tenait encore à son corps par un lien plus fort que le cordon ombilical maintenant rompu: le lien de la douleur et d'un amour terriblement exigeant.

— Et ta mère, Joseph-Télesphore? Comment est-ce que ça s'est passé pour elle?

— Ça s'est très bien passé, comme les autres fois, s'empressa de répondre la sage-femme.

— C'est un garçon ou une fille?

— Une fille. Une bien belle petite fille, murmura l'homme.

Il devait refréner son chagrin pour quelques heures encore afin de laisser à celle qui venait d'accomplir un dur labeur le temps de s'en remettre. Il ne devait pas encore dévoiler à cette femme fatiguée de la lutte pour la vie qu'elle venait de soutenir qu'une autre avait une heure plus tôt déposé le bilan de la sienne. Il n'avait pas le droit de n'être qu'un fils au chagrin immense bien que sans révolte puisque les voies de la Providence sont insondables et qu'une place toute prête attend au ciel la mère de dix-huit enfants (dont sept sont déjà de petits anges) qui a consenti à échanger sa vie contre le baptême de sa dernière-née. La sage-femme, le médecin appelé en toute hâte et en dernier ressort, le prêtre (dont la présence ne permettait aucune alternative), le mari hébété par le dénouement inattendu, avaient officié à ce sacrifice consenti par la victime elle-même. Blanche Pierrefendre s'en était allée sans une plainte, laissant derrière elle la preuve vivante qu'elle avait accompli jusqu'au bout son devoir de propagatrice de l'espèce mais aussi son devoir encore plus impérieux de catholique. En laissant extraire de son corps l'enfant qui lui arrachait en même temps la vie, elle avait rendu son âme docile aux enseignements reçus, soumise aux lois que les hommes déclaraient divines et éternelles.

Joseph-Télesphore devait à sa femme en cette journée mémorable et tragique quelque répit avant de déverser son propre chagrin. Durant quelques heures encore, il devait encercler Ida dans une sérénité dont il était lui-même bien éloigné. Mais son silence même, son attitude raide, son visage gonflé des larmes retenues, ainsi que le détachement exagéré de la sage-femme, le ton faussement rassurant de sa voix, alertèrent la jeune femme, lui firent pressentir ce que l'on désirait lui cacher.

— Non. Ce n'est pas vrai. Quelque chose est arrivé. Vous me mentez tous les deux. Je le sens bien.

Toute expression déserta le visage de la sage-femme tandis que celui de Joseph-Télesphore se couvrait d'une rougeur plus révélatrice que des paroles. Par l'intuition de sa belle-fille, Blanche devint alors extraordinairement présente, vivante même. Dans une douloureuse connivence, ils entendirent sa voix, son rire, le froissement de ses pantoufles sur le plancher; ils virent ses gestes familiers, comme de retirer et de replanter quelques épingles de son chignon, mais aussi le geste si souvent répété les dernières semaines et qui était l'indice de son épuisement, de porter les mains à son abdomen comme s'il était devenu trop lourd.

— Tu ne te vois pas, Joseph. C'est écrit sur ton visage que quelque chose est arrivé.

— Qu'est-ce que tu vas chercher là, Ida?

— Pourquoi est-ce qu'on t'aurait raconté des menteries? Parle donc pas tant, ma belle. Tu dois te ménager maintenant. Tu l'as bien mérité. Tu viens de fournir un gros effort.

— Je veux la vérité. Il est arrivé quelque chose. Je le lis sur le visage de Joseph et même sur le vôtre, Claudia. Ça ne s'est pas bien passé pour sa mère. Quelque chose est arrivé. Je veux savoir quoi.

— Repose-toi donc, Ida. Parle pas tant. Tu te fatigues.

— Ça me fatigue bien plus de vous voir me mentir. Dites-moi la vérité. Joseph, je veux que tu me dises la vérité.

Elle s'agitait, soudain effrayée: la peur s'inscrivit en plaques brûlantes sur son visage, dilata son regard qui allait de son mari à la sage-femme dans une pressante interrogation. Elle sentait dans son propre corps la menace d'une complication post-partum, fièvre puerpérale, infection ou hémorragie qui mettrait sa vie en danger, mais aussi celle de son bébé qui pouvait comme tant d'autres retourner en quelques heures au néant d'où elle l'avait tiré.

— Le bébé est mort?

Plus qu'une interrogation, les mots articulaient l'expression d'un désir instinctif bien qu'inconscient, l'alternative étant trop cruelle pour être seulement pressentie. Ni Joseph-Télesphore ni la sage-femme n'osait encore lui révéler la vérité parce que les mots leur manquaient. Et ce fut l'intensité même de leur silence qui la proclama.

— Le bébé est mort, répéta Ida.

Ce n'était plus une interrogation mais l'affirmation de son désir en même temps que l'expression du refus de cette vérité que son esprit troublé entrevoyait.

— Pas le bébé, murmura Joseph-Telésphore.

Les trois mots éclatèrent avec une telle force qu'ils en furent tous les trois secoués dans tout leur être. Ida enfonça un peu plus sa tête dans l'oreiller, remonta les couvertures pour se soustraire aux yeux de Joseph-Télesphore et de la sage-femme comme si leur présence lui devenait soudain intolérable. Elle sentit passer sur elle et son enfant un souffle glacé, comme si le printemps régressait brusquement, retournait dans un hiver encore plus glacial, pétrifiant. La sage-femme fit le premier geste inutile depuis son arrivée: elle dénoua et renoua les cordons de son tablier. Joseph-Télesphore ne bougeait pas, écrasé sous le poids des trois mots qu'il venait de prononcer et qui étaient comme une sentence de mort. Pourtant, il ne pouvait plus se taire; il lui fallait relater les derniers instants de la vie de sa mère qu'il aurait pourtant voulu enfouir au plus profond de l'oubli mais qui remontaient à la surface, tels des corps de noyés. Chaque syllabe plantait une épingle dans sa chair mais il ne pouvait plus se taire. Il parlait à voix basse, la tête penchée vers le lit où il apercevait non plus sa femme mais le cadavre de sa mère. Ida l'écouta en serrant contre elle son bébé afin de conjurer le malheur que la voix de son mari appelait. Mais comment concevoir une Blanche Pierrefendre étendue dans une permanente immobilité? Comment imaginer la maison désertée de ce rire avec lequel elle résistait contre toute adversité, repoussait toute agression du destin jusqu'à ce que la mort (et la mort seule) se fût chargée de l'éteindre? Le silence qui régnait en ce moment dans la maison d'Ubald Pierrefendre pénétra dans celle de son fils où la vie venait d'apposer son sceau. Lorsque Joseph-Télesphore se tut, le silence ne fut plus interrompu pendant un moment que par la succion du nouveau-né suspendu au sein de sa mère. Mais ce bruit si vivant, qui est l'expression même de la vie à son éveil ne parvint pas à conjurer la mort de celle qui l'avait si souvent entendu.

— La Providence fait de bien drôles de choses des fois, dit la sage-femme. Elle frappe à l'aveuglette, on dirait.

— Et la petite?

— C'est une bien belle petite fille, répondit Joseph-Télesphore.

— Plus belle que lui?

— Je dis pas ça.

— Celui-là n'est pas comme les autres. C'est le nôtre, Joseph-Télesphore.

— Comme de raison.

Joseph-Télesphore essaya de se rappeler le comportement de son père en pareille circonstance mais Ubald Pierrefendre était si souvent absent à la naissance de ses enfants qu'il lui arrivait de se trouver à son retour des chantiers et de la drave devant un bébé déjà sevré qui apprenait à parler et à marcher. Joseph-Télesphore n'éprouvait pas le mâle orgueil que certains hommes font paraître à chaque nouvelle naissance, surtout lorsque c'est un garçon. Il lui semblait que dans cet acte de donner la vie, il avait joué un rôle plus que modeste, que tout s'était accompli sans lui, d'autant plus que, ayant passé tout l'hiver dans un chantier, il n'avait pas assisté à l'évolution de la grossesse de sa femme. A son retour, l'abdomen gonflé d'Ida l'avait étonné presque autant que s'il ne l'avait pas lui-même fécondé. La continence que l'approche imminente de la délivrance d'Ida avait imposée au couple et que la naissance prolongeait lui causait une amère frustration plus que l'orgueil de sa virilité. Une si longue séparation dès la première année de leur mariage avait été pour l'un et l'autre une dure épreuve que Joseph-Télesphore avait péniblement supportée. Aussi une certaine rancune refroidissait-elle son élan vers ce nouveau-né qui était son fils.

— Qui est-ce qui va élever la petite et s'occuper de la maison? demanda Ida.

— C'est Marie-Louise, comme de raison.

— La fille aînée prend la relève quand la mère disparaît, dit la sage-femme. Marie-Louise a déjà quitté la fabrique d'allumettes.

Ce temps-là est fini pour elle. C'est une autre vie qui commence mais c'est un bien gros fardeau pour une jeunesse de vingt ans. Surtout qu'il y a Aurèle.

— Si tu voulais, Ida, tu la prendrais et tu la nourrirais en même temps que lui, dit Joseph-Télesphore.

Ida s'enfonça davantage dans le lit. Elle couvrit la tête du bébé avec un coin du drap afin de l'éloigner avec elle-même de Joseph-Télesphore, de son chagrin, du deuil et de la mort, mais surtout de sa requête. Elle refusait ce partage comme si l'enfant qui coûtait la vie à sa mère pouvait mettre la sienne en danger. En ce moment, la mort de Blanche était une réalité presque palpable que sa belle-fille ressentait plus que tout autre jusque dans sa chair. Claudia Regimbald cessa d'enfiler une manche de son manteau et posa son perspicace regard sur le visage buté, embrumé de son refus.

— Faut pas trop lui en demander, mon garçon, dit-elle en finissant de mettre son manteau. C'est son premier. Faut lui laisser le temps de s'accoutumer. Une femme qui vient de mettre son premier enfant au monde est séparée en deux. Faut lui laisser le temps de raccorder les deux morceaux. Faut pas demander à une femme plus qu'elle peut donner. Je reviendrai demain.

Ni Ida ni Joseph-Télesphore n'avaient été préparés à un tel bouleversement en un laps de temps si court. Ils en étaient troublés jusque dans leur attachement réciproque. Ils pouvaient même se changer en ennemis irréductibles si l'un des deux ne parvenait pas à desserrer l'étau que la mort venait de refermer sur eux. Le fossé qui se creusait depuis le retour de Joseph-Télesphore pouvait devenir infranchissable si aucun n'accomplissait l'effort nécessaire pour rejoindre l'autre. Ida attendait de la part de son mari une compréhension que Joseph-Télesphore était incapable de lui apporter, n'ayant pas encore quitté la maison de son père où le retenaient la souffrance et la pitié. Le refus d'Ida le déconcertait, le peinait; il jetait une ombre de plus sur cette journée déjà si chargée d'émotion.

— Non, non, jamais, répétait Ida. Peut-être qu'elle me tuerait moi aussi comme elle a tué ta mère.

— Voyons, Ida, la mère est morte mais toi, t'es vivante. Dis pas que c'est la petite qui l'a tuée. Faut pas dire ça, c'est mal. Un enfant à peine au monde peut pas commettre des péchés. C'est le bon Dieu qui l'a voulu. Il fallait baptiser l'enfant. On est des catholiques, on pouvait pas laisser mourir un enfant sans baptême. Il serait jamais allé au ciel tandis que la mère, elle . . . .

— Il fallait la laisser vivre, jeta Ida en un sursaut si violent que le bébé lâcha le sein et se mit à geindre.

D'une main qui tremblait, elle caressa le crâne mou couvert d'un duvet sombre, remit sa mamelle dans la bouche avide du bébé. Des larmes de colère plus que de douleur coulaient sur ses joues, glissaient dans son cou jusque sur le col de sa robe de nuit, sur l'oreiller.

— Il fallait laisser vivre ta mère, Joseph-Télesphore. Ta mère qui avait encore des enfants en bas âge. Et Aurèle? Qu'est-ce qu'il va devenir? On avait encore besoin d'elle, un si grand besoin d'elle, tandis que ce bébé-là, qui est-ce qui en avait besoin? Il a apporté le malheur, le plus grand malheur.

Elle pleurait de fatigue et de révolte, se sentant elle-même victime autant que sa belle-mère. Tout comme elle, elle était prisonnière de lois qu'elle n'avait pas promulguées, d'habitudes qui lui étaient imposées, de coutumes dont elle subissait les contraintes. Il se pourrait qu'elle eût un jour elle aussi à payer de sa vie l'admission de l'un de ses enfants dans l'Eglise. D'avance, elle refusait d'être immolée. Elle se sentait pleine de rancune à l'égard de Joseph-Télesphore qui ne s'était pas opposé au sacrifice de sa mère et accepterait celui de sa femme avec la même soumission. A travers Joseph-Télesphore, Ida haïssait les hommes qui s'arrogeaient le droit de décider de la vie et de la mort pour les autres. (Mais ces pensées, elle devait les garder pour elle, ne jamais les dévoiler à quiconque, même en confession, même si elles mettaient en danger son salut éternel.)

Les protestations d'Ida choquaient Joseph-Télesphore plus qu'il n'aurait su le dire. Même dans les chantiers, les bûcherons n'auraient pas osé proférer de telles paroles par crainte du châtiment qui s'abat inévitablement sur ceux qui doutent des lois infaillibles de la religion. Un arbre tombe sur un homme, une scie ou une hache ampute d'un pied ou d'une main ou encore le gel s'insinue jusqu'au coeur. Leurs blasphèmes ne mettaient jamais en cause les enseignements des prêtres: c'étaient tout au plus de mauvaises habitudes de langage que la confession au missionnaire qui les visitait chaque hiver effaçait. Qu'une femme à peine mère osât condamner la naissance de l'enfant d'une autre femme qui en était morte, dont le cadavre n'était pas encore refroidi, le jetait dans un désarroi profond, le consternait. Il ne savait plus que dire à cette Ida qu'il ne connaissait pas et qui se révélait à lui d'une manière si inattendue et troublante. Qui était-elle pour se permettre de contester les lois établies par des hommes qui recevaient de Dieu leur inspiration? Ces hommes à qui l'on devait respect et obéissance sous peine de châtiments terribles? Il regardait couler les larmes de sa femme dans un sentiment d'impuissance, trop malheureux lui-même pour pouvoir consoler.

— Ah! Joseph, ce n'est pas juste pour Marie-Louise non plus. Quand est-ce qu'elle pourra se marier à présent?

La brusquerie des événements (la vie et la mort qui se heurtaient) ne lui avait pas encore permis de dresser le bilan de leurs conséquences, d'en prévoir les tristes lendemains. Cette mort frappait l'avenir. Mais fille de devoir elle aussi, Marie-Louise ne songerait sans doute pas un instant à rejeter le fardeau qui la meurtrissait.

— Adélard l'attendra le temps qu'il faudra.

— Un homme qui veut se marier n'attend pas après une fille bien longtemps. Il va chercher quelqu'un qui n'aura pas toute une famille sur les bras. Est-ce que tu m'aurais attendue dix ans, Joseph-Télesphore?

— Le temps qu'il aurait fallu, Ida.

— Je ne te crois pas. Les hommes n'attendent pas une fille si longtemps. Mais je ne partagerai pas mon lait. Je veux que mon enfant soit fort. Je veux qu'il vive.

— C'était rien qu'une idée comme ça. Marie-Louise va comprendre.

Il écarta le drap, contempla le bébé qui tenait solidement la mamelle entre ses gencives. L'effort de la succion gonflait ses tempes que le duvet noir ombrait. Joseph-Télesphore se rappela que les tétées étaient souvent pour sa mère les seuls moments de la journée qui lui accordaient quelque répit. Ordinairement à l'heure calme du début de l'après-midi, quand les plus jeunes dormaient et que les autres étaient à l'école, elle se retirait dans sa chambre, baissait le store de la fenêtre et la tête appuyée au dossier de la chaise berçante, elle fermait les yeux. Si quelqu'un ouvrait la porte, la silhouette de la mère se profilait dans la pénombre imprégnée de douceur. Son regard luisait, arrêté aux frontières du songe. A quoi rêvait-elle dans ces moments de solitude recherchée? Dans quelle région de la conscience se réfugiait-elle, à quelle méditation se livrait-elle pendant ces quelques instants de répit que lui permettait l'allaitement de l'enfant dont la naissance alourdissait sa tâche mais qu'elle accueillait parce que telle était la volonté de Dieu? Par une grâce particulière, elle parvenait à échapper pour quelques minutes à cette réalité qui la tenait si durement et à se réfugier dans le domaine du rêve. Joseph-Télesphore était toujours sensible à cette aura mystérieuse qui émanait de la chambre de ses parents lorsque sa mère s'y retirait pour allaiter son bébé. Une ligne invisible séparait le rêve de la réalité sur le seuil qu'il hésitait à franchir. Dès que la porte s'entrouvrait, Blanche s'empressait de couvrir son sein et la tête du bébé avant de répondre d'une voix qui n'était jamais plus douce à la question ou à la requête que Joseph-Télesphore lui adressait à mi-voix, retenu par le désir de ne pas briser le charme, de garder à cet instant sa sereine quiétude. Mais en ce moment, le visage d'une femme révoltée était devant lui: une femme enfermée dans son refus, qui osait élever la voix contre ce qu'elle ne craignait pas d'appeler une injustice, ce qui risquait de déclencher la malédiction divine. Jamais Blanche Pierrefendre n'aurait douté du bien-fondé de ce que l'on avait exigé d'elle. Elle n'aurait pas non plus refusé de nourrir un autre enfant en même temps que le sien. "Quand il y en a pour un, il y en a pour deux," aurait-elle déclaré en riant, sans tenir compte de la fatigue supplémentaire. Il est vrai qu'elle savait à peine lire et écrire tandis qu'Ida, une ancienne institutrice, avait acquis dans les livres des pensées audacieuses et la capacité de les exprimer. Mais Joseph-Télesphore aurait préféré ne pas les entendre. Il désirait effacer du visage de sa femme cette expression douloureusement butée qui l'enlaidissait. Peut-être n'était-il pas juste d'exiger d'elle la même abnégation. Pour Blanche, tout venait de se terminer: aucun partage ne lui serait demandé. Ida débutait dans sa fonction de génératrice. Jusqu'où se rendrait-elle? Joseph-Télesphore ne se sentait pas capable de résoudre l'énigme que sa femme était devenue pour lui mais il eut comme un pressentiment qu'il ne serait jamais à la tête d'une famille aussi nombreuse que celle dont il était lui-même issu.

— Marie-Louise va comprendre, répéta-t-il, embarrassé et malheureux.

La blancheur du lit d'où émergeaient les yeux et les cheveux sombres d'Ida, la peau de son cou et de son visage, l'éblouissaient. Un étonnement presque incrédule persistait dans son esprit. Sa mère avait pourtant si souvent dirigé la maison de son lit, un bébé près d'elle que le spectacle d'une accouchée avec son nouveau-né lui était familier, n'avait rien qui eût dû l'étonner. Mais l'idée que cette accouchée était sa femme, que ce bébé était son premier fils ne pénétrait que lentement dans l'esprit de cet homme trop secoué par les événements.

— Je peux pas me faire à l'idée que c'est pas le père chez nous qui a fait celui-là comme les autres.

— Il te ressemble, Joseph-Télesphore. Pourquoi est-ce qu'il te ressemblerait s'il n'était pas de toi? Ce n'est pas ton père qui est mon mari.

— Il paraît que j'étais rouge itou à ma naissance. Comme lui.

— Il est beau quand même. C'est le plus beau.

Joseph-Télesphore se pencha sur Ida, l'embrassa, cacha son visage dans ses cheveux. Il aurait voulu pouvoir exprimer ce qu'il ressentait en ce moment: tendresse, fierté, chagrin. Mais l'habileté lui manquait avec les mots qui exprimaient les sentiments intimes, les fortes émotions. Parce qu'il était l'aîné d'une famille où le père ne faisait que de courtes apparitions (toujours marquées cependant par le sceau d'une conception) entre la fin de la drave ou même la conduite d'un train de bois jusqu'au port de Québec et le nouveau départ pour le chantier à l'automne, Joseph-Télesphore avait très jeune assumé vis-à-vis de ses frères et de ses soeurs des responsabilités qui l'avaient tôt vieilli. "Il faut que tu donnes le bon exemple, que je puisse compter sur toi quand ton père n'est pas là." L'impérieuse nécessité d'alléger la tâche de sa mère lui avait enlevé son enfance. L'école n'avait été qu'un lieu de passage où il avait tout juste appris à compter et à signer son nom. A dix ans, il travaillait déjà douze heures par jour à la fabrique d'allumettes. Pour une piastre par semaine, il plaçait dans des râteliers les petits bouts de bois destinés à être enduits de soufre fondu et de phosphore. Plus tard, il avait eu la charge de la machine qui coupait le bois en bâtonnets. Il avait toujours refusé de travailler dans les chantiers où le salaire était pourtant plus élevé qu'à la fabrique, parce qu'un homme devait rester auprès de Blanche durant l'hiver. Cependant, son mariage l'avait obligé à s'engager comme bûcheron l'automne précédent mais il s'était juré de ne pas renouveler l'expérience. Il refusait de marcher sur les traces de son père qui avait laissé à sa femme le soin d'élever seule leurs enfants. Il retournerait à la fabrique d'allumettes ou se chercherait un travail qui ne fût pas saisonnier comme dans les scieries.

Mais en ce moment, son amour pour sa femme, son émerveillement devant son fils n'empêchaient pas le vide de se creuser. Il aurait voulu pleurer non pas dans les bras de cette Ida révoltée mais là-bas, dans la chambre de ses parents, près du lit où gisait celle qui n'allaiterait plus jamais, qui ne rêverait plus dans la pénombre en donnant le sein à son nouveau-né.

— C'est la mère chez nous qui l'aimerait. Elle disait qu'être mémère, c'était avoir la joie des enfants sans le barda. J'aurais été fier de lui montrer son premier petit-fils.

— Elle le voit, Joseph-Télesphore. Je suis certaine qu'elle le voit et qu'elle l'aime. Elle va le protéger de là-haut.

Il n'ajouta plus rien, conscient soudain de parler de sa mère au passé, de son fils au présent alors qu'il y avait quelques heures à peine, sa mère habitait le présent et son fils était encore l'avenir inconnu. Cette journée pas encore terminée s'inscrivait déjà dans la mémoire: c'est à partir de ces heures troublées que le temps serait désormais compté.

Joseph-Télesphore servit le maigre souper de carême que la sage-femme leur avait préparé. Mais l'émotion lui serrait la gorge: il ne put avaler que quelques bouchées.

— Tu ne manges pas, Joseph-Télesphore.

— Ça passe pas.

Elle l'observait, inquiète, mécontente aussi. La mort occupait en prépondérance son esprit et son coeur. Le chagrin prenait le pas sur la joie. Son regard restait sombre, ses yeux embués étaient ceux d'un fils malheureux plus que d'un père et d'un mari comblé. Ida se sentit délaissée avec son enfant, plus seule qu'elle ne l'avait été durant cet hiver interminable dont elle avait souhaité avec tant d'impatience la fin qui lui ramènerait son mari. En cet instant où elle avait un tel besoin de sa tendresse, elle le voyait partagé, à demi absent. Avant son mariage, elle avait cru que l'amour du jeune homme pour sa mère garantissait son propre bonheur mais il était en ce moment l'obstacle qui empêchait le lien de se former entre l'homme et la femme qui contemplent ensemble l'oeuvre de leur chair unie.

— Je vais aller veiller au corps chez nous, dit-il soudain.

Elle tressaillit violemment, comme sous la surprise d'un bruit insolite ou trop brusque. Ce n'était plus l'amour d'un fils pour sa mère qui guidait son mari mais l'inconscient égoïsme de l'homme, sa profonde indifférence, son hostilité même à l'égard de toute femme qui vient d'enfanter.

— Ta place est ici, Joseph-Télesphore. Chez nous, c'est ici même. Ta mère n'a plus besoin de toi. Elle n'a plus besoin de personne. Tandis que moi, tandis que nous. . . .

Il lui fit face, le visage en feu, le regard noir, les deux mains tirant sur ses bretelles comme pour les arracher.

— Je veux voir ma mère, baptême! Je veux aller chez nous voir ma mère, tabernac! Chez nous, tu entends, Ida? Chez nous, calvaire!

Ida se rappela la mise en garde de Blanche le jour même de son mariage: "C'est un bon garçon comme il n'y en a pas beaucoup. Mais il ne faut pas le brusquer. Il n'oublie jamais un tort. Même à moi il ne pardonnerait pas si je le vexais trop. Il est rancunier, c'est son seul défaut. Je te mets en garde." Elle craignit de le voir s'éloigner d'elle à jamais comprit, qu'il en serait capable et que s'il quittait la maison maintenant, il pourrait ne pas revenir. Son absence durant tout l'hiver et la continence sexuelle forcée que l'état d'Ida leur avait imposée depuis le retour de Joseph-Télesphore avaient provoqué une fêlure qui pourrait s'agrandir. Ida se sentit elle-même sur le point de le haïr; elle eut envie de le chasser, de lui ordonner de sortir et de ne plus reparaître devant elle. En une seconde, ils étaient devenus l'un pour l'autre des adversaires. Son immobilité forcée la plaçait dans un état d'infériorité difficilement supportable, rendait la lutte inégale. En ce moment, la fatigue de l'accouchement pesa sur elle d'un poids énorme: elle eut une terrible sensation de vertige comme si elle se trouvait sur le bord d'un gouffre.

— J'ai honte de toi, Joseph-Télesphore. Comment oses-tu blas-phémer devant moi, devant ton fils?

Il se calma brusquement, passa ses deux mains frémissantes dans ses cheveux. Le feu de son visage persista un moment, puis le remords de sa colère étendit sur ses traits une couche livide. Il parut effrayé des mots qu'il avait lancés comme partent les coups d'une arme automatique. Les mots lui revinrent comme en écho pour sa plus grande honte. Son ombre grandit, grimpa sur le mur, s'étendit sur le plafond, sépara la chambre en deux. D'un côté se dressait Joseph-Télesphore dans sa verticalité quelque peu mena-çante; de l'autre gisait la femme déçue, le corps épuisé et le coeur blessé. Ida comprit cependant la nécessité, l'urgence même de retrouver l'équilibre perdu et même de retourner si possible la situation. Il fallait en ce moment même que la tension diminuât, que l'atmosphère s'éclairât. Il était devenu nécessaire, essentiel, d'encourager cet homme qui était en ce jour davantage un fils malheureux qu'un père heureux, à se rendre auprès du cadavre de sa mère, de lui accorder ces quelques heures susceptibles d'influer si profondément sur leur avenir.

— Vas-y, mon Joseph. Je n'ai jamais voulu t'empêcher de rendre à ta mère un dernier hommage. Je l'aimais moi aussi et j'ai autant de peine que toi. Ne t'inquiète pas pour moi. Je n'ai pas peur.

— Je demanderai à une des filles, à Isaure, ou à Lucie de venir rester avec toi.

— Oui, oui. Mais je n'aurai pas peur.

Elle veilla à ce qu'il se lavât avec soin, revêtit son costume de noces, sa chemise blanche et son faux-col dur, tandis qu'elle cousait sur la manche de son veston une bande de tissu noir. Elle lui fit sortir ses bottines à boutons qu'il n'avait pas remises depuis le jour de son mariage parce qu'elles lui blessaient les pieds.

— Mais il le faut, par respect pour ta mère.

Elle lui rappelait d'une voix douce et tout en l'aidant à se préparer à la quitter qu'il n'était plus seulement le fils de sa mère mais un mari, le père d'un nouveau-né et qu'il allait passer quelques heures devant le cercueil de la morte avec l'assentiment de sa femme qui avait quoi, qu'il en pensât, le pouvoir (et le droit) de le retenir. Quand il fut habillé tout comme au jour de leur mariage (mais avec le brassard de deuil sur la manche), elle le contempla avec émotion sans oser pourtant lui rappeler ce jour

heureux. Mais il s'en souvenait aussi à sa manière raide, com-
passée, rouge d'émotion, près d'éclater d'une souffrance inexpri-
mable.

— Embrasse-moi, mon Joseph.

Alors, il s'effondra. Les sanglots qu'il retenait depuis des
heures secouèrent ses épaules. Ida le serra contre elle, se jurant de
ne jamais oublier cet incident. Elle allait le graver dans sa mémoire
comme matière à réflexion, point de repère mais aussi comme
base pour raffermir sa propre volonté.

— Va, Joseph-Télesphore. Je vais prier pour ta mère en attendant
ton retour.

ALISTAIR MacLEOD

Two Winter Poems at the Graves of Children

Heavenly Rest Cemetery, Windsor, Ontario, January 22, 1979: Afternoon.

On the winter birthdate of our lost, last son,
We pause, desperately dressed for warmth, before
Cold, stone bilingual pillars. The left one reads
"Heavenly Rest" and on the right, *"Repos Celeste."*
There is other information too, given in the form
Of warnings: "No Thoroughfare," "Plot Owners Only,"

And "Gates Will be Locked at Sundown." We meet all
The entrance requirements. We are not going thoroughfaring,
And we are plot owners only (now only that) and we
Have touched the barriers of locked gates within
The Sundown of our hearts. We may pass through.

Beyond the gates, the snow is banked in drifts,
And all the graveyard roads lie buried, We read
The tracks of earlier entrants; the sharp heels
Of a woman's boots and the imprints of her knees
When she stumbled; the larger pad-like prints of
The man and the impatient, delicate steps of the
Two children who probably did not want to come.
Already the signs of these earlier death-chilled
Pilgrims are being obliterated. The snow sifts and
Whispers like fine salt across their spoor. They
Too are gone now, out and into the emptiness of white.

We fall and flounder forward, towards our own
Still waiting child. Beyond the third station
(*Jésus Tombe Pour La Première Fois*) there is no
Further sign in the barren whiteness. No single
Signal. Lost again. As anguished creatures, deep
In fur and skins, we run to the instinctive spot
And fall to dig with frenzy at the all-concealing
Snow. Seeking, perhaps, the breathing hole of the small,
Entrusted figure we were forced to leave behind on
Our past dark winter journey. Deep in cold. We
Uncover instead, a small stone marker 12" by 8"
Which is the largest size we are allowed. (More
Regulations: small child, small marker. Death somehow
To be known in inches.) It bears statistics and
A Gaelic Line: *Tamh Ar Leanabh*.* Our inland winter
Child, who, now, will never know the sea.

Beyond the barriers of this field of death,
Snowmobiles, in packs, circle and turn and

*Our child is at rest.

Hasten to pursue. Their high pitched, nasal moans
Rise to the sky above their aimless paths.
One sputters, coughs and fails, unable to go on.
A huge ungainly man in a thermal suit stands
Over it. He kicks and curses angrily at the small
And dead Ski-doo. It offers no response. In the distance
Smog rises while police sirens wail like lonely urban
Wolves. Each of us and everything seem where we
Should not be.

West Kintail, Cape Breton

Here on a windswept hill that looks down to the winter sea
The unnamed children lie in unmarked graves.
For them there are no markers, even in summer.
Silently they lie, beneath contours of snow
Shaped by the wind. Their tiny earth mounds
Have long since been levelled by the time of seasons.

When we were teenagers, it was our task
To dig the graves of our dead in the family plot.
Standing, with picks and shovels, we would wait for
Our grandfather to stake out the area. "Don't dig
Here," he would say, "That's where the babies are."
And "Not here either. Nor here." Sometimes he called
Them "children" making them seem somehow older
And more playful, although dead. We imagined their
Delicate, skeletal fingers linked together in the
Circle of a children's game deep in the darkness
Of the earth.

All of them found these small lost destinations
In a short and desperate span. Within two years
The first three came and the others rapidly
Thereafter. Most were stillborn, though some,
They say, lived for a few brief hours and one,
A boy, endured a day. In him there was the most
Hope.

We were never to know these lost potential
Children who might have been our cousins,
Playmates, friends. Perhaps they could have saved
The lives of those young and desperate teenagers
Who so yearned to give them life. Parented their
Parents: offered them directions and provided
Markers through the stormy winter landscapes
Of their lives. Perhaps they might have tossed
Them lifelines with their small but, oh so
Necessary, hands and saved them from their
Lonely fallings down the seacliffs of despair.
Born of loss and failed creation.

Here in the winter graveyard of West Kintail
There are no gates, nor barriers, nor warnings
Of any kind. One may erect monuments or stones or
markers of any shape or size, yet over these
Small graves there still are none. Beneath the snow
The quiet children lie. The winter wind sweeps from the
Cape and snow blows hard across the hill. Out on the ice,
At night, the baby seals send out near human cries.

MARILYN BOWERING

Aunt Dorcas:
on omens

for Milton Acorn

It were a death rattle,
that was it here knocking
in the old clock. I knew it was
something going wrong in the house,
and here we was sleeping all night
while it struck.
The old man snores in his underwear,
ready for anything he sez, well
I sez I'm tired of taking it
off;
its a cold skin he has
under the wool.

The cows are bawling, the fleets
out and I seen the crows fleeing
back-foremost from the sun.
I ain't looking forward to this day;
even the strong boys can't help
when things is this far. . .
And there was a dream in it . . .
he and me had less than half a face between us,
and that was more than was wanted.

I ain't saying more ——
Look at him, snorting and blowing
like any old fool. He'll fire
the stove and won't notice, won't notice
a thing's changed.

BRIAN BARTLETT

The Cure of the Lawyer's Wife

Despite the soil packed around her neck she could turn her head, looking across their yard to the well, the garden, and the boy she had asked to chase away any dogs. Their pale house stood taller than usual, seen from the bottom up because she sat there in the ground by her own design. Blankets wrapped around her to keep her dress and shawl clean built an extra layer of heat in the tree-shaded corner of yard she had pointed out for Philip to shovel up. Two or three times during the morning she had heard, more clearly than if she were walking atop the earth, a customer on a horse climb the stony path to Philip's forge beyond the far side of the house.

The boy was sitting over near the garden. Since her wedding in the spring she had thought of him as much younger than herself, though once their three years difference had not kept them from running races together. When she called, "My hat's slipping! Howard, come push up my hat!" she saw his eyes were fixed on something in the harbour below the hill. Two distant ships inched into her vision, which was stunted by the closeness of her eyes to the earth. A man in the rigging of a sail was smaller than the blades of grass around her.

Crouching with his boots in her face, Howard lifted her wide-brimmed blue hat. "No dog will come near you," he said, high-voiced. "They'll be scared of you, Chokecherry Face."

Her fingers bunched under the earth as he headed back to the garden. "You say that again and I won't tell you any stories!" she shouted. "Tomorrow you won't be talking nasty, when this gives me a new face like Philip says!" From beyond the far side of the house came sounds of a hammer striking heated iron.

He had not actually said burial would be her cure, Beth knew, smelling soil below her chin and spruce branches overhead. Mending a chair leg the previous week, he had borne with her familiar fretting about the oily spots that had plagued her face since girlhood, then mentioned a cure he'd heard from a lawyer in his native village down in Massachusetts. "He swore his wife's face was like a angel's the next day," Philip said. "Like a angel's." "For my face, I'd have to stay buried a *month*," she replied, half believing the story — she wanted to believe all stories — yet unable to picture restless herself sitting still for a day even above the ground.

Gradually, at all hours, washing their clothes or visiting her parents or reading a book of verse as small as the palm of her hand, she backtracked to the cure of the lawyer's wife and felt growing hope. That hope speeded up her heartbeat when she recalled how as a child, watching her oldest brother Mansford shake with a fever, she had heard her father cry "For God's sake, silence!" at a window-lashing thunderstorm, and her two good eyes had seen the sky settle down in minutes. The perseverance of the lawyer's wife, she convinced herself to complete the circle of belief, was no more unfounded or extravagant than her father's shouting at the storm.

The crow's beak was opening, its back feathers lifting. "You've got no business here, go away. *Howard!* Ugly bird, go away or I'll spit in your eye!" A rock curved within inches of her hat, and the crow

flew up silently but for its flapping wings. She was about to bawl
out Howard for flinging the rock so heedlessly when she noticed
his plump mother rushing past the garden, her bonnet laces
undone.

Vera didn't slow down until she reached Beth, then with her
double chin trembling she said, "Good Lord. You've done it after
all."

"I'm *doing* it," Beth said proudly.

"Who ever heard a more hare-brained —" Vera began, but she
became speechless. The wrinkles in her chin, seen from below,
were deep crevices. *I'm stuck down here but I'm young, young* Beth
thought as she said, "If you sit down we can talk better." The girl
grinned smugly while the woman, whom she had never seen
sitting without a chair, awkwardly arranged her grey dress and
slowly descended.

"Won't you get hungry?" Vera asked from the edge of the
sunlight. "I could bring over —"

"No eating is part of the cure."

"The cure?"

"There have to be rules besides just staying here for a day, don't
you think? I had to think what the rules might be."

"Did that Philip try to stop you?"

"What man wouldn't? But he worked hard this morning when I
begged him to dig this hole for —"

"So he'd see you suffer."

One of Beth's feet tried to lurch, but went nowhere. "You're all
too hard on Philip cause he's nobody's cousin and —"

"I don't suppose he's even bothered to visit you."

Beth wished she were bantering with Howard rather than
receiving unwanted, unneeded sympathy from his mother. She
said, "He has his customers, he's busy," then they heard Howard
pulling up the rope of the well, and a bird screaming in the
woods, but no sound from the forge. Her face flinched with her
suspicion that Philip had not practiced his trade for years in the
United States, that he — a decade older than she, weary of living
alone in small rooms and of some fragile or even illegal business — had picked up remnants of a long-forgotten apprenticeship, and married her to have a wife, any wife; unwillingly she
recalled Vera's report that he had shown some joke playing-card

to her husband at their bachelor friend's (Vera had told no more), so she herself had searched through his deck and found a Queen whose face had been marked, by a pencil's brutal sharpness, with little round spots. To stop flushing she said, "Why should he visit me? He knows I won't be moving an inch from here."

"I guess you won't," said Vera, her voice sinking in defeat. "So my Howard might as well be of some use and keep an eye out for you. I'll be back after supper with food for *him* at least."

At its peak, the sun was so bright she could see waves in the bay glitter, fall and foam. Howard was crawling in tall grass near the garden. "I know what you're looking for!" she shouted. "No grass snake can scare me!"

"Chokecherry Face!"

Suddenly, for once hating the fancifulness within her, she imagined *Philip* had invented that name and the boy merely echoed it.

Howard stretched out flat on his back in the shade against the house. If he wanted to sleep she would let him, so in the night he would be rested and alert. Saving all her own sleep for the dark second half of her stay in the ground, she fought an urge to let her eyes shut, which increased with the heat. Her legs, even when she shook them, seemed airy and distant; her neck felt elongated and her head felt expanded, as if she were only a rootless cabbage atop the earth.

At the end of the afternoon while she was dazed, listening to her body throb, bootsteps approached from behind. She saw Howard still lying flat on his back, and heard a familiar phlegmy cough. "Oh Philip!" she laughed. "Is half the time gone already?" As he shovelled she felt totally awake again, relieved that her one ascent back to the ground, which she had tried not to crave too intensely, was minutes away. "Why didn't I hear any customers this afternoon?" she asked.

"Because there weren't any," he said, rusty-voiced. Even on ordinary days half the time he spoke from behind her.

"Maybe you'd be better off at other work." She began laughing and said, "Like doing this," then cut her laugh short when she sensed his silence like a burned-down forest at her back. "Did that lawyer say how they celebrated his wife's new face?"

"We won't be doing any celebratin'."

"How did you know that lawyer?"

"I got caught," he said flatly; this seemed not one of his jokes, but a riddling frankness bound to haunt her without telling her anything clear.

"Walk around here so I can —" she began, only to realize by his phlegmy cough that he was further away. Turning her head, she saw him over kicking Howard's foot. The boy stood, taller than the man, then the man pushed the shovel against the boy's chest and left, his wire-tied twist of long hair swinging indifferently at her.

Howard shovelled angrily, sleep still clinging to him. "I should get all my friends," he said, "to come up here and jump on your head." She was too stranded and emptied by Philip's departure, too heavy-headed, to reply. If Howard's friends did what he wanted, she felt, her head would be heavy enough to withstand all the battering of their boots. Once most of the earth over her body had been heaved away, she took Howard's hand and lifted her bottom, the backs of her legs, finally her feet, and stood, astonished how shallow the pit now seemed.

"The ground!" she cried, forgetting Philip, then though she wanted to skip and twirl to the house she sensed she must maintain a suitable solemnity; any wild intoxication might break the cure. Slowly passing the garden, which seemed far below, she did not stretch her arms. Her shoes solidly hit the steps yet she held back enjoying their sound, as she held back glancing at her face in the bedroom mirror after she had used the chamberpot and with two trembling hands drunk one mug of water though she was thirsty enough for ten. *One mug too many* a sentence of the cure might say *and you return to the beginning*.

After Howard had shovelled the earth back around Beth, he sat against the well and started eating the food his mother had brought in a straw basket. Vera reached Beth just as Mansford came up the nearest path on the horse he had bought to honour his promotion to corporal. "Oh Good Lord, he doesn't know anything about this, does he?" asked Vera, already turning to go and meet him. He had just dismounted by the house when she tugged one of the sleeves of his striped shirt.

"I come for a visit, and what do I see?" he asked as he reached Beth. He talked loudly yet hardly moved his mouth, which was lost behind his new beard. "My own sister is . . . is bewitched. Yes, yes, if that Philip was a woman I'd say he was a witch, making you do such —"

"He didn't make me do anything. All he did was tell me the stranger's cure."

"What was this stranger, an Indian?"

"A lawyer."

"A lawyer. Ha ha, yes, yes, they're always good at making something out of nothing. I s'pose you still think there's dragons in China, like you used to." Now that he was a bearded corporal he pretended to be much older than she. Unlike her he couldn't imagine that scaly beasts might live in distant, mist-draped hills — though maybe they didn't breathe fire. "All you girls think about is your faces."

"How many hours," she asked, "do you spend shining these boots of yours — that never set foot near a battle?" (They were at war, she knew, but the real fighting was hundreds of miles westward.)

Mansford's polished boots turned away. She and Vera watched him take a short cut through one corner of the garden. Climbing onto his horse, he shouted sarcastically, "I'm going to find the dragons of China!"

"I thought Howard would get scared thinking about tonight," Vera said, watching her son eye Mansford, dust rising from the horse's hooves, "but he wants to stay. That brother of yours, I just hope he doesn't tell your poor mother. You're going to feel some foolish when this is over, and you've done it for nothing."

Beth couldn't see, but could faintly taste, dust from the horse's hooves. She shivered in and above the earth, because the sun was now shrouded by a small cloud so all ground in sight was shadowed, and because Vera had just reawakened her most monstrous fear, that it *would* all be for nothing.

"Don't you dare say that again," she snapped. "We have to say it'll happen or it won't."

Vera snapped back, "All right, it'll happen, it'll happen, it'll happen."

All defences against hunger gone, she was an empty shell ready to be filled with darkness. Dragging a wool blanket his mother had brought, Howard approached and threw an apple core down over the hill. He sat crosslegged with his back to her near the shovel stuck blade-down in the earth. "Howard, move over, you're blocking that pretty sun. . . . I'm glad wolves've been scarce this year. I never told you, did I, about the time when I was a baby? About the wolves?"

"Wolves?" he asked, moving nowhere. "I ain't seen one all summer."

"When my father and mother weren't much older'n me," she went on, hoping to kill time by talking, "they lived upriver out in the woods, where Father always had out trap-lines. One day when the cabin door was open a wolf walked right inside and started making noises and moving its head, so Father went over to the stove — the same stove Philip and me have now — and he said, 'We'll have to do without soup tonight, Hetty,' and threw all the soup in the wolf's face. A moment later it was gone. Oh, I'd like some soup myself now. *Howard*, I told you to move over." The bay was rapidly darkening, but Howard's back kept her from seeing how much of the sun was left. "That's just the first part of what happened. A year later Father was off checking his lines. Then some wolves came at him and he climbed a tree faster'n he ever had before. They growled, jumped up and hit their jaws against the tree. 'We'll have to do without soup today, Hetty,' Father said in a loud voice, and suddenly all the wolves turned their tails and ran away."

"That's cow shit. That couldn't happen."

"Yes, it did, it did. Father told me."

In the house a lamp was burning. Perhaps Philip was making a quick stew, stirring vegetables and thinking about . . . about Massachusetts. Howard began to slump. "Don't you dare sleep, get up and do something. Find some rocks, you'll need them if a dog comes by."

"*You're* the one I should throw rocks at," he said, rolling over on his side.

A minute later he returned from the well, dropped a handful of rocks into the grass and said, "Do I get a kiss for my good work? You kissed me once."

"Just to see what it's like. You could've been *anybody*." While he sat down with his back to her and flung the blanket around himself, she wanted him to turn and face her so she would be less alone, but he had spoiled it by mentioning kisses. Nearby in the woods a chorus of frogs sang with one voice. Howard slumped, silent. "Those frogs over there," she said, "are better company than you."

Branches above her, which during the day had graciously kept the sun's rays away, blocked off welcome moonlight. An hour had passed since her last words when Howard stood with the blanket around his shoulders and said, "If those frogs are such good company, let them protect you."

"Don't, Howard, don't. Stay with me." He did not pass the garden but headed directly down the hill, a loping caped shape who left with the speed of a figure in a dream. "Please, Howard, please, stay with me!" She was about to call *You can have a kiss!* but she was talking to no one. Alone, she twisted her body and lifted her legs slightly against the trapping weight. "Philip, Phil-ip, *Phil-ip!"* There was no lamp on in the house, and she was sure he was lying there listening to her.

Once she was still, hunger swept through her, sapping her strength. Something fell nearby, a body cut down or leaping from the trees. She threw back her head, again stiffening against the earth. She vaguely saw the source of the sound — the shovel had fallen over — but still she trembled. Behind her in the darkness, a few feet behind her, anything could have been lurking. She whispered, "We won't need any more soup tonight, Hetty," and desired the solace old women must find in singing hymns. Yet when she remembered the hours ahead, she suspected the most uplifting, unburdening hymn would now do no more than a child's ditty.

What almost comforted her was the memory of a piano. In the winter she and Philip had met at a dance on the edge of the village, in a house where bells hung in doorways, gold-trimmed tablecloths stretched under food, and a tiny old man with a purple birthmark on his neck played the most festive and fluent sounds she had ever heard. Piano tunes remained in her ears even when the man rested, even when she and Philip left the house and walked along a road, then away from the moonlight and off the road, their boots breaking through higher and higher snow until she feared for her dress. Philip tugged her, saying he wanted to show her a ghost. "Don't worry, it's a sad old one who just stands there and won't ever chase you." When he pointed at a spot in the darkness she saw a long, greenish, flickering form floating in the air, and clutched his arm. He held one arm around her, guiding her to the spot, lifted her gloved hand to the tree and, laughing, tore a growth from the bark and slipped it into her pocket. As frightened as she had been, disappointment — that the figure turned out to be nothing but a green growth — seized her like a rough man; she felt it more than Philip's arms. Now the growth sat on a ledge in their bedroom where until a few weeks ago, taken into her hands, it had brought back sounds of a piano.

The lamp in the house was lit again. A door swung shut. A horse snorted. Though she sensed, with an unmistakable heaviness like that in her legs and arms, what was happening, she remained silent even when his horse, no doubt laden with bursting saddlebags, reached the stony path. She ended her stillness only when stillness began out there, making not a plaintive or angry cry of a man's name but a wordless sound which soon dissolved into weeping. The one story she wanted to stay inside her head — ugly, charmless and incomplete — finally seemed the only one living outside her. Her sobbing changed into wailing, tears flowing until in her fever she imagined herself soaking the earth and weighing down her prison. All her muscles relaxed and she felt a warm wetness run down her thighs. As she subsided into silence she noticed the frogs too were silent. In a torpor deeper than fear, she only had to wait.

Sleep came now and then in the last hours of darkness. Toward morning she dreamed of a summer when she had been a small girl and her father had lifted her into a lilac tree to tie paper around branches so buds wouldn't bloom until the King's birthday. Other girls and women were there along the road-side row of lilacs, all tying paper to trees. Her father effortlessly held her up among the twigs, up in the air where, swinging her legs, she seemed taller than the ladies of the village. When she had fallen from that dream, at first she thought she was only lying atop the earth under a tree, ready to stand up and walk away.

"Oh Beth, Beth, have you been alone all this time? I just found that Howard in his bed. I'll take the stick to him, don't you worry. I ran over here expecting to find you in Lord knows what state!"

Her face itched with dried tears; her throat felt voiceless, shrivelled. "I'm so tired," she managed in a loud whisper. "Dig me out, Vera. Or will it spoil your shoes here?"

"Forget about my shoes."

Panting and grunting went on for many minutes as Vera shovelled, then the woman's hands grasped the girl's. While the woman pulled the blankets from the hole and shook them, the girl walked away with erratic strides, squinting, her itching thighs brushing each other. The garden floated by, a stream of green.

In the kitchen as she looked at the wall she let out a short cry, though she saw — for once — exactly what she had expected to see. His saddlebags and both his coats were gone from their hooks. Even in her dizziness, grasping the back of a chair, she craved to be told whether he had left on a whim, or invented everything — even the spotted angel face — to trick and torment her. She resisted lifting her hand to her cheeks. Limping, she started towards the bedroom.

"Stupid girl, stupid girl," she whispered, to keep the room from crowding against the sides of her head. As she passed the stove she saw a wolf crouched by the woodbox. He disappeared a moment later, but not before she knew that her father sitting in a tree had said nothing about soup to the hungry pack. Walking home through the woods with pelts strung over his shoulder, he was already planning to tell a story.

ARVED VIIRLAID

Take Off Your Masks

Why are you clowning,
    Pharisees,
as if you could fool me?

I can see through you
because I see myself
and undoubtedly belong among you.
Take off your masks —
We are tired of them
    in life and on the stage!
we yearn for sincerity,
    sincerity just once.

If you are snakes,
    why do you hide your eyes?
If you are devils,
    why do you wear God's face?
If you are animals,
    why do you call yourself humans?

Take off your masks,
    clowns!

Take Off Your Masks and *Strangers* were translated from the
Estonian by Taimi Ene Moks.

Strangers

Winds whisper in trees,
but we
have nothing to say.

We stand side by side.
Our bodies touch,
but still —
we are two strangers.
We hold each other
in tenderness and love;
we can read each other's minds —
we are almost one
But our souls weep:
we are two
aimless strangers.

Oh, my love,
two strangers,
two unacquainted beings,
and a strange wind whispers
in the foreign trees.

JOY KOGAWA

train trip

sitting beside the strange
man on the train I
hang my coat over his,
the hood covering
his brown collar the
blue arm bumping
bumping against the
brown elbow patch

intimate as lovers
our clothes caress
in the rock rock of
the train while
discarded on the seat
we travel together
polite as death

calligraphy

my eighty-one year old mother's
penultimate act
before leaving her house

of thirty three years
was to kill a
large black spider
that sat still as death
in the white bathtub

the calligraphy
lies on the bathtub ledge
a foreign word
of curved spider legs
delicate as brush strokes

SHIRLEY MANN GIBSON

In the next room

In the next room a woman
    is dying —
white hair,
white face above a hollow mouth,
sheets wrapped round her
    like a shroud.

My radio plays Bach.
She does not hear.
Hers is a silence no one
    (Bach, her family moving
    in and out) can break.

In the hall,
    handsome and awkward in
    his well-cut suit,
her grandson waits,
leans on the wall,
checks the gold watch on his wrist,
looks angry.

He sights me through the door.
We eye each other.
The woman goes on dying.

Necklace

(for M. A.)

You sling the teeth round your throat
    with the confidence of
    a cannibal.
The red dress backs them
    like a wound.

Whose are they, I ask.
Anyone we know?

Cow, you suggest,
    or prehistoric poet.
Anyone we know?

All evening,
    glimpsed through the crowd,
    the necklace takes my eye and
when you come near
    I finger the yellow incisors.

I think they are horse.

By midnight,
    your neck strains under
    their weight.

SUNITI NAMJOSHI

Four Fables

Case History

After the event Little R. traumatized. Wolf not slain. Forester is wolf. How else was he there exactly on time? Explains this to mother. Mother not happy. Thinks that the forester is extremely nice. Grandmother dead. Wolf not dead. Wolf marries mother. R. not happy. R. is a kid. Mother thinks wolf is extremely nice. Please to see shrink. Shrink will make it clear that wolves on the whole are extremely nice. R. gets it straight. Okay to be wolf. Mama is a wolf. She is a wolf. Shrink is a wolf. Mama and shrink, and forester also, extremely up tight.

The Giantess

Thousands of years ago in far away India, which is so far away that anything is possible, before the advent of the inevitable Aryans, a giantess was in charge of a little kingdom. It was small by her standards, but perhaps not by our own. Three oceans converged on its triangular tip, and in the north there were mountains, the tallest in the world, which would perhaps account for this singular kingdom. It was not a kingdom, but the word has been lost and I could find no other. There wasn't any king. The giantess governed and there were no other women. The men were innocent and happy and carefree. If they were hurt, they were quickly consoled. For the giantess was kind, and would set them on her knee and tell them they were brave and strong and noble. And if they were hungry, the giantess would feed them. The milk from her breasts was sweeter than honey and more nutritious than mangoes. If they grew fractious, the giantess would sing, and they would clamber up her legs and on to her lap and sleep unruffled. They were a happy people and things might have gone on in this way forever, were it not for the fact that the giantess grew tired. Her knees felt more bony, her voice rasped, and on one or two occasions she showed irritation. They were greatly distressed. "We love you," they said to the tired giantess. "Why won't you sing? Are you angry with us? What have we done?" "You are dear little children," the giantess replied, "but I have grown very tired and it's time for me to go." "Don't you love us anymore? We'll do what you want. We will make you happy. Only please don't go." "Do you know what I want?" the giantess asked. They were silent for a bit, then one of them said, "We'll make you our queen." And another one said, "We'll write you a poem." And a third one shouted (while turning cartwheels), "We'll bring you many gifts of oysters and pearls and pebbles and stones." "No," said the giantess. "No." She turned her back and crossed the mountains.

The Friends

And so, they walked through the woods; summer was over, but the sun was still warm, the leaves were turning. They chucked stones into the water and likely looking sticks. They competed amiably. It never once crossed their minds that walking through the woods in early fall was an ancient pastime for heterosexual lovers, which, even for them, might have much the same meaning. They said, "Good Night," and met two days later at a formal gathering. They drove off together and got themselves supper, they exchanged stories. They had a great deal in common: an extreme ambition, a preference for women, and a happy wit. Each was charmed by the other's gentleness and felt at ease, they parted cheerfully. Three days later they met once again. They had done some thinking. They were still cheerful and kind and friendly; but about what they had thought, they said nothing.

Nymph

The god chases Daphne. Daphne runs away. Daphne is transformed into a green laurel. What does it mean? That that's what happens to ungrateful women?

Daphne says, "Yes." She says, "Yes. Yes. Yes." Apollo is pleased. Then he gets bored. Girl chases God. It is not very proper. Daphne gets changed. Into what is she changed? Daphne is changed into a green laurel. What does it mean? That that's what happens to ungrateful women.

Daphne says, "Yes." Then she keeps quiet. Her timing is right. Daphne gets changed. Into what is she changed? Daphne is changed into a green laurel. And what does it mean? It means, it obviously means, that trees keep quiet.

GAIL FOX

Listening to Myself Sing

Because I am a stranger to this
world, I try to learn the alphabets,
the numbers of love,

And there are books and sometimes
people, or occasionally a note that does not
mutilate the ear.

But feeling continues unfamiliar, and
I am slowly dying to the intense timed
sequence of the leaves.

A tear runs down the eye. My spiritual
life is not what it should be. What is the
point of seeking Love?

Hear from the doctors I'm incurable.
O damn to the red April evenings by the lake;
I don't know why the

Sun sets and rises in a perfect shaft of
green light. I dance the intricate steps of the
music, listening to myself sing.

SID STEPHEN

An Absence

This is me
standing
in the bathroom
pale against the tile,
hair gone awry, sleep-creased
cock hanging flaccid
as a leash, my beard
becoming through
my face.

In the way
my teeth fill my mouth,
how once again
uncontrollably
I seem to possess
ten fingers, ten toes,
there is no evidence
of our having been together.

Nothing's missing.
nothing has been left.
You could at least have taken
a single keepsake. The Gideon bible
still smirks from the dresser drawer,
not even a damp towel
smells of you for me.

Too late, I tell the maid
to leave the bed unmade.
Already she has stripped
the sheets — a hair, a single scrap
of fingernail would do.
I search my body for a mark,
but you have been so gentle
that the only thing
I find is the taste of you,
like a foreign language
in my mouth.

TOM MARSHALL

Robert and Nancy (1968)

That weekend there was a party in the neighbourhood.
Nancy was always invited to these, and so Robert attended most
of them too. Everyone seemed to assume by now that they were a
couple — it was even reported to him that Neil had said something reflecting such a belief — and yet they hadn't done more
than kiss goodnight a few times. But their relationship felt so
natural, had so very little strain or tension in it, that there seemed
to be no pressure on either of them.

At the party everyone danced to "Sergeant Pepper's Lonely

From a novel in progress.

Heart's Club Band." Rebecca arrived with a Pakistani violinist she had met at a party earlier that same evening in Knightsbridge. He was quietly witty. "Guess what?" she said to Nancy, "I'm going to Paris for two weeks."

Robert had recently been in Paris and in France's chateau country for several days with fellow students from London House. It was a trip that had been planned for some time and it took him away from Nancy and her world only briefly. It was relaxing and enjoyable. He had admired in a rather detached way the cold splendour of Chenonceaux — perhaps because it was worlds away from London's seductive untidiness and disorder. Much of the countryside too had great charm — so ordered in its rows of poplar trees, so Cartesian. On the first evening in Paris, though, they sensed the anarchy at work too. They had wandered over to the Left Bank. It was a mild evening. Soon they found that the crowds in the streets were moving, flowing, in a more or less directed fashion, so that they were propelled back towards the river. Then there were glimpses of gendarmes and long-haired young people, some with signs, but it was difficult to make out in the swiftly flowing currents of people just what was going on. They made their way eventually back to the hotel. "Some sort of student demonstration," said Harvey, who was an American.

"Nothing is real," sang the Beatles now, "Strawberry fields forever."

"Let me take you down, 'cause I'm going . . . "

Rebecca danced with Robert. She chattered on in her usual way about how marvellously things were unfolding in Czechoslovakia under Dubcek's new dispensation. He called it "communism with a human face." The English newspapers were calling it the "Prague spring." Rebecca, who considered herself some sort of freelance communist — she had never been a member of the party — wanted to go to Prague from Paris but probably couldn't afford it.

"What did you mean," Robert asked her, "when you told me that Neil left Nancy because he was afraid of what might happen?"

"Don't you know, then?"

"Evidently not."

"Then I doubt if I should be the one to tell you."

"He was running out on some kind of trouble."

"Yes. He's a bastard."

"Then tell me."

She looked torn. But only for a moment.

"Not here. Let's go for a walk, I'm hot," she said.

So they slipped away into the street. Robert did not see Nancy in the front room. Outside was a world of shadows.

"You'd have to be told sooner or later. She's just been putting it off because she wants to enjoy her time with you." Rebecca was justifying herself, he saw.

"You see," she said now in the quiet street, "Nancy hasn't always been very well."

"It's her health."

"Yes. She'll be fine for the longest time, but then it will 'hit' her. And she exhausts herself, she's so foolish. She lives with a kind of desperation."

Robert thought this a better description of Rebecca herself.

"*What* 'hits' her?"

"It's called Hodgkin's Disease. They don't have a cure, though they're working on it. It lets up for months, years, but it always comes back. Nobody who has it lives to be very old."

"But she seems so well."

"Yes, it's her front, she's marvellous, she wants so to live fully. And she exhausts herself."

"Hodgkin's Disease," he repeated.

"It's cancer. Of the lymph glands. And the only treatment gradually destroys the bone marrow. So they can only hope for another spontaneous remission, another temporary reprieve. And work for a cure, or control."

"When she's happy, it's in remission." It was a question.

"Who can say?"

They were both upset. Robert found the news difficult to take in. So Nancy lived with almost certain doom, an early death. But it was Rebecca who was habitually melancholic. And yet . . . It made a certain sense. Nancy lived intensely in the present and in the world of other people for good reason. Rebecca perhaps contemplated a future that could be only more of the same unhappy past. Or so he told himself.

"There's no way," he said, "Of knowing how long she has."

"It's very unpredictable."

Then he asked: "Was she very much in love with her husband?" He could not remember the name.

"I think she is now."

"But it was so long ago. And she left him for someone else."

"Oh Robert, you're so innocent," she said, laying a hand on his arm. "Don't you know that these things are never *cleanly* over?" And thus brought things round again to *her* life, *her* pain. Her large, professionally tragic eyes demanding that he take notice.

But he only said, "Let's go back."

The party was still crowded. "I don't know why you say goodbye, I say hello," sang the Beatles, "Hello, hello, I don't know why you say goodbye, I say hello." Robert saw Nancy through a cloud of smoke talking to one or two people by the door into another room. He made his way to her side.

"Let's dance," he said.

In the dance, in which they moved separately with a certain stylized violence, not touching, she relaxed, she seemed to belong there. He wanted desperately for things to be perfectly ordinary between them, he wanted her to be her everyday responsive and supportive, even motherly self, he thought he could not bear for her to be ill. He clung to the moment, he sang along with the song: "You say goodbye, but I say hello."

But within a few minutes of the song ending he felt trapped, claustrophobic. He could not bear all these strange people. He had to get out, and he could not bear to leave her behind him.

"Let's go," he said.

"Already?" she said. But she came without further question. She saw the urgent look on his face.

They walked back, not talking much. He knew he would never speak to her of her illness unless she spoke of it to him.

"Do you want to come up?" she asked as she unlocked the outside door of the house.

"I can't," he said. "Forgive me, I'm not feeling very well." He wanted at this moment only to be alone. But he could not bear to leave her behind at the party.

She looked at him quizzically, perhaps she was even a little amused at him. She had never behaved with him as if time was short.

"All right," she said. Then he kissed her on the lips lightly. "Goodnight," he said.

"Hello, Robert," said Nancy with quiet emphasis. "Hello." And closed the door behind her.

The next day Robert felt almost normal again. He began once more to look at things with his customary detachment. If he could not actually forget Nancy's illness, he could at least put it out of his mind and behave as if he had never learned about it. That was what she would like, he told himself. They could go on being friends in the same easygoing, pleasant way. But he held her at a distance now too, try as he might to conceal this even from himself. His thesis once again reasserted a central importance that had almost shifted itself to Nancy. Now she was on the edges of things again as she had been in the earliest days of their relationship.

Some weeks of perfectly light camaraderie followed. Nancy could apparently accomodate herself quite effortlessly to anyone else's mood and rhythm. He even found this ability a little suspect now. She was like a chameleon in her obligingness. There was a profound passivity there somewhere despite the energy she expended.

Then Rebecca returned from Paris, much disturbed, it seems, by what she had seen there. She had found herself right in the middle of the student riots and was much shaken. "It must have been fascinating to watch," said Robert, self-appointed historian of twentieth century doom and apocalypse. He thought that the student revolutionaries, led, according to the English press, by someone he could think of only as "Danny the Fat", were theatrical and somewhat ridiculous. No doubt they were a symptom, though, they were so thoroughly bourgeois. "Fascinating! It was horrifying," cried Rebecca with great, round eyes. They were in The Lamb, she had by now touched him for several drinks. She was more hysterical, he thought, than he recalled her being before. "I saw cars overturned and set on fire," she said vehemently. Robert rather liked this vision — he almost gloated over the newspaper photo of burning cars on the Paris streets — but for Rebecca the sight of a burning car apparently held some deep nameless horror. Even though he was the bourgeois and she the supposed communist.

Then she said, again vehemently, "You bloody *dons*, you're just — voyeurs. Robert, you're a vulture, a jackal just hanging around so you can prey on the corpse."

A week later she was dead.

Her most recent lover, an American, broke into her flat and found her. She had apparently been dead for about four days. It was a case, the autopsy showed, of medication and alcohol, and thus perhaps accidental — one of those ambiguous deaths.

Nancy took it all amazingly calmly. Robert was a little shocked at her, even though he thought he knew why she did not express very strong emotion over the death of one of her oldest and once closest friends.

There was a cremation, a brief, simple affair, then a party in someone's garden. Everyone drank wine. Helen Tufnell came from Hampstead. And Neil, without his wife. There was a good deal of reminiscence about Rebecca's remarkable adventures and lovable characteristics. The American lover excused himself fairly early. He had known her very briefly and felt out of his depth. But the party continued, everyone got somewhat drunk.

Afterwards, Nancy and Robert went over to his room and went to bed. When they had made love they lay a long time in a kind of melancholy peace. "Nobody can find me here," was all that she said.

Later, standing naked by his side, she fingered the photo of his parents taken when they were still in their twenties, and remarked, "It's a silly thing to say, I suppose, but you look like both your parents." He always remembered that.

Eventually they went out and got something to eat. Oddly, they didn't feel closer. The event, which had occurred, it seemed, with a certain inevitability, only seemed to underline the distance between them. It was more the end of something than the beginning of something. They returned to their separate places, their separate worlds, certain of each other in some way impossible to define, but not of any future. She was going to die, and he was scarcely born.

"You'll be going home, of course, in the fall," she said to him a week or two later in The Lamb.

"Yes. I've got a job, I think."

This was an important consideration. Academic jobs were beginning to be scarce.

"Yes. I expect you can only live in your own country. And in your own view of things," she added without rancor.

"And yet," she continued, "the third year in London is the one in which you really come to be at home. It's what everyone says." She said this as if perhaps she had promised herself to make at least this much effort.

He knew all too well by now that he could succumb to London, to this pleasant death, that he could become a Londoner if not an Englishman. He even thought quite consciously, well, why not? He persuaded himself for hours at a time that he ought to do it. At the theatre with Nancy, waking beside Nancy in her grubby but likeable little flat, he sometimes felt that he now belonged somewhere as he had never really belonged anywhere before. But always he knew, somewhere, that he was called away, that he would not stay. And so did she.

Usually now they spent Saturdays together. They would wake up together in the grubby flat, grateful if it was a sunny day. Looking out the front window you could see the tops of trees, and lose yourself briefly in sunlight on the leaves, urban birds making their morning noises. They had tea and oranges as a rule, not talking much, and later bacon and eggs, toast and honey. Nancy's flat was the most peaceful place that Robert had ever been. He would go down and get the paper, and then browse in it while she made brunch. The world's disasters could be viewed here from a great distance. Often they went to the cinema in the afternoon. Of the films they saw he later remembered best *2001: A Space Odyssey* and *The Taming of the Shrew*. Later there was The Lamb, sometimes a party. Eventually bed again. It became a comfortable routine.

Her body was slim, even bony, but well-proportioned. Nakedness was more graceful and natural in her than with any Canadian girl that he had known. They seldom got dressed at all until afternoon — except in a robe to go down to the main floor and pick up the large papers — on Sunday. They read the papers at leisure, lounging around on the bed, drinking tea, sometimes reading things aloud to one another, laughing and talking, sometimes interrupting these imaginary forays to the outside world to make love, always throwing the sections of the paper on the floor when they were done with them. Their bodies became stained in places with printer's ink when their hands explored each other.

Once, he was leaving her flat late on a Sunday afternoon, when he ran into Neil coming, unexpected, to call on her. "She's got them leaving as the next one arrives," remarked the doctor with sardonic good humour. Robert could only mutter in response that he had just dropped by. And then felt ashamed of his betrayal. Of course Neil knew they were lovers. Everyone did.

"Robert, you're so ambivalent," said Nancy a few days later at the pub. "You're not committed to anything. I suppose you're a type representative of this time."

"It always comes back to that, doesn't it? Marry me, then. Marry me, and I'll commit myself to that."

But he was not committed, not to her, not to London. She saw that much all too clearly. He was "involved" for now but he was also detached, elsewhere. He wearied her suddenly, he seemed at this moment more genuinely decadent than London, more deadly in his remoteness than her illness. Probably she loved him.

"No, I've been married. I don't want that again. You'd want me to go to Canada and support you in your career."

"I don't know about that," he said. At the moment he thought he might stay in London. He had drifted so far now.

"I can't go anywhere now," she said. "I have to stay here."

Meanwhile his thesis was more or less done. Dr. Cornforth professed to like it. An oral examination was scheduled for July. It was now June.

One evening Nancy and Robert quarrelled. She was in one of her rare moods of resentment. She accused him of feeding on her like a parasite. He observed (falsely, though it seemed true as he said it) that they had got along better before they started sleeping together. She said, all right, let's pack it in if you find it so oppressive. He said again, marry me. She said no. They ended up going to bed together.

But it was a kind of climax for their "idyll." The next week she went off to the country, leaving him a note but no address. The note said that she needed time to think about things and would return before long. He supposed she was visiting relatives in Wales.

But when she came back she left again almost immediately. With Neil. He had left his wife again. "He is earthy, physical, good for me, not intellectual," she wrote in the slightly distraught note that she sent to Robert this time. "Forgive me for not being able to meet you on your ground."

Neil and Nancy went camping in Wales. When she returned she looked well, she seemed to have resolved things for herself. She spoke to Robert in an apparently unselfconscious, easygoing and friendly fashion when she met him in the pub. Even Neil was friendly. But apparently she had been ill for a day or two on the trip. Robert responded as he thought a gentleman should but he found it very difficult. He would have to stop coming to The Lamb.

His thesis oral went very badly. Cornforth was obviously under the weather, and thus not very helpful, and the external examiner, a pinched and purse-lipped youngish man with a prissy manner, decidedly hostile to the whole tenor of the thing. The third examiner tended to be swayed by this, though he had earlier seemed quite friendly. Extensive revision was demanded. They could not dismiss the piece outright, since Cornforth still had considerable prestige, but they seemed determined to water it down as much as possible with every sort of qualification and reservation. He would have either to stay on in London or to return the following summer to finish up.

He was more than a little sick with disappointment and humiliation. He could not go to Nancy. Nor could he bear to stay in London. He spent the late afternoon and early evening getting very drunk in a strange pub. The next day he had a dreadful hangover.

There was a letter that he had been waiting for from Queen's, a ray of hope. He had a job in the History Department for the next year, someone had left unexpectedly, but any further employment there would be dependent on his Ph. D. This was something, then.

He decided to go and see Nancy, to say goodbye properly, to try even to salvage something of the marvellous friendship they had had.

But she had gone into hospital a week before. And he hadn't even known of it, so absorbed had he been in his preparation for the thesis oral.

"Go and see her," said Neil. "It'll do her good." He seemed quite breezy about it all. It had, after all, happened before, and would no doubt happen again. "Don't be such a gloomy Gus, that's your trouble," said Neil, who was a doctor, to Robert.

Nancy was at the picturesque but antique University Hospital on Gower Street. He found her in a long drab room with a number of other patients. There were only curtains round her bed to create some illusion of privacy. It was terribly hot. She had some books and some lemonade on a table. She offered him a glass of lemonade.

She was pale and thinner. There were shadows under her eyes. She looked apologetically at him.

"Oh, it's so boring," she said. "I'm sorry, I'm so useless like this."

"You must rest and get well again," said Robert.

"I know. But sometimes I feel as if I'm on my *death*-bed."

Then she fell asleep before his eyes. Helplessly. He waited, watching her. Then he read a few pages of her book, a novel by Iris Murdoch.

Locating the ward's nursing sister, he tried to discover how serious it was. But she was evasive. Perhaps she didn't know.

The next day Nancy was more alert. But she tired very easily, he saw. And there didn't seem to be any treatment. Perhaps treatment was too dangerous now, and they waited only for remission or death.

He came in every day, then every other day. He was supposed to fly home to Canada in ten days. Often Nancy was asleep. One day she said again, in exasperation, "Oh Robert, I feel as if I'm on my *death*-bed," but not as if she really believed it. If Neil came to see her, it was never at the same time that Robert did. Perhaps it was too painful for him, Robert no longer felt he understood or had any right to judge Neil's behaviour.

One day Nancy seemed decidely better. She chatted animatedly and even spoke of things they might do together in future. He hadn't told her just when he was leaving. She spoke of Neil only once — he gathered from her words that things had come to a crisis between them before she fell ill, and that it was probably over, once and for all, between them. But there was no bitterness in her words.

The next day he was busy with friends who were returning to Australia. The day after that he came in, eager to see further improvement, with flowers that he had bought on the street.

Nancy was propped up on the pillows, unconscious, with her large eyes open, staring. Her dark hair was thoroughly dishevelled. She looked like a corpse, the thought was unspeakable and irresistible, or like an aged caricature of herself. It was utterly grotesque, a horror. He was transfixed by her open eyes.

Then he was aware of her breathing, a harsh, hoarse sound. A murmur of other patients in the long, dim room. The sister came wordlessly from behind him and took the flowers. Her look answered any questions he might think to ask.

It was weirdly seductive (he realized, with growing horror), hypnotic. He could not look away. The emaciated face. The breathing. The hair. The unspeakable, all-knowing, open eyes. A death's-head. That he had loved. He had not used to her or even to himself the word "love" before, even though he had offered to marry her. Now she was consort of Death. Crumbling into earth before his eyes.

After a time impossible to measure he forced himself to look away. To move, though he felt detached from his functioning and obedient limbs, down the long room. Without looking back. To the door. And down the steps. And outside into an exceptionally humid, sunny day.

He does not remember much about the next day or two. He did not go back to the hospital. On the third day after his last visit Nancy died.

There was another cremation. And another party in the garden.

Two quite elderly aunts from the country joined a group of Nancy's friends and acquaintances. Helen Tufnell turned up along with the famous Scottish poet. They all drank wine. Much was said about Nancy's courage and gallantry. "She was the perfect hostess," murmured Robert's friend from London House for what seemed like the millionth time. Robert felt very drunk. On the other side of the garden he saw Neil looking at him. For a moment Neil made as if he might come over and speak to him but then apparently thought better of it, and turned away. From a window next door, faintly, could be heard the ubiquitous Beatles: "All you need is love . . . "

Two nights before he flew back to Canada Robert had a homecoming dream. First he was on the plane, and then for no reason on a very rattly English train that swayed from side to side alarmingly. Somehow it managed to crash into a lake. But there was nothing truly frightening about all of this. It was simply interesting as a spectacle. For he was outside of events as well as inside them.

Then, somehow, he was in a darkish cave. He felt that it was somewhere beside or under the lake. At first it seemed empty and cold. It was immensely old, he felt that it must be the oldest place in the world. There was apparently no way out. But there was the beginning of a faint dawn-light from somewhere. Anyhow, he had always been able, once his eyes had adjusted, to see in the dark. Now he noticed some small stone objects on a ledge at one end. He could not say what they were, except that one, as he approached, assumed the vague outline of a female shape, as if it were a small carving, an immeasurably more primitive and ancient Henry Moore. It was abstract and utterly cold in its effect. It was tiny but it now focused his whole attention. The stone was old, he knew, it was as far back as he could possibly go. It must be, he realized then in a flash of waking consciousness (for he knew that he was dreaming), the goddess herself. Then he awoke briefly but drifted almost immediately back into sleep. It was dark and he could hear the London rain on the window.

Then he was in Kingston in the house where he had lived as a boy. Only in the dream it had become a skeleton, a frame, naked to the wind and the night rain, and he was balanced on the outer top beam, precarious, moving along by inches, one foot after the other, edging slowly along the left side of the house, which was swaying a little now and creaking in the wind, then along the back beam, and then forward along the right side, until he came, inevitably it seemed, to the child, a child sitting down on the rough beam by himself, and without surprise or foreknowledge he looked at him, the fierce wind mingling with his breath, he looked upon the child whose large eyes were open, staring back at him, the lonely child that he had once and perhaps always been.

MIRIAM WADDINGTON

Notes on Managing Death

It is not easy
to manage death
or the thought of
death our own or
that of our friends;
each friend who dies
empties the world
a little and leaves
a fainter tracing of
our carvings in stone.

It is not easy
to manage death but
it is not heroic either;
it is the piecemeal
following of hints,

the slow breaking
of this link or that
in the last quickening
flash of the iron
chain of the flesh.

It is moving through
the patchwork of light
into deepening darkness,
and the glimpsing
against our will of
the land that can only
be known by those who
are silent and blind.

The Green Cabin

The year went by
in marriages and deaths,
not least do I mourn
the death of my youth and
the death of
the friends of my youth,
and now at last I have begun
to mourn the death
of my young mother whose life
was bewildered by children,
and also to mourn the death
of the young mother in me
who still wanders so
restlessly haunting the lives
of her children.

In this year of deaths
and marriages I mourn

the death of the lover
in me who ran to meet
a world full of love and
star-blessed miracles,
but now those doors are shut
and the miserly world
has locked all the rainbows
in earth.

Where did the year go
with all its marriages and
deaths its wedding cakes
and funeral flowers?
How did the year drift out
on elegies and sail away
to foreign harbors before we
noticed its going?
Why did we continue to work
after our friends and lovers
died? Some of us sculpted
statues and others composed
life-music to each small
delicate motion while the rest
kept on painting people
in deck chairs staring at
the never-ending sea.

This year of marriages
and deaths I sit and mourn
in the green cabin
under the spruce tree,
I hear the rain on the roof
black and dark as the heart
of November a rain dark as
the heart of old age dark
as my heart of stone that
mourns the dark stone of
age itself a dark stone
in a dark dark age.

Crazy Times

When the birds riot
and the airplanes walk,
when the busy sit,
and the silent talk;

When the rains blow
and the winds pour,
when the sky is a land
and the sea its shore,

When shells grow snails
and worms eat toads,
when winters chase summers
on upside-down roads,

We'll sit by our fires
and warm our hands,
and tell old tales
of bygone lands.

JOYCE NELSON

Pastimes

In the Kingston Penitentiary
for Women, there's a woman who
can make a fine tattoo, draw

an eagle on your back
with feathered wings of blue
and talons that close in
upon your spine each time
you put your shoulders back.

She can ink a yellow butterfly
to flutter on your shoulder
and a rosebud done in scarlet
in between your breasts.
The scarlet rose is popular.
It hurts more
on that tender skin
and costs you twice as many
hand-rolled cigarettes. But
with her needles moving
slow
precise
you know you've stood the test.

The time drags by
with teeth clenched
and tears stinging in your eyes,
but then,
a butterfly,
a rose,
or part-way down your spine
an eagle flying
free.

ROBYN SARAH

Maintenance

Sometimes the best that I can do
is homemade soup, or a patch on the knee
of the baby's overalls.
Things you couldn't call poems.
Things that spread in the head,
that swallow
whole afternoons, weigh down the week
till the elastic's gone right out of it —
so gone
it doesn't even snap when it breaks.
And one spent week's
just like the shapeless bag
of another. Monthsful of them,
with new ones rolling in and
filling up with the same junk: toys
under the bed, eggplant slices sweating
on the breadboard, the washing machine
spewing suds into the toilet, socks
drying on the radiator and falling down
behind it where the dust lies furry and
full of itself . . . The dust!
what I could tell you about
the dust. How it eats things —
pencils, caps from ballpoint pens,
plastic sheep, alphabet blocks.
How it spins cocoons
around them, clumps up and

222

smothers whatever strays into
its reaches — buttons,
pennies, marbles — and then
how it lifts all-of-a-piece,
dust-pelts
thick as the best velvet
on the bottom of the mop.
                    Sometimes
the best thing I can do
is maintenance: the eaten
replaced by the soon-to-be-eaten, the raw
by the cooked, the spilled-on
by the washed and dried, the ripped
by the mended; empty cartons
heaved down the cellar stairs, the
cans stacked on the ledge, debris
sealed up in monstrous snot-green bags
for the garbage man.

And I'll tell you what
they don't usually tell you: there's no
poetry in it. There's no poetry
in scraping concrete off the high-chair tray
with a bent kitchen knife, or fishing
with broomhandle behind the fridge
for a lodged ball. None in the sink
that's always full, concealing its cargo
of crockery under a head
of greasy suds. Maybe you've heard
that there are compensations? That, too's
a myth. It doesn't work that way.
The planes are separate. Even if there are
moments each day that take you by the heart
and shake the dance back into it, that you lost
the beat of, somewhere years behind — even if
in the clear eye of such a moment you catch
a glimpse of the only thing worth looking for —
to call this compensation, is to demean.
The planes are separate. And it's the

other one, the one called maintenance,
I mostly am shouting about.
I mean the day-to-day,
that bogs the mind, voice, hands
with things you couldn't call poems.
I mean the thread that breaks.
The dust between
typewriter keys.

MARK JARMAN

Hands Cannot Cease

North Lincoln is drunk with cripples
housewives sidle through
pale queens, the muscleboys, fierce juicers
A woman in a red booth shakes her salvation
army bells her face the color
of limestone dissolving in water
Her bells sing of hymns and
like it or not we shall gather
by the river
That yellow prairie river those bells
that ring the shrinking of iron
the burning of flesh on a Bowery mattress
God hammers out each stroke
the slaughter of innocents or the hay

scythed into wet rows on the stubble
Outside the Thunderbird Tavern a loosebellied woman
pulls at a red accordion
Under an arch a man flicks bread at blinking pigeons
for hands cannot cease moving
one day, the next day
We gather by the river again and again

W. P. KINSELLA

Weasels and Ermines

"Silas, I know you're telling me the truth," Mr. Nichols say to me, "but," and his face get all red like it do when he have to say something that embarrass him, "I wouldn't tell a story like that to anyone, whether it's true or not. Not if you ever want to get out of here."

Mr. Nichols, my counselor and English teacher from the Tech School in Wetaskiwin, wear a blue suit that don't fit him very good; he got stooped shoulders, gold-rimmed glasses, and a gold tooth in the front of his face that make sparks when he smile. He is about the kindest white man I know, so I always try to believe what he tell me.

I'm in jail and the RCMP are thinking about charging me and Mad Etta with doing a murder on RCMP Constable Chretien, Wade Gaskell, and his friend Clete Iverson.

I remember one time Mr. Nichols saying to our class at the Tech

School, "Telling the truth means never having to run away from anything," but I'm not so sure. If I tell the truth of what really happened I'm pretty certain they put me in the crazy place down to Ponoka where I'd never be able to run from anything again, and I know that ain't what Mr. Nichols had in mind. But it seem to me that everytime an Indian tell the truth it get him in more trouble than if he lied.

The first bad thing was when Wade Gaskell start hanging around Florence Rockthunder. Wade Gaskell is about as bad a dude as it possible to be. He is white, come from Wetaskiwin where his daddy own a big business sell and service tractors. He's got a kind of gold colored hair come about to his shoulders, pale blue eyes set wide apart, a nose that been broke a couple of times, and a mouth of bright red, pretty as a girl's.

Wade wear tight jeans and a denim vest show off muscles what been tattooed in quite a few places. When he ain't in the bar of the Alice Hotel or at the Passtime Pool Hall in Wetaskiwin, he drive around in a customized car make as much noise as three Mack trucks stuck in gumbo.

Indian girls usually know enough to stay away from Wade, especially Wade. And if any Indian girl should stay clear of him it is Florence Rockthunder 'cause she got a secret he would sure want to know if he could.

A couple of years ago Wade's brother, Clarence Gaskell, did a murder on an Indian girl name of Little Margaret Wolfchild, and when he got only 90 days in Fort Saskatchewan jail for doing it why some of us Indians even up the score by making him dead. RCMPs never find out who rubbed out Clarence. There was only five girls who know all about it and me who guessed. One girl is dead, one moved away to Ontario, one is my girlfriend, Sadie One-wound, another is Robert Coyote's woman, Bertha Bigcharles, and the last was Florence Rockthunder.

First time I seen them together was at the Alice Hotel in Wetaskiwin. It was a Friday night and a bunch of us was having a few beers. About 11 o'clock in come Florence, Wade, and a white couple, friends of Wade's I guess. They sit down across the bar from us and order up a table full of beer. They must of come from the Canadian Legion because it is easy to see they is all a little drunk except Florence who is a lot. She sit with her legs out in the aisle and her face that is wide and flat be kind of out of focus, like a buttered slice of brown bread. Florence wearing jeans, and a denim jacket over a red sweater. She is tall for a girl, and got big hands and feet.

They laugh a lot at that table. Florence light up a cigarette, take a big drink of her beer, spill some down the front of her. Wade point at what she do and they laugh some more.

When Wade finally go to the bathroom a bunch of us go over quick to that table try to get Florence away from there. There is me and Sadie, Frank and Connie, Robert Coyote and Bertha Bigcharles, at least. We kind of form a half-circle around Florence, have our backs to the white couple at the table.

"You know who that is you're with?" we say.

Florence smile kind of silly.

"That's Wade Gaskell," we say, though we pretty sure she know already.

"Come on," say Connie, and pull at Florence's sleeve.

"I can sit with anybody I want to," say Florence and give us a mean look.

We is just about to haul her away with us when Wade Gaskell come back.

"What have we got here?" he says, "a war party?" and he give us a mean laugh.

There is enough of us to fight him and win but we don't want that if we can help it. Everybody know that Wade carry a knife and that he got at least a shotgun and a rifle in his truck, and that he is the kind of guy to use them.

"We want Florence to come to a party with us," says Robert.

"Flo here is my lady tonight," Wade say. He put his arm around Florence's shoulders and squeeze and she smile stupid at him like she can't see no one else. "Ain't that right?" he say to Florence who smile some more, then turn her chair so her back be to us.

We go away then but it sure spoil the evening for us. I remember something else Mr. Nichols say one time about a chain being only so strong as its weakest link, and that worry me.

They give to me a Legal Aid lawyer with a name I can't remember. He is only about five foot tall, look like he might be made out of bread dough. He have a little bit of curly-blond hair on the back half of his head, and tea-cup ears that be bright pink as a rabbit's. His glasses is so thick that all I see is a blue blur for eyes and the silver rims glint in the light like new polished chrome on a car.

Just for fun I tell him the story like it really happen. He don't say nothing but the blue behind his glasses just get bigger and brighter as I talk. Then he shake hands on me and trot away real fast. It been three days and I ain't seen him again.

Wade Gaskell and his friend Clete Iverson got an apartment in Wetaskiwin and it appear that Florence Rockthunder is moved right in there 'cause she don't even come home to the reserve for a change of clothes in over a week.

Sadie and Bertha say they seen her shopping in Saan Department Store in Wetaskiwin one afternoon; she been drinking already and was buying up some lipsticks and jewellery with a twenty dollar bill she say Wade gave her to spend just on herself.

"Are you crazy?" Bertha say to her. "That guy's gonna make you say things you don't want to."

"Leave me alone," Florence say back to them. "Wade don't care no more about what happened to his brother. He told me so. You just leave me alone," and she take a sample perfume bottle from the counter and spray herself good. "Wade likes me and I'm gonna live in with him for as long as he wants," and she turn her back and walk away.

It is only a day or two later that Constable Chretien from the RCMP come nose around the reserve ask questions about who rubbed out Clarence Gaskell. And this time he talk to Bertha Bigcharles and he ask her about Sadie but by that time we had her hid away at Firstrider's cabin. You can bet Constable Chretien didn't get the idea to start asking questions again all by himself. Even for an RCMP Const. Chretien is pretty dumb. He is from Quebec and he speak English about as bad as we do, and he always have a kind of surprised look on his face like he just been kicked in the ass by a big boot.

"What are we gonna do?" we ask Mad Etta our medicine lady. Etta don't have to be told when there be trouble around; she smell it like a coyote smell a trap or a gun barrel.

"I worry for you," Etta says.

RCMPs mainly believe what white men tell them and like to make as much trouble as they can for us Indians. Looking for a good RCMP, Mad Etta say, is like looking out over a field of skunks for as far as you can see and trying to figure which one of the whole bunch ain't gonna make a bad smell when you get up close to it.

Every couple of days Frank Fence-post borrow Louis Coyote's pickup truck and drive Sadie up to see me. I worry some each time they do cause Frank don't have a driver's license and he have to travel right up to the middle of Edmonton and even park near the police station.

One time I get to teasing Frank that he should have the good name of Ermineskin, like mine, instead of Fence-post. "Ermine skins is beautiful and worth lots of money," I tell him, "while fence posts is just dull old wood and not exciting at all."

"Fence posts is good and real," says Frank, "I'd rather be one of them than something that don't even exist, like you."

And Frank is right, there ain't really no such thing as an ermine. I'm not sure how to put it, but it is kind of like old Miss Waits, a teacher up at the Residential School. All fall, winter, and spring she is a teacher, but in the summer she ain't anything except herself. Ermines is only around in the winter, in the summer they is just plain brown weasels. Peoples a long time ago didn't even know they wasn't different animals.

In winter ermines turn to the same color as fresh snow, all except the tip of their tail which is black and shiny like a little nugget of coal. Ermines is only about a foot long and got a body like one of them rolls of sausage that hang in butcher shops. When it runs the middle of its body bend up to make a loop like the top of a paper clip. In winter they is beautiful, in summer they is ugly. All year round they have an ugly disposition. Ermines is one of the animals that do wasteful killing. One of them will break into a hen house and kill off every single hen, just for the fun of it.

It was Frank who found Florence Rockthunder; she was just wandering around down by the highway in Wetaskiwin. Her nose be broke for sure and both eyes black and swelled almost shut. She lost too a couple of teeth from the side of her face.

"He told me he loved me," she keep saying over and over. "He said we was gonna get married so it was alright for me to tell him about his brother. He told me he didn't care about it no more."

"Did you tell him everything?"

"Everything," say Florence, spit out some blood on the floor of Mad Etta's cabin. "He was so nice to me until . . . "

"What's he gonna do?" ask Etta.

"I hear him call and ask for Constable Chretien," Florence says, "then he told Clete he'd have to wait until tonight 'cause the constable was away to Edmonton until then."

"So we got about 6–7 hours," I say.

Florence start to cry again. "Said he wasn't gonna make the mistake his brother made of killing an ugly Indian whore."

"Be quiet," Mad Etta say to Florence. But then she look sad at her and give her a cloth, soaked in some bluish stuff been boil on the back of the stove, to hold on her face, then lay her down on the bed at the back of the cabin.

"What are we gonna do?" I say to Etta. "If Wade get to the RCMP they arrest Sadie, and Florence, and Bertha. And I bet Florence don't be able to keep her mouth shut . . . "

"This is too big a medicine for me to work, Silas. I'm gonna have to try something. I only seen it done once, back when I was a girl. Old medicine man named Buffalo-who-walks-like-a-man called up the Fog Spirit to help his little daughter who was awful sick. Ceremony take a long time to prepare for even though he was afraid every minute his little girl was gonna die. He boil up strong medicine that he put into bags that he tie to trees all around a small meadow. It be summer and I remember the meadow was yellow with cow slips. The fog was thick as white ketsup in the early morning.

"Buffalo-who-walks-like-a-man take his medicine stick and carve the shape of a woman in the fog, then there be a gust of wind even though it been still as death. That wind move off the rest of the fog and there stand the grey shape of Basket Woman, the most famous Cree medicine woman there ever was.

"She got a voice as soft as a cat walking on damp grass.

" 'Why have you called me in from the hills?' she say to Buffalo-who-walks-like-a-man.

" 'My daughter burns with a fever I cannot cure,' and he point to where little Margueretta lay on a pile of moose hides, her eyes sunk and what breath she got sounding like a cat's purr. 'I have been told that if my medicine is strong enough to call you here,

that you do what I ask. I ask nothing for me. You can even take
my life if you want it, but make my little girl better.'

"'I will have to take her across the space between your world
and ours,' Basket Woman say to the medicine man. 'Wrap her
warmly in robes and bring her to me.'

"Buffalo-who-walks-like-a-man, though I bet he six and a half
feet tall and have hands like bear traps, cover up his little
daughter like she was made of butterfly wings and carry her to
the arms of Basket Woman. "'You are a good man, I will do what I
can,' say Basket Woman. Then she walk off across the meadow
and into the scrub tamarack of the muskeg."

"So what happened?" I ask.

"I'm here ain't I?" say Mad Etta, first smile, then laugh, and I
notice that there be big dimples on the backs of her brown hands.

"You mean you was Margueretta?"

"Little sister of mine couldn't say my name right is how come I
get called Mad Etta."

"I never knew that, I thought . . ."

"It was 'cause I was always mad at somebody?"

"Yeah," I say, which seem to get me out a lot of trouble. I guess
Etta know that 'cause she waddle over to the corner and get us
each a bottle of Lethbridge Pale Ale from the washtub that sit
there half-full of rusty water.

"Sometime I tell you what I remember of the other side."

"I'd like to hear," I say.

"I been teached the ceremony to call up the spirit of Basket
Woman, but I never until now had something serious enough to
use it on."

"You sure you want to use it for us?"

Etta's face get solemn as a cow's.

"You're good young people."

"You think Basket Woman would care about us. These is kind of
what would be called worldly problems . . ."

"Basket Woman have a good heart," say Etta, and she turn her
buffalo big back to indicate that the conversation be over.

Frank say that all the guys from the pool hall at Hobbema:
Eathen, Robert, Rufus, Charlie, and some others put together
their money and call the office of Martin Prettyhand, the Indian

lawyer in Calgary. Mr. Prettyhand be off to Halifax for a con-
ference on Human Rights and stuff like that.

"We ask that when he get home that he come to Edmonton to
get you out of trouble," Frank says. "His secretary want to know
what you been charged with, and when we tell her that they
figure you might of killed a couple of white men and an RCMP
she say if Mr. Prettyhand run around the country defending every
Indian who killed somebody he wouldn't have time left to work
on important things like Human Rights."

"I have to think about that for a while," I say.

When they leaving, Sadie always hug as much of me as she can
through the bars. Sadie ain't beautiful or make a lot of laughter
like Frank's girl, Connie Bigcharles, but Sadie like to kiss me, and
there ain't never no doubt about how she feels about me. Sometimes when I'm loving her and we been together like one person
for a long time, I look down at her face and she have her eyes
closed and her face relaxed. Then she is more beautiful than
Connie Bigcharles or any other girl I know. I have this tender
feeling for her and it make me feel so good to know that I am the
one who makes her beautiful.

I never knew Mad Etta could move so fast. She have me and
Frank and Sadie stuffing wood in her stove and borrowing sauce
pans and when they run out gather up soup cans, and she mix up
so many different kinds of stuff to boil on the stove that I don't
know how she keep track of it all.

"What if Basket Woman ain't around no more?" I say. "Spirits
must get old, or retire and move away to the city."

"You got a better plan you let me hear it," say Etta.

About supper time she give me some instruction that I have to
pass along to Bedelia Coyote. "We can't trust Florence to help us,"
say Etta. "First, she ain't very smart, and second, she is hurting
both inside and out right now."

Bedelia get on the phone at the Hobbema Texaco Garage and
call up Wade Gaskell.

"I'm calling for Florence, she wants to see you."

I guess he ask why she don't call herself.

"Because you broke her jaw, you asshole," Bedelia yell. "All she
can do is write down what she has to say. But she's still in love

with you. I can't imagine why, and she says she don't tell you the whole story, whatever that means, and she wants to see you right away. She's at Wolfchild's, that's the last cabin on the right after you drive up the hill."

He must give her some more argument.

"Look, I'm just passing on a message. If you're too fucking scared to come out to the reserve then it's no skin off my nose." There is another pause.

"Like I said, I don't care whether you come or not or who you bring with you. Florence just says she has something real important to tell you." Bedelia hang up the phone.

"He'll be here," she smile. "Yellow bastards like him can't stand to be called yellow."

The car come roaring up the hill to our cabins, spreading out clouds of dust on both sides of the road. Wade is driving and his friend Clete Iverson is beside him, a shotgun poking out the passenger window. Clete is about Wade's age but is tall and thin and have red hair and a pointed face like a fox, a face that be mostly pimples and not much else.

Wade step out of the car and he is holding a sawed-off shotgun. He look around real careful. The door to Wolfchild's cabin open real slow and while they is both looking at that I sneak from the tall grass until I'm behind the car. Then Bedelia Coyote step out of the cabin and she is wearing a red dress what was give to Sadie by a white woman one time. The dress let most of Bedelia's breasts hang out. I don't ever remember seeing Bedelia in a dress before.

"Don't point that thing at me," Bedelia say and push the gun to one side just like it was maybe a broom he was holding. "Florence is laying down," she says. "You really worked her over. You know you are kind of cute. I can see why Florence likes you," and Bedelia turn and walk into the cabin wiggling her bottom at him. The shotgun is pointing at the ground as he disappear into the cabin.

I slip up the side of the car walking like I got an inch of air between me and the ground and stick the nose of my .22 gun right behind Clete Iverson's ear. He jump like he been poked by a cattle prod and his shotgun shoot off at the sky.

"Don't kill me, Don't kill me," he say and throw his gun the rest of the way out the window. Then he put his hands on the dashboard, look at me for a second and his mouth snap shut make the same sound as closing a locker at the bus depot.

Inside the cabin Mad Etta and Bedelia got Wade tied up like he been the loser in a calf-roping contest. We tie Clete up the same way and then get busy with making up medicine bags, and helping Etta get dressed in her medicine woman outfit with mean paint on her face, beaded leggings, and fox tails pinned all down the sleeves of her five-four-sack dress.

We go out to a meadow a mile or two back of the cabin and pin up the medicine bags in the trees all around so they look like tiny bird nests in the crooks of tree limbs. We also pick whatever wild flowers we can find and scatter them in a circle what Etta drawed in the lowest part of the meadow.

We are all real glad that we caught Clete Iverson 'cause it worried us how we was going to get Wade to make a telephone call. But Clete is scared whiter than he ever been before and he agree to anything as long as he figure we don't kill him. He start making the calls about nine o'clock and every fifteen minutes from then until Constable Chretien get back to his office.

"I'm out at the reserve," he explain when he finally reach the constable. "Wade's rounded up the Indians who killed his brother. He's got a gun on them and wants you out here right away. I've got to get back to help him watch them but there will be a friendly Indian meet you right by the culvert in the road and show you the way."

Bedelia and me we wrote that out on a piece of paper for Clete to say. He don't read it very good but it is enough for Constable Chretien to believe him.

I wave my hand at the RCMP car as it drive up and I'm real happy to see Constable Chretien is alone. I get in and direct him to the meadow. He ask me a lot of questions but all I say is "White man give me five dollars to meet you. I gonna buy some fire water and have a happy time. Get good and drunk," and I smile at him, stupid as I know how.

We can only get to within a hundred yards or so of the meadow. The constable stop his car at the top of a knoll and the lights shine down into the night fog.

Constable Chretien walk slow, carry a rifle over his arm. In case we need him, Frank Fence-post is hiding off in the tall grass with a rifle of his own. I bet he is as scared as I am.

"Wade?" Constable Chretien call out.

From down in the meadow Wade answer, "Yeah, I'm down here. Everything's okay."

I don't know what Etta done to get him to say that, and I probably don't want to.

Constable Chretien let his gun point at the ground and walk a little faster. I pick my own gun up from where it been hid in the grass, point it at him, tell him to drop his gun. Then we walk down to where Etta, Wade and Clete is. They both sit on a tree stump with their backs touching and I see that their hands ain't even tied. They both smile like the constable was just a friend what walked into the pool hall. Boy, my whole body shakes like it twenty below and I got no shirt. I don't even want to think about how many years in jail I get for point a gun at an RCMP. I'm glad he don't know that I wouldn't shoot him. If he wanted he could just turn around and take the gun from me. We tie up his hands and sit him next to Wade and Clete. Mad Etta toss his rifle and hand gun way off deep into the slough.

"Get away from here, Silas," Mad Etta say to me. "Take Frank and Bedelia too. This is my business now."

Constable Chretien's eyes be most popped out of his face and I guess he be scared too 'cause he talk a lot but mostly in French which none of us understand.

We walk back up the hill. When I turn around about half-way up I see Mad Etta holding a coup-stick which she say belong to her father, and she drawing with it what appear like the shape of a woman. Then there is a blast of wind, cold as January and the fog roll back as if it been pushed and Etta is left facing an old woman of fog, stooped in the shoulder, wearing a long dress and with a cloth covering on her head. I swing around, finish climb the hill and turn off the lights and motor of Constable Chretien's car.

I send Frank and Bedelia on by themselves and for one time they listen to me without arguing. In fact I think they glad to get away. I lean on the car and look down at the meadow.

Last I seen, there was Constable Chretien, Wade Gaskell, and Clete Iverson, running off over the meadow toward a poplar grove, only I couldn't tell which one was which — they was just three brown weasels, their eyes glowing rose-red in the moon-light, and their middles making loops like some kind of fancy handwriting, squishing together and then straightening out just like the slinky-toy my littlest sister got one time for Christmas.

It ain't long before other RCMPs come out looking for Constable Chretien 'cause he told them he was going to the reserve to meet Wade Gaskell. And Wade told somebody from town that him and Clete was coming to the reserve to meet Florence Rockthunder. We sent Florence off on the midnight bus, visit her cousins at Little Pine Reserve in Saskatchewan, and nobody around here admit there is even such a person as her. Trouble was I touched Constable Chretien's car while I was riding in it and RCMP arrest first me and then Mad Etta. They got us up here at Edmonton and since I can't explain why my fingerprints are on the car, and Mad Etta can't explain why her fingermarks was on Constable Chretien's gun what they dug out of the slough with a metal detector sound like a fast-working woodpecker, they claim we is both gonna be charged with murder.

Frank on one of his visits to me ask if there was a little tiny RCMP hat on the weasel what used to be Constable Chretien, but that kind of thing just don't seem very funny anymore.

"Have a little patience," Mad Etta tell me today, after we got to sit together in the same room waiting for RCMPs to take us to court. "It take two months before them guys come back, and when they do they'll have forgot all about us, Florence Rockthunder and Clarence Gaskell. They'll be gentle as babies. Oh, maybe they'll get a little excited when they walk past a hen house," and Etta laugh and laugh, shake like a pup tent in a strong wind.

"What if they get killed in the meantime?" I say. "Or what if things don't work out like you planned?" Mad Etta shrug her buffalo big shoulders.

"We're lucky it ain't trapping season," she says. "Hardly nobody shoots weasels in the summer. Hey," and she smile at me 'cause she see I'm scared. "It ain't so bad here — the grub's good and they got me a special bed 'cause when I lay on the bunk it pull right out of the wall. Have a little faith, Silas," she say and take hold of my arm with her big brown hand. "Everything's gonna be okay."

I read somewhere that faith is, "Believing something that

nobody in their right mind would believe." I'm not sure I want to but it don't look like I got much choice.

DOUGLAS BARBOUR

story for a saskatchewan night: for robert kroetsch

"Picnic in a coulee in a cow
pasture. . . . But I couldn't tell a
story. The novelist unable to tell
a story. The ghost of my father,
there in the shadows — the
story-teller."
               The "Crow" Journal
               Friday July 25   1975
               Qu'Appelle Valley

i

coyote's maybe hidden   nearby   i
am silent   the ghost in
the shadows waiting to speak   but
i am silent   listen

no   there is
no story   that
is what i have to tell you

i have to tell you   there

is no story tonight   there
is no story here   listen
there are all too many stories
clamouring   &
i have to tell you   i
cant tell them

if the cowshit could speak it would tell you
nothing   no   well
nothing you dont already know
& the grass
talks on of dying   of dying
to feed the goddamnd cows

            (this isnt narrative   hell
            it's not even complaint)

the flames die too
& their story wont stay still
you cant follow
the changes   modulations

                              the sky
is full of stories   those bright
eyes looking down
on the prairie   i
cant begin to tell you about

listen   all
the stories you wont hear
about that train now
its long roar fading in the dark

no   now that we know
there's no story at all
we can begin to tell it

listen

ii

what the silence said
was nothing   nothing
we could listen to

we could *hear*

the silence   it
wasnt saying anything
but the stories   stars
spatter on the night sky

that train   dopplers away
WHOOEEEE   whooeeee
we hear that tale
everyday   each night
of its retreat   running
like the storyteller   not
saying a word
into the darkness   & away
from some
                place

or the cows
no longer seen   but
listen   their stories
are   shumpff   mumchpht   chumpff
the chewing over of what vast
metaphysics   the grass
also refuses to speak
or the crickets

the writer refused
      to tell a story
or   no   the writer
told us   he
      couldnt tell us
a thing   &

we listend   again
to the silence   no
silence   &

all it had
to say

iii

or some other
possibility:

the yawning air
says   open
wide   like the sky   now
swallow it all
                    empyrean

there   curved high above us
as the darkness deepens

more stories   appear
                              silent
insistent
              listen

        & sky
        tells another blue story
        of fucking sweet earth
        down there   way off   where
        they meet
        in utter silence as usual
                              (can you
                    see it   where
                    one darkness   solid
                    touches another   clear)
        at the end of the road
              end of the valley
              end of the lake
              end of the   world

or the story
so   far   away
& not telling it   again
of course

iv (31.10.79)

the sky   opening
the land   the land   the sky

they keep repeating   they
have nothing to say   &
they say that   they
say   we say
there's nothing here
can you hear it

each time they
repeat it   each time
i believe it   i believe
there's nothing more to say

there's more nothing to say

there's more

or   driving
the point home   driving
again along the prairie
seeing what has not been   said

& saying it
's saying it

that there's nothing to say
& *that* grows

i said

listen/

or look

it's all around you
all those stories   you
want told
or it does

     listen

          : one moon   only
  a howling below

all that emptiness filling
with the stories we dont believe
we can tell

& we're telling them

v

plenitude   0
prairie /   plenitude

                              there is no room for
it unfolds   a short space   a
                              short poem here   you
          nothing   must expand   to fill
                              the space with words

is what it says

the sky   eg.   un
folding   blue   stories   youll
               no   never tell   yes
thing   crisscrosst
labyrinths of cloud
unspeaking   un
speakable   grey   rain

                              but he wouldnt 'sing'
                              either?   he said only
                              i have

the lines of
        type perhaps
that rush against the window

nothing to say
the rain says
dont   listen

the prairie   unfolds
so much   expressive shading
tone   say   in
spring   fall
a loss or   abundant
shifts of   (tone)   mud
soakt in rain
fall   saying
             nothing

it didnt hurt
you dont have to say
anything   you
mustnt cry

it unfolds   then
now   unfolds   mystery

& that is what it wont tell
& that is what it cant tell
& that is what it
tells you

an abundance of
absence

nothing
        to say

ssshhshshshshsh shsh sh

a few colours   hey
is it spring   or
fall   which
few colours   what
signs

that hasnt been said
or you werent listening
or it *wasnt*   a story

that time

say will be held against you
all that   pain
you cry   why
me   so far from
comforting   sky   or
grassy hills   or
not
that horizon
split with light
a way   off

silence

you know   you forget
                            the catalogue
                            of desire

                            it grows

                            the seeds
                            grow   it
                            opens
                            wider
                            it   refuses

                            to speak

vi

this is not
absence   simply

                                    the presence
                                    of absence

there's a story here   unspeakable
not to be told   i cant
                                    tell it

nothing to say   of black earth
nothing to say   of the crops   tall
nothing to say   wind-swept   waves
nothing to say   of wheat   say   the
nothing to say   harvest   coming

                    in silence
                    say   silence
                    again

BERT ALMON

Signs Taken for Wonders

Waiting for the airport bus
in the MacDonald Hotel,
I notice the bell hop
lining up white letters
on the announcement board.
The Christians (Reformed)
are meeting in one room,
The Lions in another.
The Rotorians (Misspelled)
hold the line between them.

Riding the bus in the dark
I see the red luminous sign
over the driver's head:
Watch Your Step.
I always will. We pass
the red grain elevator,
painted with JESUS SAID,
WHAT SHALL IT PROFIT A MAN
IF HE GAIN THE WHOLE WORLD
AND LOSE HIS OWN SOUL?
Floodlights keep the message
shining in the darkness,
and I agree, without believing
in Jesus or the soul.

When the sign in the cabin
says Fasten Seat Belts,

I do. And think how careful
the bell hop should be,
with every word in the language
resting in his tray of letters!

GEORGE WOODCOCK

The World of Time:
Notes towards an autobiography

These notes towards an autobiography relate to one aspect of my life between five and eleven, and bring on stage only a few of the people who were important to me during that period. After taking me in infancy from Canada to England, my parents lived first for five years in the small Shropshire town of Market Drayton. Afterwards we moved away, to Cheshire and then to Buckinghamshire, but all my school holidays were spent in Market Drayton, so that between the ages of five and seventeen I was living in two quite different worlds, the time-bound world of the school term in a Thames-side resort town near to London, and the world — where I was little conscious of time — of a rural Shropshire that was still in many ways a Victorian society.

The notes I reproduce relate to the world of time, and mainly to the kinds of education, formal and informal, which during that period of early boyhood shaped the cast of mind that would in turn shape my later life.

When my father first left my grandfather's business, we went to Altrincham in Cheshire, a kind of remote suburb of Manchester, where he worked as book-keeper in a flour mill. We lived in a terrace of houses beside a main street where tram lines ran and there was a great deal of traffic, mainly horse-drays, steam wagons and a few early motor trucks. By this time I was four, becoming five while we were still in Altrincham, and I must have been allowed a certain freedom of wandering, for once I caused a great commotion when a blind man asked me to guide him over the street, which I at once proceeded to do as if the street belonged to me. By the time we reached the middle of the road there was a great shouting, a driver reined his horses to a halt, and, as I and the blind man reached the farther pavement, my mother and a woman neighbour came racing over to take me back. Desperately relieved as she was, my mother's code of strict behaviour forced her to slap me, especially as my crime had been complicated by the fact that the blind man had offered me a penny and I had accepted it. I puzzled greatly over the fact that it was wrong to take rewards for helping the unfortunate, but that there were also times when it was wrong to help them even without reward. I do not seem to have taken the physical danger I was in very seriously.

It was wartime — the Great War as it was then called — and my memories of Altrincham are largely associated with it, for this was the centre for a number of military camps, and there were always columns of soldiers marching through the town headed by military bands, whose noise I detested so much that when one drew near I would run to hide in the cellar. But I remember vividly one bandless march. It was a long, silent column of prisoners-of-war on their way to their special camp a few miles out in the country; the authorities seem to have thought it would boost local morale if they were displayed. There were many British soldiers as escort, but it was the prisoners in their field-grey — or sometimes navy-blue — uniforms who drew everyone's attention, and the desperate melancholy, the sense of helpless defeat that emanated from them impressed itself even on my child's mind, as I think it did on the minds of all the women and old men who came out of the houses to stand and stare silently without a single sound of triumph.

At that time I was a very fair child, with corn-coloured Saxon hair that in later years, perhaps as my Celtic inheritance asserted itself, turned into a dark brown until, in my early twenties, I became — like my mother's family — prematurely white. On that day in early 1917, as we watched the prisoners march by, my mother was holding me in her arms, and one of the Germans looked at me with his tired eyes and suddenly smiled, and then said a word to the man marching beside him, and looked again, and smiled a second time, with a great sadness. I knew by an immediate insight that I had reminded him of his own child, and I have remembered the incident more vividly than anything else from that period.

I do not recollect much about the house in Altrincham, except the great bath — as it seems in memory — enclosed in a polished wooden surround, where I would play with celluloid fishes, and the cellar where I hid from the military music. It smelt of earth, potatoes and coal dust, and had a long slate slab where, in those pre-refrigerator days, we kept perishable foods in the cool darkness. Fishes are linked in my memory with the cellar as well as the bathroom, for it was here that my father gave me an early lesson in natural history by showing me the swimming bladders of some roach an angler friend had given him, and explaining how these kept them upright in the water.

The passion for natural history that by the age of ten had me reading books like Darwin's *Voyage of the Beagle* and Bates' *Naturalist on the River Amazons* and W.H. Hudson's *British Birds*, must have had its roots in this period, for I also spent a great deal of time with a boy and girl a few houses away whose names I do not remember but whom I always think of as the butterfly children.

They caught splendid insects like Red Admirals and Peacocks and Tortoiseshells and Hawk moths, and kept them in large glass jars whose tops were covered with pierced paper. When — and if — the butterflies laid eggs on the leaves put in the jars, they let them go, but kept the eggs, and the caterpillars that hatched, and the chrysalids that followed. I knew the children long enough to see the metamorphosis completed by another generation of butterflies struggling free of their cases, and so, even before I went to school, I had understood one of the great natural cycles.

Apart from the butterfly children, two people stand out with vivid clarity from those Altrincham days. One was an old Scottish baker named Anderson, who came to the back door every morning with his big square basket of bread. My father had done him some favour in getting him extra flour from the mill in the difficult wartime situation, and this gave a special flavour to my Saturday, since when Anderson came that morning he would always add an iced cake, usually a brightly pink one, "For the bairn!" I was always present in time to receive it.

Mr. Skelhorn, the house painter who lived next door, held with no such offenses against nature as pink icing; in fact he was the first health food fanatic I encountered. He had a great belief in the therapeutic value of dandelion roots, and sometimes fed me those bitter tidbits, which I ate out of affection for this large and rufous man who treated a child as an equal, until my mother found out, was shocked, and put an end to the practice. Once I imagined I had discovered Mr. Skelhorn occupied in preparing something more delectable than dandelion roots, and ran into our kitchen to shout that: "Mr. Skelhorn is mixing blancmange in a bucket!" I had a passion for that dessert more for its intriguing wobble when it was taken out of the mould and carried on to the table than for its flavour. But Mr. Skelhorn was only mixing whitewash.

My father's job in Altrincham was only temporary, and he would lose it if its former occupant returned from the war. Besides, he wanted to be taken back by the Great Western Railway, for which he had worked before going to Canada. He saw security there, and the alarming state of his health made security seem necessary. Influence — or "pull" as we called it — counted then, and a boyhood friend who had risen in the railway service got my father appointed goods clerk at Marlow, almost two hundred miles south, beside the Thames. But he never gained the security he desired, since he never passed the company's medical examination, and so he never became a permanent employee with the right to a pension. He remained always in a temporary status, from 1918 when he reached Marlow to 1926 when he died there, and this gave our life a curiously provisional quality which was enhanced by the matter of the house we lived in.

My father preceded my mother to Marlow and did his best to find us somewhere to live, but he was not very successful. The town — a little riverside resort place, was crowded with people who had come down from London thirty miles away to escape from the air raids. The kind of good housing that remained available was beyond my father's income, for from this time onwards his salary never rose above £200, which was then equivalent to $1,000. Eventually he did find a place that was cheap and near the station, but it was a small terrace house so modest — so positively mean — in every way compared to our houses in Market Drayton and Altrincham that my mother wept when she arrived with me and saw it. Both she and my father regarded our presence there as only temporary, and so in this way also our life was provisional. Eighty-two Station Road was a kind of camping ground; we were always going to move away, but the will and the money were both lacking, and there we stayed until my father and mother had both died, which meant twenty-two years from 1918 to 1940, when I finally left the house for good and only once, in the long years since, went back to take a look at its crumbling brick exterior.

It was the eighth house of a terrace that must have been built early in the nineteenth century, with a little shop at the end, highly priced as they always are where people are hard up. There were no front gardens, and people walking along the pavement passed before our window. Behind the house was a garden as narrow as the building itself, with worked-out soil that seemed to grow only coarse irises whose roots were inhabited by enormous snails. Next to our house stood a long wooden building which when we arrived was a factory where a round jolly little man in rumpled tweeds named Joey Rumbelow made "antique" furniture out of oak taken from old ships, which was said to be beaten with chains and drilled with simulated worm holes to make it look authentically ancient. Its presence meant that the sound of hammering and of the circular saws continued for five and one-half days every week, and when it was closed at the onset of the Depression — which meant that there were no longer any American customers for Joey's fakes — it became an even worse noise producer, since children from streets around found their way in and made an incessant din racing over its wooden floors.

Eighty-two Station Road had two rooms below, a "front" room we entered right from the street and never had the heart to pretend was a drawing room, and a kitchen in which we lived most of the time, with a pantry under the stairs and a scullery behind with a lead sink and a copper for boiling clothes. Upstairs there were two bedrooms and a tiny room over the scullery that served as a box room and had space for a camp bed. There was no bathroom; the john was a little corner bitten out of the scullery and reached from outside through the coal shed.

The kind of amenities we had known elsewhere just did not exist here. There was neither electricity nor gas nor piped water in our cottage. We cooked with coal in a Victorian cast iron range, and burnt sawn up railway ties in the front-room grate; I can never remember the bedrooms being other than bitterly cold in winter, with ice forming in the chamber pots. We lit the house with candles and a brass paraffin lamp, which had a tall glass chimney that was always either cracking or blackening when the lamp smoked, and a pearly white globe that gave a rather soft and harmonious creamy light. We levered away at a hand pump over the lead sink, always being careful to have a full bucket beside us to prime the pump in case it choked dry. The water was hard from the Chiltern chalk that underlay the valley alluvium, and we kept a rainwater butt for soft water to wash our hair. It was also not very pure, and often in a glass one would see tiny but visible translucent grey creatures and small vivid worms like fragments of scarlet thread; God knows what microscopic menaces accompanied them in that water which tasted so fresh and cool as one drew it up from the depths on a summer day.

However, apart from the "summer diarrhea" everyone in England suffered periodically in those days, we never came to harm from all this, and I am sure it was because we lived a far less hygienic life than people today, and built up better immunities. Certainly the sewage arrangements were bizarrely primitive. Our john was a magnificent Victorian creation in blue and white willow pattern porcelain, but since we had no piped water we flushed it by hand from a bucket. Though it was a resort town of some repute with wealthy residents — including prosperous writers like L. H. Myers and Jerome K. Jerome — Marlow had no public sewers. Each house had its own cesspool, and whenever one's cesspool was full one called the mobile town pump. When we first arrived this was a hand pump on wheels at which two men worked vigorously to transfer the contents of the cesspool to a horse wagon that took it to the sewage farm where the best tomatoes in the district were grown. It was a smelly process, and some houses with no back lanes had to have the leaky hose running through from the front door to the back yard. At some time in my boyhood this primitive method was replaced by a motorised pump, but not until the 1930s did the town put in sewers, and about the same time we got piped water and electricity.

As a child I did not find all this so appalling as my parents did. There was a novelty to it which I enjoyed, and it was not until I was nine or ten that I really became aware of what troubled my parents most — that we lived in a row of houses where all the other residents were manual workers, and not even very high in the complicated caste structure of the English working class. In other words, we were isolated in a world out of our class, and all our shabbiness, by the pressure of circumstances, turned into a soured gentility; on a lower scale we were like the impoverished upper middle class of Orwell's world, and perhaps similar embittering experiences in our different families helped to induce similar outlooks in us so that when I met Orwell we understood each other easily.

The result of our situation and my parents' reaction to it was an almost complete atrophy of any kind of social life as a family. I cannot remember our formally entertaining anyone during the whole period of eight years until my father's death. Once I remember our going to dinner at the house of one of his colleagues, but we never returned the invitation. My father had a wide circle of acquaintances, but I can think of only two friends he made in Marlow, and both of them were odd men out who understood his predicament.

One was a florid sporty man named Artie Porter who bred horses and had a staggeringly beautiful wife who drank. Artie and his father, the most prosperous farmer in the area, recognized in my father a man who had seen better days, and did their best to bring them back in some minor way by giving us pheasants and partridges in season, and chickens from the farm, and sometimes one of the great Thames eels they caught in their weir. The first of these eels caused an exciting kitchen drama, for, skinned and decapitated though it was, it began to leap about the table from the reflex actions of its dying muscles, thoroughly scaring my mother as she tried to put it into the stewpot.

My father's other friend was old Dr. Bath, the hunch-backed

organist from All Saints' Church and a notable figure at the Royal
College of Music, who was intrigued by my father's youthful links
with Edward German and was the only acquaintance with whom
he could talk about books and music and ideas. Sammy Bath had
a son Bertie who looked like the spitting image of the Prince of
Wales, and was a chronic remittance man, being sent out to some
colonial job, failing, returning, and departing again, for Ceylon,
or Kenya, or Assam. Sammy Bath also had a daughter whom
everyone called merely "Miss Bath," typical of the self-sacrificing
young women, doomed to churchy spinsterhood, who were so
common in small English towns of that period. She was much like
the heroine in Orwell's *Clergyman's Daughter*, always dashing
around on church and charity business, a whizzing figure tumbling off her bicycle for breathless conversations and then speed-
ing on to the next class or meeting or the next deserving poor
person. I think she had a crush on my father, for when he was
dying she appeared every day at the hospital, carrying expensive
gifts for England of those days, like freesias and grapes, and when
he died she wept in a way which, as a boy of thirteen, I felt
affronted the privacy of our own grief.

However much they seemed like friends to my father, the
Porters and the Baths would never ask us to their houses, and my
mother would have been filled with consternation if they had
done so, for how in our wretched cottage could she have returned
their hospitality in sufficient splendour? This situation had its
inevitable effect on my own life, and it amounted to a great deal
more than the absence of a family social life.

Though my parents could not entirely stop me playing with the
"low class" children in our street, they tried to restrict my contact
with them as much as possible; I might pick up wrong ways of
speaking and God knows what proletarian habits! In a different
way, when I went to school the attachments I formed depended a
great deal on the status of the children's parents. A crisis would
immediately blow up if I were invited to a party at some relatively
prosperous house. My mother would feel it shameful that if I
accepted she could not possibly offer the same kind of hospitality
in return; no birthday parties were given for me lest children from
better-off homes would tell their parents how poorly we lived. Yet
when I did make a real friendship, a casual kind of in-and-out-of-

the-house relationship was allowed. My parents seemed to know the kind of boys to trust, and so, I suppose, did I, and I do not think I entirely lost by the situation, since the boys I did associate with tended to be outsiders like myself: Gino Boscetti, the marvellously sunny Italian son of the chef at the Compleat Angler Hotel; Louis Heftel, whose mother was a French mystery woman living in a glittering mist of town gossip against which my parents took it on themselves to defend her; George Nicholls, whose parents had come from India and must, I realized later, have been Anglo-Indians, or Eurasians as we called them in those days, and in whose untidy, curry-smelling house my passion for India must have awakened. I cannot say I had a solitary childhood, but it was a childhood less populated than most, and I learnt to play alone and to work alone, relying on myself, as I have done ever since. And certainly the untypical and often un-English households into which my few friendships led me gave an introduction to ways of life outside my own that I would never have got if I had moved all the time within the circles of provincial respectability and prejudice that despised the foreign as well as the poor.

Remembering those very first days in Marlow, when I was not yet six, I recollect perhaps most vividly the wide gracious sweep of the Georgian High Street, with its beautiful Regency houses, and of course the Thames, far larger than any river I had yet seen and on which life in Marlow so largely centred. (My experience with waterways up to then had been confined to the narrow Industrial Revolution canals of northern Shropshire and the little river Tern that ran stinking out of the tanyards under the sandstone cliffs of Market Drayton and purified itself winding through the meadows until you could sometimes catch trout three miles downstream.) On the day of our arrival we walked over the old Brunel age suspension bridge at Marlow, with the water flowing blackly underneath in the early dark of a winter evening, and the way across seemed endless. I could hear the thunder of the weir beyond the bridge, and next day, when I saw the water tossing and pouring through the open sluice gates it seemed more stupendous to me than Niagara does today. Beside the weir was the lock, and all through my childhood I would go there, particularly on luminous summer evenings, to see the water raised and lowered and, later on, to help push the great beams that opened the massive wooden gates. I was fascinated by the river steamers — for I had never seen anything larger than the gaily painted canal barges that cart horses towed along the Shropshire canals — and not long after reaching Marlow we went on one of them down the river to Windsor and Eton, and for the first time, among those grey and ancient towers and cloisters, I began to understand that history had its physical symbols which unite one age with another. And as soon as I realized that history lived outside books, it became a dominant interest and my favourite subject in school.

Other early memories? First of all, the racing shells practicing on the river even in winter with the coxswains bellowing through megaphones strapped to their faces, and the regattas to which all this led. The first I attended must have been 1919, for these events were suspended during the war. I got caught in a crowd on the towpath, tall pressing bodies cutting me off from my father and pushing me towards the water until I screamed in terror. I was consoled that evening with the marvels of the fireworks and the river all aglow with reflected light from the Chinese lanterns suspended on the swaying punts.

And Armistice Day, 1918, when the sirens sounded and the bells rang in tumbling notes and guns were fired down at the Rowing Club and we all went into the High Street to see the parade of whatever aged soldiers were in the neighbourhood and the local firemen and boy scouts and land girls and anyone else who had a right to a uniform. I had just recovered from the Spanish influenza, which almost killed me with delirious dreams of foxes slaughtering chickens, and was a pale little shrimp, worn down to half my infant chubbiness, as I tried to see through the forest of legs. A tall man with a white mane was standing beside my mother; he picked me up and put me on his shoulder to see the parade go by. I do not remember much of the parade, but I remember the man, for he was Jerome K. Jerome, and this, apart from the portentous backs of all the books in my father's shelves, was my first contact with literature. During the next few years — he died in 1927 — I would often see Jerome around the town, and for some reason he remembered me and always greeted me. One winter, when I was perhaps ten, Jerome and L. H. Myers and a few other literary people decided to arrange a series of improving lectures for the people of Marlow, and one night Edward Carpenter came, and my father, who by this time had become very reclusive, as if he were conscious of his approaching death, broke his asocial habit of never attending local functions, and we all went together. Jerome was in the chair, but Carpenter was much the more striking figure, and I can still recollect his looks, dignified but androgynous, the silky quality of his hair and beard, the powerful softness of his voice. He talked of a secular hermit, a man who had cut out from civilization, had gone to live as the Indians did, making his own clothes, gathering or cultivating whatever he ate, and, for the good of his spirit, living a life without any manufactured thing. I think most of the Marlow audience was either puzzled or bored, and louts guffawed in the back seats, but both Carpenter and his subject deeply impressed themselves on my imagination. Curiously, I cannot remember the name of the man on whom Carpenter lectured, except that I think he had a French name which was certainly not Thoreau; even more curiously, I have never since that time come across any hermit record that quite fits my memory of what Carpenter told. Yet that, I know, was one of the epiphanic evenings of my life.

I am writing, of course, of one side of my education, quite different from the side that school represented. School was an experience I was already partly prepared for when I reached Marlow, in the sense that I knew my alphabet and had begun haltingly to read before I entered a classroom. What school immediately gave me, above anything else, was a sense of time; suddenly the days, which had seemed unbroken continuities, were divided into sections of time, and the school terms became like prison terms in which I would count, marking them on a calendar and even scratching them on my classroom desk, the days until the end of term. I suppose this preoccupation with time was accentuated by the fact that every school holiday, which meant a total of three and one-half months a year when I went to grammar school, I spent with my grandparents in Shropshire, living a curiously unchronological country life, and so my years, from six to seventeen, were divided, in a way of which I was highly conscious, between life in time and life outside it. The two ways were so different that, writing now about my time-bound life in Marlow, I have to leave aside for later writing my timeless life in Shropshire.

I never wanted to go to school, and though I learnt quickly and enjoyed much that I learnt, I never liked schools as assemblages of human beings. I feared, disliked or despised most of the other children and most of the teachers; I loathed the organized sports that played so great a role in all English schools, and from the beginning I was a truant from the much exalted team spirit. If there had been any means by which with a few kindred spirits I could have acquired the power of expressing myself in words and a knowledge of subjects that interested me, like English and history and geography, there was no time in my school days in which I would not have chosen it in preference to what I endured. From the beginning it seemed to me that school, like any other massing of human beings, brings out more of the bad than of the good in them, and this in spite of the fact that though I was not sporty enough to be popular, I was never greatly bullied and had enough friends.

Though — or rather because — we lived in a poor street, my parents believed they could not send me to the "rough" public elementary schools attended by the boys of the neighbourhood. They could not even aspire, in their own poverty, to send me to a boarding school, and I was certainly fortunate to escape that special hell of English middle-class youth. I was sent instead to the only private school in our little town, a dame school which the Misses Illsley kept in the big tall-windowed Georgian rooms above the Post Office. One Miss ran the school, another gave courses of shorthand and typewriting in the evening as a local substitute for a business school, and the third Miss, the most genial of all, kept the house.

A succession of young and not so young women earned wretched salaries as assistants while they waited for something better to turn up, and most were inclined to take out their frustrations on the children whom their parents' snobbery had put in Miss Illsley's charge. I do not think Miss I. herself really meant to exploit either her teachers or her pupils; she provided a good basic training in the three R's, with painting and drawing on the side and — somewhat eccentrically — knitting for both girls and boys; after painful hours I did finish a scarf, but I never graduated to three-needle items like socks and gloves. But there were perpetual difficulties during the three years I attended the school. Town councils were becoming conscious of standards of accommodation for schools and similar institutions, and before I had been there long we were expelled from the sunny rooms above the Post Office and moved around like a clandestine immigrant English school in Québec, first into the basement of the Wesleyan Church and then into the Sunday school of the Baptist church.

I cannot remember a great deal that was actually taught during these fugitive progresses from building to building, but clearly a great deal that characterized my later life was fostered by my encounters with Miss Illsley's acerbic assistants with their ever-ready rulers to beat at errant knuckles, for most of the incidents I remember from that period have some flavour of deviousness or rebellion. I developed early — perhaps under my father's influence — an eye to the artificial in literature, and when I was picked to recite Wordsworth's "The Daffodils" at a school event for the edification of the parents, I immediately recognized the silliness of the poem and developed a dislike for Wordsworth I have never shed. So I got my own back by reciting the poem perfectly at every rehearsal and then, on the day itself, playing the bumpkin, fluffing my lines clownishly to the amusement of the audience and the fury of the teachers. I became a fluent liar. One day a girl brought into class a beautiful seashell for which I felt a sudden and irresistible desire, so when the opportunity came I quietly pocketed it and took it home, declaring I had found it in the road. I now regarded myself with a mixture of pride and perturbation as a thief, and felt a kind of smug satisfaction the next time one of my parents said: "You can lock up from a thief, but you can't lock up from a liar." I was both, and for a while pursued the two careers to the point of rashness, which came when I passed off a watercolour sketch of snowdrops which one of the young teachers had done hurriedly in class as my own. It was a nice little piece of work, and my grandparents framed it and hung it in their house as an earnest of my artistic powers. Foolishly, I allowed myself to be convinced by my own lies, and proceeded to do some more paintings — the great artist working on demand — which aroused such suspicion in my shrewder relatives that I retreated and reserved lying for self-defence.

This did not mean that I retreated from creative fantasy, inspired largely by books like *The Swiss Family Robinson*, which gave me ideas about ways in which small boys might transcend the possibilities of their limited everyday lives. I invented situations in which I and my friends built huts and performed other feats of craftsmanship, and took advantage of my double life by attributing these to my Marlow life when I was among my Shropshire friends, and vice versa. But I think my highest level of small-boy fantasy, approaching the verges of literary creation, was achieved in connection with my truancy from church when I was between ten and eleven. My mother thought it would do me some good and my father felt it would do me no harm if I were sent off to church every Sunday morning, and I chose the village church of Bisham, about a mile from Marlow. I was going to school in the village (of which more later), so that there was a plausible connection, and I knew my father never went into a church except to look at the architecture, while my mother was too busy cooking the most elaborate meal of the week, the big Sunday mid-day dinner, to check on what I was doing in a village church a mile away to which none of her acquaintances went. So I would pocket the pennies, buy a surprise packet of stale sweets at the general store down the street, and spend three Sunday mornings out of four wandering in the woods around Bisham, munching licorice and gob-stoppers. On the one Sunday out of four I really would attend church and listen to the sermon and carefully watch the vicar of Bisham, who was noted for his extravagant gestures in the pulpit, for his outlandish similes and for the absurd anecdotes with which he illustrated his points. This would give me enough material to make up accounts of fictitious sermons for the rest of the month, which I would recount on my return, elaborating the oddities of the vicar's behaviour. My father would listen in anti-clerical delight, and with a certain paternal pride in my powers of expression, and if he suspected I was romancing he never let me know. I was beginning to learn the power and the joy of manipulating words.

My links with Bisham — the church and school — were precipitated by an act of sheer rebelliousness, my participation in the strike at Miss Illsley's school. This was some time in 1920, when there was a good deal of talk about strikes circulating among our parents and in the newspapers, whose headlines I was reading and understanding at the time. A new teacher had angered us with the capriciousness of her punishments, and one day, when she had committed what seemed to us some intolerable injustice, news of it spread quickly from class to class in the one big schoolroom, and we older boys of eight or so got up and ran out of the class. Some of the more tomboyish girls joined us as we shouted, "Strike! Strike!" and stampeded out of the school, bashing with our pencil boxes the monitors — goody-goody boys chosen for the task — who tried to stop us. Once we left the school we had no idea what strikers did, so we roved around the railway yards in a shouting gang, and then decided to go back to school to pick up the coats some of us had left behind. By this time the teachers had sent the small children home and closed the school, so we battered the door, running against it en masse to try and break it in, and then one of us broke a window and we all ran away.

The strike did not last, for the parents applied divide-and-rule methods. My father had seen me from his office among the gang in the station yard, and when I got home I was duly cross-examined and caned. I imagine in one way or another his fellow parents applied similar methods, for the strikers all turned up at school next day, and neither we nor the teachers mentioned the incident, though the one who had precipitated it soon left. And so did I, for my parents decided that I had outgrown dame-school teaching, and as I was not yet old enough for grammar school, and they still did not wish to send me to the "rough" public elementary schools in Marlow, I was sent to the school in Bisham, a riverside village of thatched flint and mortar houses, with a manor house — Bisham Abbey — said to be haunted by the hand-washing ghost of Lady Mary Hoby who smothered one of her children in Elizabethan days, and a beautiful Gothic church with medieval brasses and crusader's tombs.

The school, opposite the church, was run by an arrogant and sharp-tempered Welshman, Jones, who happened also to be a rather good teacher. He and his wife took the upper classes, and the lower ones were taught by two young women we called Teacher Sylvia and Teacher Dorothy. Sylvia was a pretty and sweet-natured woman, but I was too old for her to teach me and went immediately into Dorothy's class. She was a florid, genial, expansive woman, who had the natural power of discipline that comes from being able to deal with any situation without allowing the equilibrium of one's good humour to be disturbed. There were some rough characters among the children from outlying farms, but it was never Teacher Dorothy who fell foul of them. She was the first teacher I really liked, and under her encouragement I began, at about nine, to show the facility in prose that ended up eventually in my becoming a writer.

Going to Bisham school would probably be regarded as a hard assignment by a modern child used to school buses and school lunches. It was just over a mile from my home, and I would walk there, in all weathers, for the first class at nine, walk home for the mid-day meal, walk back to school for the afternoon classes, and then go home again at four o'clock. A group of us, boys and girls, went together, earnestly hurrying on the way to school and larking and scrapping on the way back. Sometimes we could jump on the back of horse-drawn delivery vans, but often the drivers were malevolent and would flick at us with their long whips until we jumped off.

Again I cannot remember a great deal of what we were taught at Bisham, though I do recollect becoming strongly aware of history at this time, perhaps because it was congealed, as it were, in the neighbouring church and abbey in a concrete form I could easily apprehend. More than what was taught, I remember the feel of the place and its look: the big room where the higher classes all sat together — always, in memory, a room filled with sunlight; the great playground with the line of poplars beside the road, the corner where the small children played hopscotch under the thorn bushes, and the big area of grass where the older boys and the wilder girls played rounders and touch and some kind of improvised football.

There was a difference we all recognized between the town children like me and George Nicholls, and the foreigners like Gino Boscetti and Louis Heftel on one hand, and the country children on the other. They represented to us a different world of experience and values. Fred Rogier — we pronounced it Rozha — seemed to me, for example, the height of rustic barbarity. Coming from a distant farm, he always wore smelly corduroy clothes, his red hair was always uncut and unkempt, and he spoke in a broader accent than anyone else when he talked about shit, as he constantly did, and enlarged the strange concepts small boys developed about procreation in those days before sex education with exaggerated accounts of the sexual life of farm animals. He was always inciting the other village boys to make the town boys eat horse dung, but nothing came of it.

More formidable, because it was large and tended to act as a cohesive unit, was the Frith clan, a great interbred family of cousins who seemed to constitute half the population of Bisham. They were poor and tough, their parents ordinary labourers and hard drinkers. When I was at Bisham the leadership of the clan — in the school at least — had been seized by a girl, Ethel Frith, a loud-mouthed tomboy with tousled hair who — like her sisters — wore the kind of long smocks, halfway down the calf, one sees in pictures of late Victorian girls. Ethel was extremely hard to control by any of the teachers, and Jones, who was a great disciplinarian, decided he must take the situation in hand.

Jones caned one on the hand with painful skill, so that one's palms ached for hours after three of his best. But he had never before caned a girl. Girls were regarded as naturally more good than boys, and if Jones did not use his cane on them, it was due not to a sense that female flesh should be left inviolate, but to a knowledge that girls in general responded to less severe measures. Not so Ethel, who treated with contempt any ordinary kind of discipline, and finally Jones decided to break precedent by caning her and to emphasize the lesson by doing it in public, before the whole school.

It was a disastrous enterprise. The feeling in the assembly was hostile to Jones from the beginning. The girls all supported Ethel out of sexual loyalty, and the boys out of a sense that what might be proper for them was not proper for girls. And then there was Ethel, who had no intention of letting the occasion increase the dignity of authority. Among the boys there was a code of accepting one's punishment and showing one's contempt by not flinching as the cane cut down upon one's flesh. But Ethel recognized no such code. When Jones tried to take her hands, she snatched them away, and when he seized her by the arm, she struggled, screamed, kicked and scratched, and Jones, in a white rage, manhandled her across his knee and beat her on the legs, arms and back with a fury that even to our innocent eyes seemed unnatural and perverse. By the end of it all, Ethel was weeping, more dishevelled than ever, but still defiant. Jones was sweating, with a red streak from Ethel's nails across his cheek, and, I believe, thoroughly aware of the silent disapproval of the whole school, for though he declared that he hoped we now realized that nobody was exempt from punishment, he then turned and walked away with a set face and was not seen for the rest of the day. Authority had shown its weakness to us, and we fostered the lesson, while Ethel became a heroine, which perhaps she did not wholly deserve, for she was just about as stupid as she was intractable.

Ethel's cousin Tom Frith was the ferryman's son, and nearer a friend to me than any of the other village boys, yet it was with him that, at the age of ten, I was provoked into accepting the challenge to fight seriously. Tom would occasionally challenge me and, when I did not react, push me into a corner and pummel me, not very seriously. One day, when there was an audience, I felt I had put up with enough, and advanced on Tom with flailing fists. Had he known anything about boxing he would have slipped in under my non-existent guard, but as it was his nose was bloodied and he never tried to pummel me again. The news seemed to spread, for after that Fred Rogier no longer talked of feeding me horse dung, and I lived the rest of my time in the village school, until I was eleven, in peace.

More of my real education took place in the house than in the school. The kitchen was the place where we carried on the business of daily living; the front room enshrined my father's interests, and it was a surprising room to anyone who happened to step in from the pavement. In that primitive cottage it seemed to throw into relief our shabby gentility, how we had come down in the world so far as to live in what would now be regarded as a slum, but had kept our pride and the material symbols of it. The furniture was the best kind of fake Jacobean, which even Joey Rumbelow admired. On the massive sideboard stood my father's collection of old English pewter, and on the marble mantelpiece and the tops of the two built-in cupboards his collection of Staffordshire china with a few other oddments like Neapolitan figurines (which I still have on my bookshelves). The cupboards contained his stamp collections, mainly from the Commonwealth;

he spent a good deal of time with these, belonging to exchange clubs and actually making a little money out of speculating in rare issues.

If the pewter and the pottery, and my father's books about them, gave me my first insight into the importance of craftsmanship and interested me in the lifestyles of the eighteenth century, to which most of his collection belonged, the stamps helped to educate me in exotic ways of life, in tropical scenes, in unfamiliar fauna and flora, leading me on to areas of interest I might otherwise have ignored. Later, when I travelled, particularly in Asia, I found that much in the countries I visited were at least partially familiar to me from having pored over my father's stamps and the illustrations in Stanley Gibbon's catalogues.

But most important were the books that filled one wall of the room. My father coveted well-bound and well-printed books; he loved facsimiles and limited editions. A book for him was a sensual as well as an intellectual experience, a visual as well as a literary artifact. He had most of the monumental turn-of-the-century series, the Tudor Translations, and would spend hours poring over Montaigne and Heliodorus and the King James Bible and early translations of Machiavelli — both *The Prince* and *The Florentine Wars*, which especially fascinated him. Much of his time he lived mentally in the Elizabethan and Jacobean ages, and apart from the Tudor Translations I remember a collected edition of Sir Thomas Browne and one of Isaak Walton, *The Closet of Sir Kenelm Digby*, facsimiles of Nashe, Greene and other lesser Elizabethans, Captain John Smith's accounts of the settlement of Virginia, and William Lithgow's *Rare Adventures and Painful Peregrinations*. To begin, I liked the wood block illustrations to Smith and Lithgow (particularly the latter's lurid drawings of the tortures of the Inquisition), and later, in my *Robinson Crusoe* phase, I was fascinated by Smith's detailed practical accounts of voyages and settlements. A little later, when I took to fishing, I spent a great deal of time with Walton, and stage by stage I read all the other books.

Outside the sixteenth and seventeenth centuries my father's collection was rather patchy. Before I could remember them he had sold from need items like his complete collection of Wilde's books (he was a great defender of Wilde, which took some courage in his time and place). But he still had a good many books by Frank Harris, whom he admired, most of John Davidson's books of poetry (which I liked from the beginning and still do), Clive Bell's books on art, some Bernard Shaw, and the books of that rather good but now entirely forgotten Edwardian poet, Richard Middleton. There were novels by Frederick Niven, including *The Lost Cabin Mine*, which gave me my first idea of the British Columbian terrain and a desire to experience it, and the historical romances, which I devoured when I was about twelve, of Maurice Hewlett. I was encouraged to read any of these books that I could understand, and to talk about them when I could not.

My father also bought in a sale a set of *Chambers' Encyclopedia*, in an old leather binding that was falling away into dust, so that it must have been quite outdated, but for me it was a source of endless hours of fascinated reading. I did not read it all through, as Huxley is said to have read the *Britannica*, but I made several efforts and became extraordinarily knowledgeable about aardvarks and Afghanistan, about beavers and bison and Bolivia, but more sketchily so about subjects that came after D. I always enjoyed and still enjoy good reference books, and would read county directories of Shropshire and Buckinghamshire from end to end, so that I had from about eleven a good idea of the immediate regions in which I lived, a habit I have followed ever since and which has undoubtedly fostered my strong regionalist predilections. *Whitaker's Almanac* I read almost every year and thus I taught myself a great deal that appeared in no school curriculum about the complexities of the British political and social systems and much about the politics of other countries in the period between the wars. Nor can I forget the collection of issues of the *English Review* from the early Ford Madox Ford days which my father had kept in a trunk in the box room, and which I would dig out and read, though this was mostly after my father's death, when I was thirteen. Here, just when I needed them at the ages of fifteen and sixteen, I first encountered D.H. Lawrence, Ford himself, Norman Douglas, the Powys brothers, and a great deal of Conrad, whom I had first read as an adventure writer.

We took the *Daily Mail* and the *Sunday Telegraph*, and my mother would borrow *The News of the World*, which my father detested, from our next-door neighbour, so that I followed in detail the more sensational murders of the era, on which the English rather prided themselves, and gathered hints of strange crimes in public lavatories, often involving distinguished gentlemen, which I did not then understand. I took my boyhood politics from the Tory *Daily Mail*, and believed in Empire Free Trade, in turning the commonwealth into a closed, self-contained federation. Perhaps my father's sustained interest in Canada, and my own pride in being Canadian-born (a point of difference from my schoolfellows which I cultivated) had a good deal to do with this attitude, which was fostered by another source of reading. One day in the 1920s a touring coach arrived in Marlow, sent by the Canadian authorities who were — in those expansive days before the Depression — actively seeking immigrants. My father paid his visit, talked nostalgically with the Canadians about his own experiences in the prairies, and returned loaded with a mass of literature that gave us months of reading and a great deal of matter for discussion. Though he could never recover his health, and indeed was doomed to die very shortly afterwards, he still elaborated projects, into which I entered zestfully (not quite realising the true situation), for settling on homestead land on the Peace River in British Columbia. We studied leaflets on growing melons, on beekeeping, on house construction, all of which appealed to the Robinson Crusoe streak in my nature; I never grew melons or kept bees, but a quarter of a century afterward I did build two wooden houses with my own hands in British Columbia.

My father was politically conservative, and rather simplistic in his attitudes to world affairs, as people were in those days before the totalitarian nightmares revealed themselves. Because he passionately loved Beethoven and Handel, he admired Germany, and always declared that in World War I Britain had chosen the wrong side; it should have elected to share the hegemony of the world with Germany rather than support corrupt France; especially it should not have allowed the Americans to gain a position in world politics which everyone, he believed, would regret. He thought Mussolini and early fascism were good for Italy, but I think he saw merely the trains running on time and had no idea what fascism meant in practice. He was like many people who were appalled at the chaos of the post-war world and longed for a return to order, to the predictable world they had know in their youths, having no idea that the totalitarian creeds would lead the world into even deeper chaos. He knew Oswald Mosley in the earlier part of his career, for Oswald's mother had a house near my grandfather's in Market Drayton. Mosley's fascist phase was then far in the future, but my father was rather fascinated by his conversion to socialism and emergence as a Labour M.P. The audacity of it stirred one maverick side of his nature, as did the intellectual audacity of Bernard Shaw. And he reserved judgment on the Russian Revolution, saying that Lenin must be given a chance to prove himself.

But this, I suspect, was largely to annoy my grandfather, who was both scandalized by Mosley's apostasy and passionately incensed over the Russian Revolution, largely because he had been foolish enough to buy Tsarist bonds. For a while, indeed, the Revolution loomed large in family concerns. At church services the sonorous Tsarist hymn, *God the All Terrible*, would be sung, and I remember at the age of six being taken to a lantern lecture on events in St. Petersburg in which the lecturer emphasized the Bolshevik atrocities. I still retain very clearly in my mind's eye two of the slides, one of dingily clad Russian soldiers standing packed in railway trucks, and the other of fighting in a square, with people running and some lying dead on the pavements. I was introduced early to the realities of our time.

Apart from his own library and the books — largely biographies and memoirs — which he took out of the library and encouraged me to read, my father very consciously tried to direct my education by buying what seemed to him the right kind of books. He gave me the *Swiss Family Robinson*, which perhaps encouraged my utopian bent, and the usual Marryats and Hentys and Ballantynes, among which *The Coral Island* was perhaps the favourite book of my early childhood. I had *Alice in Wonderland*, but I was a very concretely minded boy, even in my fantasies, and did not appreciate it until much later. I soon got taken up with books of natural history and of Latin American travels, particularly Bates, Waterton and Belt. My father was delighted in my interest in natural history, which stemmed largely from his own emphasis, whenever we went walking together, on the need to use my eyes and ears, to be aware of the world around me, to observe and then to think, a lesson that has remained with me throughout my life and has combined with my natural curiosity to make me the kind of writer I have become.

My father greatly admired Kipling, as I now tend to do. He bought me most of Kipling, but not, strangely, *Kim*, perhaps because India never had the kind of fascination for him which it has held for me since I first heard it talked of with nostalgia in the Nicholls' untidy home. His travels in Canada and briefly in the United States seem to have sufficed for him. I cannot remember his expressing a desire to see any country in Europe, and his literary interests were essentially English, for even with the Tudor Translations it was the resonant English through which the originals were filtered that fascinated him. He saw the world from his armchair, and became more and more a recluse as he drew near to death in my early teens.

I can indeed remember him during our first years in Marlow working on a summer evening in the allotment on railway land where he grew excellent vegetables which we would eat fresh in their seasons. And I remember especially the walks by the Thames when we would watch and identify birds and fish. But from the final years I remember him mostly sitting in his chair poring over his stamp collection or, more often, over *The Florentine Wars* or Montaigne or *Religio Medici*.

He rarely went to the pub, for his doctors had forbidden him to drink, and he rarely attended social occasions or entertainments. He detested anything mechanical, would not have a radio in the house, never went to the cinema; he carried an enormous amount of music in his head and in his later years did not seem to need concerts. He even avoided going to church, claiming that the noise would bring on headaches from which he periodically suffered. I suspect the real reasons were his reaction against the sanctimoniousness of my church warden grandfather and the fact that his own faith had worn to nothing. He never said anything, at least in my hearing, that expressed either his disbelief or his belief. I am sure, at the same time, that he was an agnostic but did not want to influence me in that direction. It would have been in his nature to wish me to reach such a conclusion in my own mind.

GEOFFREY URSELL

The Bends

as we are lowered in the deep
we tip the face-plates of helmets
down to darkness, down to cold:
yet even in the pressure of ten
centuries find glowing creatures
nuzzling at our shrouded bodies

when we have come this far nothing is
strange to consider: heart urchins, rock
fish, pulsating pale anemones, lobsters
without eyes, & the sediment of history
settled on the bottom almost undisturbed,
thick powdery level of lives & days

& only if, taking fright at a quick silence
in the steady hiss & remembering the fragile
hollow cords holding us to breath, we fight
with the element, drive ourselves upwards into
light & open air, then the unused carrier of
oxygen foams inside our veins & the bends
pull us in upon ourselves, clutching every
where at once as they tear apart the logic
of our blood & pain bubbles through the brain

: oh, most find choppy waves
icebergs, calms, massive storms
occasional sunny days, enough, but

diving, we deliver words to them
to help them know in what it is
they float & swim & finally end

W. D. VALGARDSON

Climbing Mt. Finlayson

So, this is resurrection,
This slow healing of old wounds.
Here, in the crevice, where I plucked
The columbine, taking three flowers
To thread your buttonholes,
It blooms again, defiant pink.
Here, where we slipped and slid on slab,
Our feet digging deep in shaggy moss,
Where reddish soil spilled down,
Dry and soft, decaying cedar dust,
Resilient stems, soft whorls and spirals,
Intersect. Here, British soldiers march again,
Red caps high on green-grey stalks.
No marks of boots remain.
The past is done, except in memory,
That vague, uneasy, waking sleep.
Slow healing eases pain,
And gives me paths to climb again.

NOTES ON THE CONTRIBUTORS

Bert Almon (1943–   ) teaches English at the University of Alberta. His fourth collection of poetry, *Blue Sunrise*, was published in the spring of 1980.

Douglas Barbour (1940-   ) lives in Edmonton. His seventh book of poetry is *Shore Lines*. With Stephen Scobie, he is a member of Re: Sounding, a sound poetry ensemble, which performed at the opening night of the 12th International Sound Poetry Festival in New York last April.

Brian Bartlett (1953–   ) now lives in Montreal. He spent most of his youth in New Brunswick, where his ancestors settled before 1776 in the southwest, the region he imagined as the setting for his story in this anthology. He has published three chapbooks of poetry, and other fiction has appeared in *Stories from Atlantic Canada* and *78: Best Canadian Stories*.

Doug Beardsley (1941–   ) was born in Montreal and received his B.A. at Victoria, B.C., and his M.A. from York University, Toronto. He has published six books of poetry. Two new books, *The Marie Poems*, and *A Sweet Circle of Fire*, will be published next year. He is currently general editor at Gregson Graham Ltd., a marketing and communications firm in Victoria, where he also teaches a creative writing workshop.

David Blostein (1935–   ) was born in Flin Flon and grew up in Transcona, Manitoba. He was educated at the Universities of Manitoba, Oxford and Toronto. A musician and illustrator, he teaches English literature at Victoria College, University of Toronto.

Marilyn Bowering (1949–   ) was born in Winnipeg and educated in British Columbia. She works as an editor and teacher and lives near Victoria on Vancouver Island. She has published a short novel and three books of poetry. A new book of poetry, *Sleeping With Lambs*, is to be published in the fall of 1980.

J.D. Carpenter (1948–   ), a former journalist with *The Daily Racing Form*, lives and teaches in Toronto. The author of two books of poetry, *Nightfall, Ferryland Head* and *Swimming at Twelve Mile*, his work has appeared in *Canadian Literature, The Canadian Forum, The English Quarterly, The Fiddlehead, Waves*, and *Aurora 1979*. At present, he is beginning a novel and completing a manuscript of poems.

Jim Christy (1945–   ), who was born in Virginia and became a Canadian citizen in 1974, has recently published *Rough Road To The North: Travels Along the Alaska Highway*, and is currently at work on a novel called *Streethearts*.

Michael Cook (1933–   ) emigrated to Newfoundland in 1966. He is best known as a dramatist and has written over forty plays including *The Head, Guts & Soundbone Dance, Jacob's Wake, The Gayden Chronicles*, and *Therese's Creed*. His work has been performed in Germany, Switzerland, Mexico, the U.S., and currently in Sweden. A director, journalist and associate professor at Memorial University, he is currently working full time on *The Island of Fire*, a novel in progress.

Terrance Cox (1950–   ) was born in northern Ontario and grew up there and in eastern Ontario. Educated at Brock University and the University of Toronto, he has taught in Africa, at Brock, and most recently, at Birzeit University in the occupied West Bank. His poems have appeared in a number of Canadian magazines and he has published a chapbook, *In Local Orbit*. Living now in Toronto, he is at work on *Falastin*, poems from under occupation.

Gary Michael Dault (1939–   ) has taught at a number of Canadian universities. He is a frequent contributor to CBC television and radio and has written extensively about the visual arts in Canadian and international journals. For the past six years he has contributed a weekly art column to *The Toronto Star*. He is at present executive producer of CBC Radio's current affairs magazine show, "Don Harron's Morningside."

David Donnell (1939–   ) was born and educated in Ontario and has worked at a variety of jobs since 1960. He writes art and book reviews, gives readings and works as a freelance editor. His third volume of poems, *Dangerous Crossings*, came out in April 1980. He is working on a new manuscript of poems and a novel set in Toronto.

Gail Fox (1942–   ) was born in Connecticut, but has lived in Canada since 1963 and is a Canadian citizen. She has published five books of poetry, among them *God's Odd Look*. She is the editor of *Quarry*.

Northrop Frye (1912–   ) was born in Sherbrooke and has taught at the University of Toronto since 1939. He is widely recognized as one of the foremost literary critics of this century. His books include *Anatomy of Criticism, The Educated Imagination, The Modern Century* and *The Bush Garden: Essays on the Canadian Imagination*.

Robert Fulford (1932–   ) was born in Ottawa and moved to Toronto at an early age. His reviews, articles and essays have appeared in a wide variety of publications. He writes a weekly column for the *Toronto Star* and has been editor of *Saturday Night* since 1968. His books include *Marshall Delaney at the Movies, Crisis at the Victory Burlesque* and *This Was Expo*.

Shirley Mann Gibson (1927–   ) was born in Toronto and makes her home there. She worked with House of Anansi Press for six years and since 1977 has been the director of Playwrights Canada. Her first book of poetry, *I am watching*, appeared in 1973 and a new collection, *Bloodlines*, will be published in late 1980. She is currently completing a book of short stories.

Susan Glickman (1953–   ) grew up in Montreal and now lives in Toronto where she is doing a Ph.D. in Renaissance drama and teaching an undergraduate seminar on Shakespeare. Her work has been published in numerous periodicals, including *The Canadian Forum, The Fiddlehead, The Antigonish Review, The Dalhousie Review, Matrix,* and *C.V.II*.

David Helwig (1938–   ) worked with the CBC from 1974 to 1976. He recently left a teaching position in the English department at Queen's University. A book which he edited, *Love and Money: The Politics of Culture*, will be published this fall.

Greg Hollingshead (1947–   ) grew up in Ontario. He went to school in Toronto and London, England, and now teaches at the University of Alberta in Edmonton. In the past few years his stories have appeared in a number of Canadian magazines and anthologies, including *Aurora 1978, Best Canadian Stories 79, The Story So Far, periodics,* and *The Dalhousie Review*.

Bill Howell (1946–   ) is currently employed as a radio drama producer for CBC Radio in Toronto. Since *The Red Fox*, his poetry has virtually disappeared from the public page, but lately he has been quietly compiling a second collection, tentatively titled *Famous Inside*.

Mark Jarman (1955–   ) was born in Edmonton, Alberta, and studied at the University of Victoria. His fiction and poetry have appeared in *The Fiddlehead*, *Prism International*, *Waves*, *From an Island 1978*, *Descant*, and *Cross Country*.

Bill Kinsella (1935–   ) was born in Edmonton, Alberta. He has a degree in creative writing from the University of Victoria and an MFA in English from the University of Iowa, Iowa Writers' Workshop. He has published three collections of stories, *Dance Me Outside*, *Scars*, and *Shoeless Joe Jackson Comes To Iowa*. Some 50 of his stories have been published in Canadian and American literary magazines and his work has been widely anthologized. He currently teaches fiction at the University of Calgary.

David Knight (1926–   ), born and formed in Toronto, an academic and a believer in craft. Teaches, writes, teaches writers, once wrote about a teacher (*Farquharson's Physique and What It Did to his Mind*). No nationalist. Mythical landscapes include Holland Marsh, Nigeria, and a Protestant orphanage in Pòrtici. Married to M. L. Knight. Three sons.

M. L. Knight (1924–   ) is a Toronto housewife who experiments with poems, banners, collages, and combinations of same. Her work has appeared in *Aurora 1979* and in *Indirections* (magazine of the Ontario Council of Teachers of English). She had an exhibit of banners and collages at Victoria College, Christmas Season, 1979.

Joy Kogawa (1935–   ) was born in Vancouver and now lives in a co-op in Toronto. She has worked as a writer in the Prime Minister's Office and as writer-in-residence at the University of Ottawa. She has published three books, *The Splintered Moon*, *A Choice of Dreams*, and *Jericho Road*. Her poems and short stories have appeared in a number of magazines.

Alistair MacLeod is a native of Nova Scotia's Inverness County. His poems and stories have been published in various magazines and anthologies. A collection of his fiction entitled *The Lost Salt Gift of Blood* was published in 1976. At present he teaches English and creative writing at the University of Windsor.

Tom Marshall (1938–   ) is the author of the comic novel *Rosemary Goal* (1978), of *Harsh and Lovely Land* (1979), a study of Canadian poetry, and of *The Elements* (1980), a poetic quartet organized around the four elements of fire, water, earth and air. He teaches English at Queen's University.

Eugene McNamara (1930–   ) teaches English at the University of Windsor. Born in Oak Park, Illinois, he is a Canadian citizen. His short stories have recently appeared in *Saturday Night* and *Chicago* and in *79: Best Canadian Stories*. His last collection of poems was *Screens*.

Bruce Meyer (1957–   ) was born in Toronto and graduated from the University of Toronto. He is former editor of *Acta Victoriana* and the *University of Toronto Review* and currently editor of *Nimbus*. He was winner of the 1980 E. J. Pratt Medal and his poetry has appeared in *Dalhousie Review*, *Tributaries*, *Aurora 1979*, *Intrinsic* and other magazines.

Susan Musgrave (1951–   ) has spent most of her life on the west coast of Canada. She has published a number of books of poetry, her most recent being *A Man to Marry, A Man to Bury*. Her first novel, *The Charcoal Burners*, will be published this fall, as well as a children's book, *Hag-Head*.

Suniti Namjoshi (1941–   ) was born in India. She has taught English literature at the University of Toronto since 1972. The Writer's Workshop, Calcutta, published *The Jackass and the Lady* in the summer of 1980.

Yvette Naubert (1918–   ) was born in Hull and has lived in Montreal, Ottawa and Aix-en-Provence. She has written for radio and theatre, and has published five novels: *La dormeuse éveillée; L'été de la cigale; Les Pierrefendre, Volumes I, II, and III*. She has also published three books of short stories: *Contes de la solitude, Volumes I and II; Traits et Portraits*.

Joyce Nelson (1945–   ) is a freelance writer and broadcaster living in Toronto. Her poems have appeared in *Quarry*, *Prism International*, *Malahat Review*, *Saturday Night*, *This Magazine*, *Branching Out*, and *The Canadian Forum*. Her first book of poetry, *Battlefronts*, was published in 1978.

Marilyn Powell was born in Toronto, where she still lives and works as a freelance writer and broadcaster. "A Psychological Story" is her second published story. Her first, "Home Grown in the East End" appeared in *Toronto Short Stories*.

John Reibetanz (1944–   ) was born in deepest Brooklyn, is finishing a sequence of monologues set in rural Suffolk, lives in Toronto and various other imaginary places, and teaches at Victoria College, University of Toronto. Poems and criticism have appeared in *Aurora 1978* and *Aurora 1979*, *Contemporary Literature*, *Poetry* (Chicago), *The Ontario Review*, and other magazines.

Suzanne Sandor-Lofft is a Hungarian-born, Toronto-based writer. Her work has appeared in *Saturday Night, MacLean's, The Canadian, The Toronto Star, Rune* and *Descant*.

Robyn Sarah (1949–   ) was born in New York and grew up in Montreal, where she studied at the Quebec Conservatory of Music and at McGill University. Since 1972 she has taught at Champlain Regional College. She is co-founder (with her husband, Fred Louder) of Ville-neuve Publications, a Montreal small press. Her first collection of poems, *Shadowplay*, was published in 1978.

Stephen Scobie (1943–   ) was born in Scotland, came to Canada in 1965, and now lives in Edmonton. He has published several volumes of poetry, a critical study of Leonard Cohen, and a scattering of short stories. His most recent book of poetry is *McAlmon's Chinese Opera*. Together with Douglas Barbour he forms the experimental poetry group, Re:Sounding, which performed last spring on the opening night of the 12th International Sound Poetry Festival in New York.

Carol Shields (1935–   ) was born and educated in the Chicago area and has lived in Canada for many years. She has published two books of poetry, two novels, and one book of criticism. A new novel, *Happenstance*, is scheduled for publication this fall.

Francis Sparshott (1926–   ) was born and raised in England and has taught philosophy at the University of Toronto since 1950. He has published four books of philosophy and four books of poetry, most recently, *The Rainy Hills* (1979).

Sid Stephen (1942–   ) was born in Halifax, N.S. A career military officer, he has lived in almost every province of Canada, in Europe, and in the Middle East. At present he is completing a M.A. programme in English at the Royal Military College in Kingston. A new collection of poetry, *Down the Dark Ladder*, will be published in the spring of 1981.

Peter Stevens (1927–   ) was born in England and is now a Canadian citizen, having come to Canada in 1957. He has taught at McMaster University, the University of Saskatchewan, and is currently teaching at the University of Windsor. He has published seven books of poetry, edited three books and compiled a book-length bibliography of modern Canadian poetry. He is currently working on plays and a novel. He writes a weekly jazz column for *The Windsor Star* and was a regular contributor to the CBC's "Jazz Radio Canada" series.

Geoffrey Ursell (1943–   ) was born in Moose Jaw and now lives in Regina. His play, *The Running of the Deer*, won the 1977 Clifford E. Lee

Award. He wrote the songs for the plays *Superwheel* and *Number One Hard* (they may be heard on the album of the same name). At present, he is working on a musical play, *Saskatoon Pie!*, and a novel, *Perdue*.

W. D. Valgardson (1939–   ) was born and educated in Manitoba. He currently teaches creative writing at the University of Victoria, B.C. He has published three books of short stories, a book of poems, and a novel, *Gentle Sinners*.

Guy Vanderhaeghe (1951–   ) was born and educated in Saskatche-wan. He has published short fiction in various journals including *Aurora 1978*, *Aurora 1979*, *Canadian Fiction Magazine*, *Malahat Review*, *Journal of Canadian Fiction*, and *Wascana Review*. One of his short stories will appear in *80: Best Canadian Stories*.

Arved Viirlaid (1922–   ) was born in Estonia and now lives in Toronto. He attended the State College of Fine Arts in Tallinn before the Second World War and became a partisan in Estonia and a volunteer in the Finnish army during the occupations of his homeland by Nazi Germany and Soviet Russia. In exile in various countries he has worked at a number of jobs. For the last twenty-six years he has been employed as a compositor in a printing firm. He has written five collections of poetry and seven novels. His work has appeared in twelve languages.

Miriam Waddington was born in Winnipeg and educated there and in Ottawa, Toronto, and Philadelphia. She now teaches English and Canadian literature at York University where she holds the rank of Professor. She has published ten books of poetry, the last three of which are *Driving home*, *The Price of Gold*, and *Mister Never*. She has also published many critical books, reviews, and articles.

Tom Wayman (1945–   ) has four books of poems scheduled for publication in 1980: *Living On The Ground: Tom Wayman Country*; *A Planet Mostly Sea*; a U.S. selected poems, *Introducing Tom Wayman*; and a new anthology of contemporary North American work poetry, *Going For Coffee*.

George Woodcock (1912–   ) was born in Winnipeg and brought up in England, returning to Canada in 1949 after establishing himself as a writer in England. He has published more than fifty books in many fields. A new book, *The World of Canadian Writing*, will appear in the spring of 1980.

Morris Wolfe (1938–   ) the editor of *Aurora*, writes a column about the media for *Saturday Night* magazine, regularly contributes to CBC radio programmes such as *Arts National* and *Ideas,* and teaches film history at the Ontario College of Art. He has edited (or co-edited) six books and *A Literary Map of Canada.* He is Editor Emeritus of *grub* and *crap.*